GROW RICH
With eBay Consignment

Christopher Matthew Spencer

GROW RICH with eBay Consignment, 1ˢᵗ Edition
Published by:
The Spencer Company
PO Box 1862
Beverly Hills, CA 90213-1862
www.spencercompany.com
Copyright © 2014 by Christopher Matthew Spencer
Facebook, Instagram, Twitter and Vine: @borntodeal
Published by The Spencer Company, Beverly Hills, California
Published simultaneously in Canada

This book is available at special quantity discounts to use for sales promotions, employee premiums, or educational purposes. Please email borntodeal@gmail.com or write to the address above.

Library of Congress Control Number: 2013916950

ISBN-10: 0615888348
ISBN-13: 978-0615888347

Manufactured in the United States of America

Lifestyle photography (including art direction and styling) by: Kyle Jackson
Models: Elise Christian, Paris Dylan and Anthony Usewicz
Hair and makeup: Erin Nakashima and Joelle Pitts
Location manager and property master: Jake Fehres
Production assistant: Carlos Ortiz

GROW RICH with eBay Consignment aspires to liberate you from your financial challenges and open doors to an exciting new career, full-time or part-time, working with cool people and interesting items. You will soar in this new adventure once you uncover the clear path explained in this book!

Chain of Events
A story of love, loss and recovery
By: Richard McGee

My purchase of a gold watch chain on eBay helped bring healing to a painful situation. Flash back to 1974. My fiancée Laurie & I are preparing for our wedding celebration. We broke tradition and did everything ourselves. We chose to have an outdoor reception in my future in-law's backyard which encompassed a large, sprawling property with weeping willow trees, a Japanese gazebo and large pool. A beautiful setting for our special day. This required a lot of help and preparation since we invited 280 people and were preparing all the food ourselves. With the support of two families behind us, we decided to proceed.

In planning our day, we wanted to be unique in our other choices. My fiancée helped me select an all-white three piece linen suit which was unusual for a groom at that time (this was three years before *Saturday Night Fever*). The suit had a vest and watch pocket. Alas, I had no pocket watch. As a surprise wedding gift, Laurie presented me with a beautiful gold pocket watch, which I wore on our wedding day.

On our first anniversary, she followed up with a stunning solid gold serpentine watch chain. It was a magnificent gift for the start of our young lives together. The wedding and reception went off without a hitch, well into the night, and is fondly remembered by our families and friends to this day.

Flash forward to the present. For our 40th anniversary celebration, we will renew our vows and celebrate our lives together. We want to preserve as much tradition from the first ceremony as possible, as well as the blessings we have shared with our children, family and friends since. I decided it would be appropriate to wear my pocket watch for this important milestone.

Unfortunately, I discovered that my watch chain and fob were missing from their box. Stolen? Only my watch remained. As our search broadened, we discovered that many additional pieces of jewelry were missing. We realized how this theft must have occurred.

We had welcomed the son of a friend into our home. He had difficulty adjusting to his parents' divorce and financial crisis. During his ten month stay with us he encountered many problems, which we attempted to resolve as if he were our own family. Little did we know the theft was by his hands.

A painful loss of something extraordinarily sentimental that we felt could never be replaced.

Despite this, we decided to move on and attempt to replace the chain. We searched in jewelry stores and then on eBay. No luck. Good pocket watches and chains are scarce. As fate would have it, I decided to give eBay a second look. I discovered a chain which was both appropriate and elegant. I purchased it. It arrived and I added it to the watch, along with my grandfather's 18 karat gold fob. This purchase has proven to be a great solution to our problem in helping us to restore what was lost and to move ahead with renewed faith in life's possibilities.

Richard discovered the watch chain he purchased from me as a result of eBay Consignment. This wonderful antique chain belonged to a client who no longer needed it and it discovered a new home with Laurie and Richard McGee who filled a significant sentimental loss in the process.

Laurie and Richard Then and Now

Contents

Author's Acknowledgments

Writing this book has been a wonderful experience for me. But no part of it has given me more pleasure than this page, because so many friends and colleagues kindly walked beside me during this journey. I'd like to thank:

My mother, Dr. Carol Anne Rizvi, whose sacrifices raising me, and whose unconditional love and support throughout my life, have always inspired me to become the happy, successful man that I am today.

Kathy Ireland and our mentor Jason Winters, for their love and support. And all of my kathy ireland Worldwide colleagues for kindness and acceptance.

Marsha Collier, who stood beside me on many prominent stages and flew with me to cities large and small all across the country to evangelize eBay in its early years. She is an accomplished businessperson, incredible author and a truly amazing friend. Her wedding cake was the *best* I've tasted!

Kyle Jackson, an incredibly talented photographer who also served as art director and stylist in capturing the lifestyle images accompanying this book. Models Elise Christian, Paris Dylan and Anthony Usewicz. Hair and makeup artists Erin Nakashima and Joelle Pitts for ensuring the models looked flawless. Location manager and property master Jake Fehres, who came as a personal favor and is the bassist in the world-famous rock band The Calling (and his bass was used as a prop in the shoot). And Carlos Ortiz, a personal friend who helped inventory, organize, setup and strike; before, during and after the photo shoot.

Frank Dorman in the office of Public Affairs at the Federal Trade Commission, who provided the incredible content you'll find in the Appendix.

Jeff Chase, who while president of The Chase Group, was the general contractor for eBay tradeshows and show director of eBay Live! user conferences from 2000 to 2006, my close friend and brilliant mentor. Jeff single-handedly changed my world and moved me into a bigger and better direction with my life. As a result of his cajoling, I wrote this book.

Mike Richards, my best friend in the world, who gave me the first six items I ever listed on eBay selling on consignment.

Matt Wagner, literary agent extraordinaire, whose guidance, encouragement and insights continue to inspire my work. And for his rock-solid consistency.

Stephen P. Olejniczak, the author of *Telecom for Dummies*, who generously put me in touch with Matt Wagner, his agent as well.

All the eBay consignment sellers across the country who generously shared their stories—you'll see them at the top of each chapter.

Special thanks to Sally Milo for reaching out to many of those eBay users cited above and getting their wonderful stories.

Donita Woodruff, my research assistant and a published author in her own right, for her intelligence, hard work, and terrific way with people.

Craig Weeden, an accomplished author and screenwriter in his own right, who provided substantial and invaluable input and editing skills for this book.

All the eBay executive staff, directors, category managers, and product managers who asked me to act as eBay's official spokesperson at over a hundred conferences and tradeshows.

Special thanks to Jenny Henriques and Monique Svazlian who kept me so actively involved in public speaking for over five years at eBay University. Their kind support secured my position among the leading speakers for eBay.

My friends and colleagues who graciously agreed to read and critique sections of this book as I wrote them.

The many reviewers from all over the globe who provided correctness, clarity and course correction during the writing and publishing process.

A very appreciative thanks to every one of my students and eBay community members who educated and inspired me with their personal successes.

And thanks to Meg Whitman, former CEO of eBay and current CEO of Hewlett-Packard. Meg was one of my first customers and bought my Army Corps of Engineers compass on eBay. I had the pleasure of sharing a table with Meg for lunch and the conversation was inspirational and amazing.

And I'd like to thank my mom again for being the last person to review *GROW RICH with eBay Consignment* before it went to press.

Introduction

The $74,330.60 Garage...

"I wanted to throw it out—it was so ugly. And, of course, I thought it was worthless," she said.

"And I," drawled her husband, "almost dropped it—right out there." He nodded towards the Burbank, California, sidewalk in front of my store. "But I talked her out of trashing it."

The young couple and I peered down at what they had just brought to my eBay consignment store. There, on my counter, was a porcelain figurine of a whimsical nude woman sitting on a pear. The item, standing about ten inches high, was in mint condition and well-marked with "Lenci," the date 1930, and the artist's name. Didn't look like much. The three of us gazed at it with a mixture of skepticism and wild hope—it was an odd piece.

"I figured maybe $100," the young man said, referring to what I might be able to get for it on eBay on their behalf.

The young man's father had recently passed on, leaving a Burbank garage crammed with the fruits of 40 years of collecting with a very interesting eye. The couple was moving to Oregon and wanted to give me the entire contents of the garage to list for them on eBay.

I listed the Lenci figurine on eBay with a starting bid of $9.99. In a spectacular example of eBay magic, seven days later it brought $17,100 and went back to a collector in Italy, where it was made.

The contents of their garage brought $74,330.60.

I'm not going to say, "Just another day in the life of an eBay consignment seller." That garage was an extraordinary treasure. But if you decide to become an eBay consignment seller, I guarantee that every day there's surprise, gratification, and good old-fashioned creative work.

And my simple eBay consignment business has made me a millionaire.

The Streets Are Paved with Gold

First of all, I would like to thank you for taking the time to read my book. I am delighted that you have made the commitment to explore the world of eBay consignment. Not only have I created a successful business for myself on eBay and made lots of money in the process, but I have also taught thousands of people all over the world how to make money easily on eBay. And with this book, I will help you learn this new kind of entrepreneurialism. This can lead you on the path to financial freedom and a better life filled with interesting, fun and profitable surprises!

eBay consigners use eBay to help other people sell their items online, without the risk of having to actually purchase and hold inventory. Being your own boss is fun. Your clients need you, and you're their hero—generating cash from something they don't need. If you have a computer, an Internet connection, and a digital camera or smart phone, you can easily set up shop as an eBay consignment seller. And you won't need to spend another dollar to get started, because you'll be able to sell your clients' items before eBay charges you a single cent.

The Pokemon Incident

I started selling on eBay in the summer of 1998. While I was visiting my brother Buck and his family one evening, my nephew Matt proudly showed me his Pokemon trading card collection. Pokemon was quite popular at the time, and Matt had acquired these fun collectibles on a relatively new website called eBay. His father was helping him learn the art of using this innovative new online service, and Matt was simply thrilled by the whole experience—the eBay experience. Even on a sluggish dialup connection, eBay was cool and Matt was thrilled to be using this neat site to do something really awesome…connect with people in a safe and social way to trade nifty stuff.

This little random event changed my life forever—it gave me an idea for a new and exciting business venture.

Starting as a teenager, I had held various sales jobs and worked in public relations and special events production, and by 1998 I had become a very successful personal manager of actors. The money was fantastic, and I was good at making it. But I am a person in constant need of mental stimulation, and being a personal manager had become routine. Though I worked in the heart of the entertainment industry and was in constant contact with celebrities, I was in a rut. And I wanted to be the master of my own destiny—not a well-paid slave to the whims and demands of my clients.

The little Pokemon incident at my brother's house started the wheels turning in my head. My best friend in the world, Mike Richards, is a Beverly Hills antique dealer. One of my very first jobs as a teenager was working as an intern for his company, writing letters, running errands and handling his book work. By 1998, I knew that his business, the antiques business, was on the verge of dramatic changes.

The Expensive Doorstop

For many years I had tried and failed to get Mike interested in using a computer for his company. I actually forced him to buy a personal computer in the early 1990s, but this state-of-the-art device quickly turned into an expensive doorstop. But now the Internet had really taken off—its growth could only be described as explosive.

Shortly after learning about eBay from my nephew, I suggested to Mike that we try selling a few of his antiques on the eBay website. He agreed to consign me six nondescript war medals, in rather poor condition, to photograph and list on eBay. They were just a few bones that Mike threw me as a completely risk-free test case.

At the time, I owned a cool Sony Mavica digital floppy disk camera. Though very expensive then, with a resolution of 800,000 pixels, my camera was a mere toy by today's standards. I took several pictures of each medal and listed them on eBay. A week later, I returned to Mike with my findings. I sold all the medals for between $60 and $80 each.

Mike was stunned.

But now Mike was a believer. He promptly prepared another 60 items for me to photograph and list on eBay. Between actor/client phone calls and my regular business meetings, I handled the 60 eBay auctions: answering e-mail questions from prospective buyers, collecting payments, and shipping orders. Quickly this hobby turned into a real enterprise, and Mike, my only client, was bringing me between 100 and 400 items to list on eBay each week.

By 1999, I was shipping well over $30,000 a month in merchandise that I had sold on eBay. This was getting serious! I was now selling a wide variety of items for many new clients besides Mike, and I was getting paid on commission. Most of these clients came to me by word of mouth.

No Joke

One day, while I was busily handling my eBay hobby (that was still the way I thought of it, though it was certainly becoming a lucrative hobby), I got an e-mail from one of my eBay buyers who said that a relative of hers was a writer for *Time*. The magazine was preparing an Internet-themed edition with some stories about selling online, my buyer told me, and the writer wanted to interview me. Frankly, I thought this e-mail was a joke, but I played along. The next thing I knew, my entire office was taken over by a *Time* photographer who set up lights and tons of equipment to photograph me for this story. The writer, Sally B. Donnelly, conducted a very pleasant interview, and a few months later the phone was ringing off the hook.

People I hadn't spoken to since grade school were calling to congratulate me on being in *Time*. At that moment I realized I had really started something precious, wonderful, and amazing.

Substitute Teacher

The phone rang, and it was a man named John Slocum. John had written a computer program called Auction Assistant Pro—a listing management tool for eBay that automated and facilitated multiple auction listings. John knew that I had been using his program for my eBay business. He told me that someone from eBay would be calling me shortly, because they were looking for a substitute instructor for a class on Auction Assistant Pro at an event called eBay University. One of their instructors had fallen ill, and they knew that I was an avid user of eBay and this listing tool. Eventually, I found myself speaking in front of hundreds of eager students who yearned to learn eBay.

I believe this convergence of events happened for a reason. Fate (or something) was making a major change in the course of my life. I quit my job as an actors' manager and started selling on eBay full-time with a new, second job of teaching regular seminars for eBay University. Today, I have successfully listed more than 200,000 items on eBay, and I have spoken in front of tens of thousands of students at eBay University events. I have authored so many eBay-related educational presentations and technical manuals, and even produced instructional videos, that I have lost count. I now have a trusted staff that helps me run my eBay consignment business, and they are my invaluable allies.

My eBay consignment business started with zero personal investment. I did not have to quit my day job, although I wanted to and finally did. The money I have earned from my eBay sales has enabled me to purchase investment properties such as apartment buildings, houses, condos, a motel, a hotel, a bar and a restaurant. My eBay business has generated great wealth for me and given me the freedom to do whatever I want whenever I want.

Not an Easy Decision

And now I have to speak frankly about my decision to write this book—it did not come easily. I have had no problem sharing my eBay success tips with students these many years, and I believe that there is so much business online that there is plenty enough to go around. I do not feel you're going to somehow jeopardize my business by becoming a success story like me.

There are many, many how-to eBay books on the market, and much of the material needed to start a successful business is already in print. My dear friend and colleague, Marsha Collier, has written arguably the most successful how-to books on eBay with her *Dummies* series, and I would strongly urge you to buy her *Starting an eBay Business for Dummies* (Wiley Publishing) as a companion to this book.

However, I saw a void in the marketplace on the subject of eBay consignment. Nobody had really captured the true nuts-and-bolts essence of starting a "hired-gun" consignment business from scratch.

Model T Time

If you're wondering if you're starting too late and that eBay has already matured— nothing could be further from the truth! This book could be your passport to financial freedom. Online retailing is still growing impressively, and actually you're seizing this opportunity at the perfect time. If you compare the Internet to the auto industry, we are still in the "Model T" years. There will be plenty of business out there for you. With some determination and patience, you will reap the rewards of consignment trading for others on eBay, and you can be as successful as I have been. You will reach any level of success that you choose, because now you have the tools to achieve it.

Nuts and Bolts

I'm a nuts-and-bolts kind of guy. I wrote this book for anyone interested in starting their own eBay consignment business. Maybe you're a mom thinking of starting at your kitchen table. And maybe flipping through this book, you saw a chapter heading about buying a commercial building and thought, "This book's not for me—I'll never buy a building!" Or, "Employees! You have to be kidding." Well, Mom, this book is for you. In fact, I wrote it just for you. And everyone else interested in eBay consignment.

This book doesn't have chapters on photography or how to write great eBay listings—plenty of other books out there cover topics like these, and eBay's own help boards and free tutorials are a great resource for these subjects and a lot more.

This book is nuts-and-bolts—a nitty-gritty blueprint for running an online eBay consignment business. It takes you step by step through the entire process of setting up your business and making it a fantastic success. If you think you'll never buy a commercial building or have even a single, part-time employee, feel free to skip those chapters. But Mom, you and everyone else who wants to *GROW RICH with eBay Consignment* will need to know about contracts, about how to find and keep great clients with great (and profitable) merchandise to list on eBay, about how to set your fees, about wonderful software specifically designed for consignment . . . it's all here—the nuts and bolts of starting and running your own successful business. So have a seat, whether at your kitchen table or the desk in your 4,000-square-foot warehouse, and read on.

In this book, you will find:

- Proven, step-by-step techniques for planning, starting, and executing a successful, profitable eBay consignment business
- Great ideas for finding the best clients who have valuable items they don't want or need
- Low-cost marketing programs to help even the most cash-strapped entrepreneur get immediate and highly profitable results
- The secrets of unlimited free publicity
- Tips for avoiding technology pitfalls
- Routines for streamlining day-to-day operations, including packing and shipping secrets, inventory handling techniques, accounting procedures, and much more

- Indispensable guidance on client and employee relations
- Profiles and case studies of the most profitable eBay consignment successes, both home-based and brick-and-mortar

My Bumper-to-Bumper Guarantee

I am so very confident about this mission, so convinced of your ability to *GROW RICH with eBay Consignment*, that I will personally guarantee your satisfaction with my book. If, after applying the techniques and tips I have provided, you're not completely satisfied, I will personally refund 100 percent of your purchase price. Simply send proof of purchase and the book to:

Christopher Matthew Spencer

PO Box 1862

Beverly Hills, CA 90213-1862

I welcome you into my circle of friends. Please feel free to write me with your very own tips, ideas, and personal success stories. Please know that I am *accessible.* I welcome interaction with you. Not only can you find me on social media, but you are always welcome to email me. My email is borntodeal@gmail.com.

You have begun a unique and fascinating journey, and I'm honored to be your guide through this valuable educational experience. We'll have plenty of fun working together as I show you the ropes. With your enthusiasm and a bit of patience and determination, you, too, will be trading online for friends, coworkers, and clients with your very own eBay consignment empire. You will become your own boss. It is time to claim your piece of this growing opportunity.

Remember that Lenci I sold for $17,100? Those deals are *really* out there and you can grow rich helping your very own clients make mega-bucks on the items they no longer want or need.

1. The eBay Consignment Business

A woman brought me a Walt Disney Mickey Mouse light bulb that was made in the 1930s. She had purchased it at a garage sale for $0.50. I sold it for $463.88! My husband started on eBay with baseball cards, and he enjoyed it so much he suggested I talk to businesses around town to help them sell as well. I used to clean offices for a living, and now I own my own business that takes great care of my family. I have five kids and really enjoy the success we have with selling for other people on eBay. I started working from home and eventually opened my own eBay drop-off store.

—Amy Reedy, Lowell, Michigan; eBay user ID "globalduk"; trading on eBay since December 19, 1997

The Name of the Game

In October 1999, just when *Time* magazine was talking about eBay success stories, including mine, I had started doing something—selling for others—of growing interest to others at eBay.

eBay University had been formed, and by the fall of 2001, I had started working regularly as a guest speaker at hotels across the country. eBay University was developed to educate buyers and sellers about using eBay effectively and safely. eBay had seen my article in *Time* and asked me to join the ranks of their instructors. Students eager to learn how to sell on eBay flooded these classes by the thousands. Many of my students were curious about my particular eBay business—selling on consignment—and asked for tips on how they could start their very own business like mine.

eBay management noticed that a lot of people seemed to have merchandise they wanted to sell on eBay but, for a variety of reasons, couldn't or wouldn't sell it themselves. Many of eBay's top sellers, also known as PowerSellers, were doing a good percentage of their business by selling items on consignment.

Everyone has unwanted items lying around. I certainly do, even though I am an active seller on eBay. If you can't find items of your own right away, then start by asking family members, friends, and coworkers. After all, this will be one of the primary ways you will get business for your new enterprise—by asking people!

This book is not an eBay selling book—it is an eBay consignment book—so you will find few eBay 101 tips here. However, the basics of selling on eBay are free and readily available on the eBay Seller Information Center. You can find these selling (and buying) resources at pages.ebay.com/education. eBay makes selling easy—that's why millions of people are doing it. Just take the eBay tutorials and you'll be up and running in no time.

You will need digital pictures of your items, and hopefully you can borrow a digital camera if you don't have one. Today's smart phones take truly phenomenal photos and pictures captured with a phone are certainly going to work well. Remember, the goal here will be to get started and gain some selling experience and momentum. Don't obsess or get bogged down because of analysis paralysis. You're fully capable and ready to start selling. You will learn with practice and a bit of trial and error.

Getting to 100

Feedback is the heart of the eBay system. Each eBay member can leave another member a feedback comment in connection with an actual transaction between them on eBay. So you must be either the buyer or seller to leave a feedback comment.

Feedback on eBay is straightforward and easy to understand:

- +1 point to your feedback score for each positive comment and rating left for you
- 0 points to your feedback score for each neutral comment and rating left for you
- -1 point to your feedback score for each negative comment and rating left for you

Selling items at high prices will require a reputation and that reputation will be developed by selling items. It's a bit of a catch-22, but selling your own items will be your springboard. Let's try to get to 100 before selling anything too valuable. Buyers of more expensive items will scrutinize your feedback more carefully than those individuals buying something inexpensive.

You can reach a feedback score of 100 not only by selling items but also by buying. Because not all eBay community members automatically give feedback comments following a transaction, it is important to communicate with the other member after a successful transaction and ask for feedback if they have not left any for you already. Clearly, maintaining a good relationship with your trading partner is important as a seller (and buyer) during the transaction, so feedback is the natural result of a successful trade. (Chapters 18 through 20 deal with various aspects of customer service.)

Also, note that the feedback score is actually the net sum of all the positive comments you receive from unique eBay members, less the sum of all the negative comments you receive from unique eBay members. In other words, you can't get a score of 100 if all your feedback comments are from the same member. Each member can only affect your score by one point, so while building your initial feedback rating, you'll want to trade with at least 100 different eBay members.

If you're an honest person with good manners and you treat your trading partners on eBay well, you will never even have to worry about poor marks. When you trade often enough on eBay, the possibility always exists that another member may give you negative feedback. You can't make everyone happy all of the time. The key here is that you have to make sure that most of your trading partners are happy with you. Something important to mention…only buyers can leave a negative comment for sellers. Sellers can never leave a negative feedback for a buyer.

eBay's top sellers, PowerSellers, must maintain an overall positive feedback score of 98 percent or greater to maintain their PowerSeller status.

As an enhancement to the buyer's ability to rate you with a positive, neutral or negative transaction score, eBay also permits buyers to leave detailed seller ratings (DSRs) for item as described, communication, shipping time; and shipping and handling charges.

eBay Rules

Staying on eBay's good side is also a requirement for being a seller. Being an eBay seller is very similar to having a driver's license. The privilege can be taken away from you if you don't navigate eBay's roads lawfully. If you break any major rules, you can find your account temporarily or permanently suspended. When eBay suspends a user, eBay is suspending the individual, not just a specific account, so you cannot simply walk away from a suspended account and start a new one.

Keeping an account in good standing is easy, if you take the time to understand the basics. Of course you should sell only legal items, and be sure that none of your items are prohibited on the eBay site. There are a lot of rules, but most of them were implemented by eBay to protect consumers and avoid bad experiences and, therefore, require only common sense to follow. For example, you may not list items that promote or glorify hatred, violence, racial or religious intolerance or items that promote organizations with such views. For example, KKK items are prohibited on eBay and would result in your listing being removed.

Linking from your eBay listing to another website is generally prohibited as is selling controlled items such as tobacco, alcohol, or drugs. There are other types of restrictions as well. If you use the words gold, silver, or diamond, or other words that describe precious metals or gems, for instance, you have to make certain you're accurately describing the materials that exist in your item. And you can't sell a fake Rolex or a counterfeit Louis Vuitton handbag—or anything counterfeit for that matter. Using your noggin will help here, because you already know these items are illegal and eBay does not allow the sale of illegal or questionable items.

This can all sound rather daunting at first, but in the most basic terms, be honest in your listings and take some time to read eBay's policy about a particular item before making your listings. That way, you'll be in fine shape and out of harm's way. The link to eBay's Rules and Policies can be found at pages.ebay.com/help/policies/index.html.

With a little care and prepared with the right information, you will be able to keep everything "smooth sailing" and trade safely and securely on the eBay marketplace.

Before Going "Pro"

When I first started, I had only one client, my best friend Mike. As my business grew, I found that having more clients kept a steady stream of merchandise coming in, and my sales grew along with the acquisition of new clients. There are lots of ways to acquire new clients. Before you jump into the pool, toe-test the waters. Become a proficient seller with your own items and those of your family and friends. Master the art of eBay and get good at it before you start reaching out to develop new customers.

Cat Got Your Ming?

If you don't plan to open a brick-and-mortar store, you will most likely conduct your new business from home. If you live with others, it is important to share the details of your new business with your housemates or family. What may seem like a harmless venture to you may be viewed as an annoyance by roomies who don't share your vision (or your profits).

You will want dedicated space to handle storage of items for sale, and keeping fragile items out of harm's way will be crucial. The last thing you want is to find that a very expensive painting has a big yellow stain from your faithful dog, or to come home and discover that a pricey vase has been knocked over by your feline pal. It is important to think ahead and avoid these unfortunate possibilities. Maybe you have a spare room, a spot in your basement, a corner in the garage, or some other suitable place to use for your clients' items.

Be sure your family or housemates understand and approve of your use of the living quarters for this new enterprise and don't find your new activity intrusive. You will want everyone's blessing. Keep in mind that items of good quality and in demand will sell quickly and be out of the house pretty fast. (On the other hand, shabby, useless items could be around for a while!)

You will also have to convince some clients that you can be trusted with their valuable items, and in some cases, the most skeptical of clients will have the best items for sale. You don't want to sell junk (I will drive this point home quite a few times in this book), and a clean, well-organized work space will allow you the possibility of having clients over. Looking professional and on top of things is very important, even when working from home. It's not mandatory that your clients meet you at your residence, but being well organized will help with your sanity and make the business more enjoyable and efficient for you in the long run.

Tip: I strongly suggest you maintain physical possession (and therefore control) of the items you are selling on your eBay account for others

But maybe you already have a business of your own, or perhaps you have a really cool boss who will let you set up your shop part-time at your job (perhaps in exchange for occasionally selling the boss' items for a reduced fee). If so, the same organizational concept will not only still apply but will be even more critical, because as a businessperson, you probably have many other tasks to handle in the course of a day, and you won't want to lose track of things or fall behind in any way. If you have customers or clients coming to your own place of business on a daily basis, their visits will be golden opportunities for you to sell your new eBay consignment services to them. After all, they already know and respect you.

Your Toolbox

If you have already been selling on eBay, you probably have most or all of the basic equipment you need to start your business, such as:

- Modern computer system (with an Internet connection)
- Printer
- Copier
- Scanner
- Fax
- Digital camera or smart phone
- Tripod (optional)
- Backdrop or background for photography
- Photo lighting equipment

Each of these (and a lot more) is discussed in depth in Chapter 13, "Technology."

Don't Doubt Yourself

American households have approximately $3,100 worth of unused items lying around (A.C. Nielsen, "Survey of Unused Household Items," April 2007).

Okay, I really think the time to ask this question is now and not later: Are you really sure you want to do this? My eBay consignment business has been one of the best experiences in my professional career. It taught me so much about business and life. It took me in many directions and introduced me to many amazing and helpful people. And it earned me a significant income. However, what I'll be teaching you isn't a gimmick; I won't be waving a magic wand that somehow turns you into a millionaire.

The reality is that this business, like any business, is going to involve study and work. Are you up to the challenge? I am totally confident that I am taking you down the path of success, if you follow my techniques and tips, but your success is measured by you, not by me or anyone else. Your idea of success is all that matters. Perhaps you want to sell a few items here and there for your friends in your spare time and keep a tidy flow of extra money coming in on the side. Maybe you love your job and have no interest in quitting. If you need a hobby, this is a great way to try something fun, interesting, and new.

Perhaps you already run a business and want your customers to keep coming to you to buy new "stuff," and you want to help them get rid of their old items to keep the upgrade cycle going. After all, you sold them what they have now and want to keep on selling to them.

Maybe you want to set up a dedicated drop-off store and sell items full-time as a brick-and-mortar business. This is a very big undertaking, but if you have the working capital, it is a lucrative and relatively low-cost proposition when compared to many other business opportunities out there.

Whether you're a businessperson, lumberjack, lawyer, accountant, homemaker, sanitation worker, teacher, cab driver—it really doesn't matter—you have made a decision to do something new in your life, whether full- or part-time. Remember, however, that you will be handling other people's items, and even though you will be charging them a fee, at the end of the day you will have to give them the lion's share of the proceeds from the sale of their items. This means handling and accounting for money. You're their trusted eBay listing professional, and you have to earn that trust by delivering consistent and quality work.

If you have absolutely no work ethic, it is time to start playing the lotto or asking mom and dad for some dollars. If you have a reasonable amount of determination, a great attitude, and the necessary time, however, you will be well on your way to helping other people relieve themselves of clutter, while pocketing a tidy profit at the same time.

Are you ready to keep going? I thought so! Put aside any fears you may have right now, because I'm going to empower you with the tools, tips, and tricks to make this a great experience!

2. Writing Your Initial Business Plan

I sold $21,500 worth of IT equipment, servers, computer monitors, and other items for a New York corporation. I earned $4,300 from the project, which represented my 20 percent commission. The client was in a skyscraper with limited space, and they really appreciated my pickup service. We were both very happy from the sales.
—Jack Cheung, New York City; eBay user ID "ebargainnow"; trading on eBay since December 18, 1998

Hold the Mayo . . . Where's the Plan?

Before you run out of the room screaming in terror over the idea of writing a business plan, it's time to relax and take a deep breath—it's really not hard or complicated to plan your successful future pursuing an eBay consignment business. If you're a seasoned businessperson, this chapter can serve as a review; or if you're already familiar with writing business plans, you can certainly meander on to the next chapter. You may also be asking yourself "Why in the world do I need a business plan, if all I want to do is sell a couple of items a week for close friends and family?"

If your new business will serve simply as a fun adventure and handling and making a lot of money is not part of your future ambitions, then a professional and formally written business plan won't be terribly important. But even when you make the decision to buy a computer, invest in a camera, or purchase supplies for your new business—or basically make any decision about money—you have made a plan. A business plan can be a simple set of notes or guidelines you use in your everyday activities or it can be a comprehensive written guide prepared for securing outside financing to start a brick-and-mortar eBay drop-off consignment store. Whatever your goals, however large or small, you'll need a plan to be successful. Establishing fees for your work and budgeting expenses will be part of some form of real, practical business plan to keep the operation running smoothly and profitably. And a business plan may be required if you seek financing from someone else, unless you have a rich uncle who loves to write you checks.

The nuts and bolts of a professional business plan will accurately establish your business model, set goals, and create a "resume" for your business. Using a business plan for your operations will help you to allocate resources (money, employees, time, etc.)—incalculably important decisions when the unexpected inevitably happens. A great business plan will be a critical part of taking your eBay business to a higher level.

Roll Up Your Sleeves

As a consignment business, your customers will need to understand your hours and days of operation, areas of specialty, languages spoken, services, fees, and terms and conditions.

As part of your research, it would be a good idea to start a three-ring binder with a set of tab separators to help you stay organized. Some logical tabs to create for this binder might be:

- Company information
- The competition and fee-pricing ideas
- Management/Employment
- Marketing
- Operations
- Financials

These tabs are suggestions which you can change or add to as your needs dictate. If you're a product of the computer generation, you can certainly develop and store these documents on your computer. I generally place all my important files on Google Drive, which is a cloud-based computing system offered free with Gmail.

Company information. In this section, you will want to add information regarding your planned business structure (we'll chat about this in Chapter 3), possible licensing requirements, registered business/trade name paperwork (your d/b/a or doing-business-as name), and anything else that might relate to your new company's formation.

> Tip: Research eBay for packing and office supplies. Use eBay's distance-based search to help find local sellers and cut down on shipping costs—you can even pick up your purchases if the seller offers this convenience.

The competition and fee-pricing ideas. Here you can keep notes on your competition's fees and how they charge. You might consider that your competition also includes consignment shops, consignment malls, co-ops, auctioneers, etc. You can regularly update this information as you survey the competition quarterly, biannually, or however often you feel is helpful. This might well be one of your most important tabs, because you will be keeping "tabs" on the competition.

Management/Employment. Here you will keep any documents relating to people you hire, if and when you decide to hire employees. You can also add information on any outside experts who might join your team part-time to help list specialized items for you. My company often uses such experts, and we keep a list of them. These resources can come in very handy. You can also add the contact information for any accountants, attorneys, or other professionals who will eventually make up the management team of your business.

Marketing. This can be your ideas tab, where you keep marketing ideas, plans, and programs. You'll want to cast a big net here. Fill this section of your binder with as many good free and paid marketing concepts and ideas as you can. Anytime you receive inspiration for a marketing idea, jot it down in this section immediately so that you don't forget it.

Operations. You'll often need supplies, and lists of vendors, price lists, and other details can be retained here. I find it very helpful to keep a master list of my suppliers. I spend a great deal of time finding the best prices for the everyday things I need; and with a busy company to manage, I like to keep good records so that I can quickly determine where I obtained the best price on photography backgrounds or bulbs or just plain old staples, printer paper, and the like. Ordering online is quite a time saver, so I keep website addresses as well as vendor names and phone numbers. Vendors that offer online ordering and free delivery are at the top of my vendor list.

Financials. Eventually, you will set up a separate bank account for your business, and you may also want to retain monthly financials to help you track your income and plan taxes. Remember that you're now your own boss, and any money you make is income upon which you most likely will have to pay taxes to Uncle Sam. Keep receipts in envelopes and put them in this section. An easy way to do this is simply to punch holes in the envelopes and secure them in your binder with the receipts securely inside. If you're a QuickBooks user, you will find a wealth of QuickBooks-compatible apps and services at appcenter.intuit.com/category/mobile to help you capture receipts, track expenses and interface seamlessly with QuickBooks.

Know Your Neighbors

I encourage you to research as many consignment shops, auction houses and estate sales companies as possible. Focus on the competition within 10 to 20 miles of you. This includes any eBay consignment businesses. Google, Bing and Yahoo! are your research friends. Study their scope of services and determine how you might be able to set yourself apart from them. Here are some questions you might want to ask yourself:

- How much experience do they have?
- How long have they been in business?
- Can you offer better hours?
- Would you be willing to pick up items from your clients? Does your competition offer this service?
- How do they structure their commissions and fees?
- Are their fees easy to understand or too complex for the average person?
- Do they charge an up-front listing fee for accepting an item and listing it in addition to a fee for a successful sale?
- Do they pass along the cost of eBay and PayPal, or other expenses in addition to their commission, or are their fees all-inclusive?
- Are their fees graduated (i.e., do they vary depending upon the final sale price of the item)?
- Do they have restrictions on the value, size, or type of item they will accept?
- Do they specialize or generalize?
- Do they have a drop-off location (physical store), or do they work from home?
- What is the quality of their photography and listing descriptions?
- What are their strengths and what are their weaknesses?

Take the time to thoroughly understand your competition's operation and try to think of ways you might be able to compete with them. If you're not a competitive person by nature, you will eventually develop a sense for these details; but in the meantime, seek out other business owners and ask their opinions. Mentoring with business veterans is a treasure. But don't forget that simply offering great service itself goes a long way: referrals from happy customers are the lifeblood of any company.

Your Reconnaissance Mission

You have uncovered a great number of secrets about your competitors through research. Let's try something a little unorthodox and perhaps a bit scary—let's pay them a visit! Commit yourself to an entire day to visit and evaluate every competitor you've found nearby.

I have dropped into the physical stores of many eBay drop-off businesses and learned a great deal in the process. One of the great confidence-building elements of this concept is that most eBay traders are real people, not big corporations with fancy equipment and elaborate marketing campaigns.

Drop into each of your competitor's stores. Be sure to review the checklist of questions (noted above) before arriving and have a positive and open-minded attitude. As you walk in the door, prepare to mentally answer all of the questions we posed earlier. You may want to write each question down on an index card for quick reference. Before you jump into a conversation with your competitor and get butterflies and knots in your stomach, be sure to see if they have brochures on display and, if so, immediately ask if you can have one.

Visually scan their operation and see how it is run. If you're planning to open a brick-and-mortar store, analyze the store layout, the equipment in view, and the supplies being used.

Introduce yourself and explain that you're starting your own eBay consignment business. Take the temperature in the room and determine if you're being perceived as friend or foe. You might be delighted to find that most businesspeople are friendly and willing to help someone who is starting their own business. The average businessperson has worked hard to start their business and, in actuality, they respect anyone willing to try to make a go of it. But if you sense that you're not welcome, thank them for the brochure, mentally scoop up all your observations, and make a courteous exit. Then immediately write down everything you observed and discovered while visiting.

If you're met with a smile, chat a bit and gather some tips and ideas. Many of the eBay consignment shops, as well as local businesses near me, provide client referrals. Amazingly, a good deal of my referrals come from other eBay sellers who feel I am more knowledgeable or better qualified than they, or who simply have too much business and cannot handle all of it. Smart businesspeople view a competitor as a potential ally. A nice person attracts other nice people, and in business you will need friends. Be sure to keep written notes so that you will be able to recall quickly which folks were friendly and who was not.

> Tip: If you are not met with a friendly face when you visit your competition, perhaps you can recruit a friend or family member to act as your very own secret shopper. Your secret shopper can then go to the competitor with an actual item in hand and experience their process firsthand.

Spend as much time as you can talking with your new friend and let them do as much of the talking as possible. Pay close attention to any mention of challenges that come up in their day-to-day operations and, again, when you leave their store, immediately write down everything you have learned for later reference. You may find that many of these observations fit into your Competition tab, but some of the informational jewels you carry out might become ideas for your Marketing tab.

Some possible questions include:

- How seasonal is your business?
- Do you get a lot of referrals?
- What are some of the ways you attract new clients?
- Do you get a lot of repeat business from existing clients, or are most one-shot deals?
- Have you run into any pitfalls? What were they?
- How much could a person expect to earn in the industry working full-time?

The last question might be getting a bit personal, but with the right amount of diplomacy, you can often get a straight answer about how much they are netting from their operation. Any such information must be kept in perspective, however, as sometimes people boast, or they may be overly conservative.

After you have spent the day visiting with the competitors in your local area, review your notes and transfer the best ideas onto index cards. You will appreciate having taken the time to do this when you write your final business plan.

Who Else Is on Your Heels?

As mentioned earlier, eBay consignment businesses are not your only competition.

One possible source of competition will be trade-in programs at local retailers. Many retailers offer to take used merchandise as a trade-in towards the purchase of something new. In most cases, your would-be clients would not get nearly as much in value for their trade-in as they will receive when you sell it—even after your commission is deducted. You could also leverage this to your advantage and offer these retailers your services. Having them in your corner will cut down on prospecting for new clients, allowing you to focus on listing and selling!

Nonprofits in your local area pose an interesting situation, as they are both competitors and prospective clients. Often, items donated to local nonprofits are then sold at costly and time-consuming fundraising events. Many items are even disposed of, because the organization has no suitable way to convert them into cash. You can form a symbiotic relationship here. Help the nonprofits by having them direct their patron saints to you and then sell their donations for them on eBay. In this way, the nonprofits will ultimately receive more in real dollars by benefitting from your tech savvy and eBay expertise.

Some individuals want to make a donation, but the nonprofits cannot accept the types of items they have to offer. You can help the philanthropist give cash to the nonprofit instead by converting the item into dollars on eBay.

Promote yourself vigorously or you may be left out of the loop simply because people aren't aware of you and your services. One very prominent nonprofit here in Burbank used the services of an out-of-area eBay consignment company, because they didn't know I existed. Generating awareness is a top priority.

Auctioneers and consignment shops may also become valued clients. Friendly auctioneers and consignment shops can be great sources of top-quality merchandise. Auctioneers often have unsold items, and in your capable hands, this "dead stock" becomes fast cash. Consignment shops also run into this situation, and a heavy mink coat hanging in a shop in California might do better on eBay. There aren't many cold days here!

You may also educate customers by generating a need where there was none. Many of us don't think of the money sitting idly in our garage or attic. Many families let valuable stuff go for cheap prices at garage sales.

Keeping It Real

Let's bring all of this into focus and have a reality check. An eBay consignment business, like any other business, requires patience and time to develop. Don't quit your day job until you've explored and tested the waters. If you're still reading this section, you obviously consider a business plan important. If you're becoming a bit overwhelmed at this point, don't worry—that's natural. Bookmark this section and come back after a day to digest everything you'll do to collect the data, ideas, thoughts, and notes on your business plan.

If you're seeking financial assistance to start your business, especially with a brick-and-mortar drop-off store, you will be pitching your idea to family members with money, investors, or banks. It is imperative that you express, in fair and real terms, the risks inherent in this industry. You will have acquired quite a bit of knowledge at this point, and you will be able to articulate these risks in realistic terms. Remember that anyone investing in you will not believe that this or any other business is a "sure thing." A solid business plan will include an explanation not only of the competition but any other potential risks, such as seasonality factors. Giving due consideration to the downside will display your forethought and risk-planning ability. Your business plan must also foresee all working capital requirements and a contingency allowance to cover any margin of error. If this is your first business, it is very easy to underestimate the total costs involved. Be conservative until you have a handle on both the income and expenses associated with this endeavor.

Walking in the Shoes of Those before You

Unlike a lot of what you were taught while growing up and in school, it is perfectly okay to copy another business plan. (But not to steal one!) If you know of anyone who has successfully obtained financing through investors or a bank, ask if you can review their business plan and tailor it for your own use. Many business plans are simply repurposed from other plans, and there is no point in completely reinventing the wheel. I seriously doubt you will get much resistance from most businesspeople when asking for this permission, because their mission is accomplished. They won't need that plan again, and they will very likely be willing to help out a fellow entrepreneur. Repurposing a successful business plan also prevents repeating someone else's past mistakes.

Copying the plan verbatim is not a great idea. You will want to start taking out those index cards, comparing your notes with the sections in the plan you're using as your model. It is never okay simply to take someone else's document from the Internet (or anywhere else) without permission. Ask for permission, however, and you will probably get it.

Some superior ideas on business plans come from the United States government. The Small Business Administration (SBA) has great tips on writing your plan, which you can find at www.sba.gov/category/navigation-structure/starting-managing-business/starting-business/how-write-business-plan.

If you hate typing long Web addresses, you can simply enter the phrase "business plan" into Google and find the same page in seconds. Take the time to review the SBA's best practices for business plans, just to start generally absorbing the concepts. There's a large amount of information on their website, and it can become a time bandit if you're not careful. Don't obsess too much about it; simply review some sample business plans. There's also a commercial website that provides hundreds of free sample plans called Bplans.com, found at www.bplans.com.

You may have noticed that I'm referring you to a lot of websites. It's important to realize that there are literally millions of websites that provide resource materials for virtually any topic on small businesses. I'm recommending my favorite sites, but if you know a better resource for a particular subject, please use it.

"Hey, wait a minute!" you exclaim to yourself. "Wasn't this chapter about writing a business plan? What's going on? You haven't shown me an actual written business plan for an eBay consignment business. Why not?"

The business plan is like an uncarved piece of marble—you grab your hammer and chisel and start slowly chipping away until a fabulous statue eventually appears—and this is how you will develop your plan. Don't rush it, and it isn't necessary to hold up your new enterprise while you formulate this plan. You can go ahead and test the waters. In fact, starting to sell items for other people right away will clarify the needs of your business and the possibilities for future growth, and it will help you to develop that beautiful piece of artwork on paper that will help to convey your ideas to an investor or a bank.

But if you don't intend to seek financing for this new business enterprise, you have already created a basic business plan! Remember that a professional business plan is typically used when you're asking for money. A much simpler business plan is all that's needed to help you organize your daily operations, and you will be able to add more valuable information to your binder about financial projections, company legal structure, insurance, and many other details as you progress through your journey.

What goes in a formal business plan to seek financing? Much of what you have already garnered from your research will become the puzzle pieces that make up your plan.

You will need to cover:

- Description of the business
- Marketing
- Finances
- Management

You can and should add your resume and a concise autobiography to the plan, as well as any documents to support your theories and projections. The plan should be neatly typed with proper spelling and grammar (thank you, Spellchecker!). There is no right or wrong way to write your professional business plan, as long as it contains the essential elements—who, what, where, when, why, and how—of what you will be doing and why you need money to get started. When you sit down and start typing this all up, you will want to speak in your own voice, without fancy language or complicated terminology. Remember that your target audience (e.g., a bank) may not be an expert in your field. You're the expert, and you should write with confidence and in an informational and educational voice.

Detailing Your Plan

The core elements of a business plan are summarized in this outline. Each section is already supported by much of the factual research you conducted earlier. After you have drafted your first plan, you will want to share it with "safe" individuals, such as other businesspeople, family, and friends, and get their feedback.

Be sure to include:

- A cover sheet with the proposed company name and
    - your complete legal name;
    - address;
    - telephone number;

- o fax number (optional); and
- o e-mail address.
- A mission statement, explaining why you're venturing into this business
- A complete description of the business operation, including the definition of the eBay consignment company's core activities and the benefits to your clients
- A section on your marketing plans and how you intend to keep customers coming. If you have prospective clients already lined up, it is helpful to mention it here and give a complete list of everyone from whom you have a client commitment. If you have a list of existing clients, ask for permission from them to give out their contact information as references.
- A list of your competitors and why you feel you will be able to do better, and/or how you may be able to work with the competition
- A detailed technical explanation of your operation—how you plan to handle photography, listing, storage, shipping, etc.
- A list of the employees you intend to hire and their job descriptions (nothing fancy, just what they will do for you)
- A list of insurance companies who are willing to provide liability and hazard insurance (and, if you hire employees, worker's compensation insurance)
- A list of all the equipment purchases you will need to make, as well as estimates of the costs of improvements on your business location
- Your personal financial statement (the standard form from the SBA can be found at www.sba.gov/sites/default/files/tools_sbf_finasst413_0.pdf or you can find many helpful templates at office.microsoft.com)
- A spreadsheet that shows the break-even analysis of your business (the amount you will have to sell to cover all your expenses)
- Income projections to show the future potential of your business operation as your sales grow
- Your personal tax returns for the past three years
- Your business tax returns for the past three years if you presently operate another business or businesses
- Copies of your proposed lease agreement with a landlord or purchase contract for your building

- Copies of any business licenses which you presently hold
- A copy of your resume and bio

If you're not familiar with making spreadsheets and financial projections, it's okay! These projections do not have to be fancy or complex, and in general your services are rather simple and easy to understand. You sell an item and deduct your commission. You know your expenses, such as your rent or mortgage, utilities, miscellaneous office supplies, etc. You can easily put together some basic assumptions and then share them with your peers for evaluation.

SCORE It

America is a great country. The powerful benefits of living here include all of the wonderful organizations that exist merely to help small businesses, of which the SBA is just one. Another tremendously valuable resource is the Service Corps of Retired Executives (SCORE), comprised of successful business owners and executives who provide free and confidential counseling face-to-face and via e-mail. This priceless resource is available to anyone who asks (within a few simple guidelines—see below), whether starting or already in business.

SCORE volunteers will not write your business plan, fill out your tax returns, or run your business for you. Their entire mission is to provide mentoring and education to you as a small business owner. You can visit their website at www.score.org and locate a local SCORE office that services your area, or you can request a consultation by e-mail. Because the SCORE website (like the SBA's) provides a plethora of resources, as before, I caution you to avoid the time bandits and stay focused. A volunteer from this fine organization can review your business plan and give you comments, a valuable step before you present the plan to others.

On the SCORE home page you can enter keywords and locate volunteers who have experience in the specific kind business you're starting. You have discovered gold, my friend! Imagine getting free help from the retired CEO of a major company in reviewing and critiquing your business plan.

To use SCORE's services, you must be at least 13 years of age (yes, they teach them young!) as well as a U.S. citizen or holder of a Resident Worker visa (green card.) Also, as a condition of your free consulting with the SCORE volunteer, you will be required to review and accept their terms and conditions:

- That you will cooperate if selected to participate in surveys designed to evaluate the SBA's small business assistance programs (SCORE is a Resource Partner with the Small Business Administration.)

- That the counselor will ask relevant information from you about the business operations and will agree to keep this information in the strictest of confidence

- That the counselor will not recommend any resource, vendor, or other service for which they have a vested financial or other interest (to avoid conflict of interest)

- That the counselor may not accept fees or commissions in exchange for providing you with their time

- That you will waive any right to bring a claim against SCORE or their related organizations in connection with the advice that they have given you (e.g., if they tell you to jump off a bridge, you can't sue them for the medical bills, pain and suffering, etc.)

Scan the Plan

I have found that scanning documents and converting them into Adobe Acrobat PDF (Portable Document File) format make life much easier, and when distributing your business plan, it will speed things up quite dramatically. Acrobat is a software program that converts documents from a scanner and a myriad of other document file formats (including Word, Excel, PowerPoint, etc.) into the PDF format, which can be viewed on virtually any computer. With the current standard version of this program costing a small fortune, you will probably not want to make the investment in owning your own copy just for this one project. I suggest collecting any notes, ideas, and comments you garnered that may help to sell your business plan. Take them down to your local copy shop, Internet café, or other computer business and see if you can rent time with a scanner and do the conversion yourself, without the cost of buying the program. There's a powerful, free PDF converter tool called pdfcreator that you can download by visiting www.pdfforge.org.

For Apple computer users, visit the Apple Store and check out PDF Converter Free by Wondershare Software. PC users can try OpenOffice (www.openoffice.org), which is a free, robust office suite and a very good substitute for Microsoft Office. I'll talk more about this program later in the book. Any document that is prepared in Google Drive can also be exported into a PDF. OpenOffice and Google Drive are not capable of converting paper documents into a PDF, but they can save any document that is prepared within the program to the PDF format.

If you intend to e-mail your plan, the scans will be invaluable—you can always make hard copies if you're mailing or hand-delivering your plan. And remember, you will come across as a complete pro when you include the printed profiles of your competition. This shows that you did the work to investigate your business thoroughly and will help to seal the deal with prospective investors.

Get Two Cents from Others

I'll admit it: the business plan chapter is rather dull and dreary for someone who hates homework (and that's just about everybody), but we already agreed that if you got this far into this section of the book, it's because you wanted to use someone else's money to start your business, and reading this section was a necessary evil. Don't worry—if you feel as though you're strapped in a dentist's chair, the pain is just about over.

After you've created an initial business plan and had it reviewed by a SCORE counselor, it's time to distribute copies to your family, friends, and business peers. One purpose this serves is gaining their support for your new [ad]venture. Moral support is helpful when starting a new business. Additionally, your peers in business for themselves can comment on the plan and give you feedback. Keep those index cards handy for all the comments, and you will start to see what may need to be changed.

Your business plan will develop gradually as a living, breathing document. You will add to it as you read through the rest of this book and talk to others along the way.

If your friends and peers have given you the green light and you feel you're ready to go, be sure to check grammar and spelling, then get it all into one PDF document or make a master copy that you can use for photocopying. Avoid putting this into your binder, because the three binder holes you would make will show up on the copies. Keep your master plan clipped with a large binder clip or paper clip and protect it in a large manila envelope or folder. If you have absolute confidence that you're ready, it is now okay to send out copies to your prospective investors and/or banks. But if you plan to start a brick-and-mortar store, you may want to hold off just a bit and discover the rest of what I have to say on the requirements of opening a physical drop-off store.

3. Considering Your Legal Structure

I have been a live auctioneer for 15 years. I opened up my own auction gallery and was struggling with regulatory problems. My 18-year-old assistant showed me that items we were selling were doing better on eBay. He taught me how to use eBay, and my first auction, of tools and equipment, ended up selling on eBay for over $40,000. We now use eBay to auction off virtually all of the items we sell. Where I would hire seven to nine people to run a live auction, I am able to hire just two and put more money in my clients' pockets.

—Michael Odell, Edmonds, Washington; eBay user ID "tradermicksgallery"; trading on eBay since March 10, 2004

Massive or Mini—Keep it Legal

I have been doing my duty to keep you motivated by constantly reminding you that nothing about starting a business should really scare you. That being said, if you're a business newbie, you should consider all the angles and make sure that you do things right the first time. Your legal structure (i.e., the way you manage your business and the legal entity you use for that business) is a key decision. When working as a house dad or soccer mom, you will be keeping things simple and doing business as a sole proprietor, which means no fancy paperwork and nothing revolutionary at tax time. If you decide to own a brick-and-mortar business or if your work-at-home eBay consignment job becomes massive, you'll want to consider a legal structure to protect yourself, your family, and your personal assets from possible legal liability in the event something unforeseen happens. And, of course, it's very important for potential investors to be aware of the legal structure you have chosen for your business. Many of them will want a personal guarantee of repayment regardless of your company's legal structure.

Since the day I started on eBay, no buyer has ever sued me for a transaction gone afoul, and no client has ever taken legal action because they were disappointed. In all probability, this will never concern you either, but it would be unfair to you if I failed to mention all the possibilities. If you take on a partner or decide to take plunge into a physical store, you'll want to do some soul searching on whether to form an entity such as a limited liability company, a corporation, or the alternative S corporation. If you own a lot of assets, I can't stress enough the importance of getting good accounting and legal counsel, as personal liability can be a risk, depending how deals and contracts are structured.

Legal Structure Options

In the business world, there are quite a few common legal structures with which you can operate a company. Some (but not all) of the types of entities are:

- Sole proprietorship
- General partnership
- Limited partnership
- Limited liability partnership
- Corporation (including the S corporation)
- Professional association
- Limited liability company
- Business trust
- Professional corporation

For our purposes, it's not necessary to define each of these entities, and personally, I find a lot of talk about legal structures dull and dreary. We're here to have fun, while of course making certain that you're operating with the correct type of business structure to meet your goals. So let's keep it lean while still covering what you need to know. The following issues primarily determine the type of organization you'll form:

- Taxation
- Liability
- Risk and control
- Continuity of existence
- Transferability
- Expense and formality

I'll focus on the four most popular ways to do business: sole proprietorship, limited liability company, corporation, and S corporation (the S is from the Internal Revenue Service code). The rest of the above ways of forming a company are not really applicable to you, but if you feel we don't adequately cover your situation within these four areas, it is time to call in a CPA, and possibly an attorney, for some further advice.

Two websites that help entrepreneurs with preparing corporate documents are www.legalzoom.com and www.incorporate.com. I have used the services of both companies and was satisfied. I have done all the legal work to form entities without a third party and did equally well, with a bit more effort in the process.

Sole Proprietorship

The simplest and easiest way to start your new business will be as a sole proprietor. My accountant informed me early in my business life that anyone grossing less than $175,000 from all business activities should operate under this type of business entity. Much of the consideration here is the inherent additional expense of operating a separate legal entity. In addition to the costs of forming the organization and filing additional tax returns, accounting may also cost you more, especially if you hire a bookkeeper to help.

As a sole proprietor, you can simply start doing business—and you're immediately a company. You may need to contact your state and local city licensing agency regarding appropriate licenses or permits (even when working from home), and you may wish to file or register a business name (also known as a d/b/a or doing-business-as name). Many local newspapers run the mandatory printed publication notices required when filing a d/b/a, and they may also keep copies of all the paperwork required to file. My local paper not only had the forms, they even filed them with the appropriate government agency, published the required notices, and returned my conformed and certified copies back to me. Your local chamber of commerce can also help, even if you're not yet a member. I strongly suggest that you open a distinctly separate bank account to keep your business separate from the rest of your life.

Not all areas have mandatory d/b/a notices. With the growth of the Internet, you'll want to check if your city/state permits you to fulfill any publishing requirements online via a searchable database (as Alaska does).

As a sole proprietor, you have total control—and total responsibility. You get all the profits from the business, you can hire any number of employees, and, as the owner, you're fully responsible for all taxes, claims, and debts of the business. You will need to claim the revenue from your business on your tax return. Your accountant (or you) will simply add the additional revenues to a schedule on your normal tax return called a Schedule C (Profit or Loss from Business). Bear in mind, you cannot simply tuck these earnings under the pillow. Here's a quote from the www.irs.gov website that tells what information PayPal will be sharing about your earnings:

Internal Revenue Code (IRC) Section 6050W states that all US payment processors, including PayPal, are required by the Internal Revenue Service (IRS) to provide information to the IRS about certain customers who receive payments for the sale of goods or services through PayPal. PayPal is required to report gross payments received for sellers who receive over $20,000 in gross payment volume AND over 200 separate payments in a calendar year.

With the sole proprietorship, all your business expenses will be in your name, with vendors and banks requiring a personal guarantee on any credit extended to the business. You will also need to pay estimated income tax to the government quarterly, and you may be required to pay your own Social Security, Medicare, and federal unemployment taxes for the additional income. Because you're the employer of yourself, you're required to handle the employer's portion of the taxes on your net income. The business is you. And you will be responsible for all debts, even if you decide to discontinue the business.

If you don't want or need to create your own company name, a d/b/a is not a mandatory part of the process; you can simply start your eBay Consignment business and bank your profits. If you start making some good money, you will want to speak to an accountant about handling the taxes. There are some great software programs out there to help you with the process of estimating and filing taxes, but use caution—if you're not comfortable using such programs, seek professional help.

If you hire employees, you will also need to apply for a Federal Employer Identification Number (FEIN), a number given to you by the IRS to identify your business that can be thought of as analogous to your Social Security number. The IRS uses this number to track the activities of your business, including your collection and payment of payroll taxes. In most states, you will need to apply for a state identification number for handling employees' tax withholdings as well. Don't worry: it's not as complicated as it may sound, as you will see in Chapter 21 about employees.

For now, if you think all of the above sounds like you, you're probably going to start off small and keep it simple—be a sole proprietor. To review:

- Taxation. You will be taxed once. You will simply add Schedule C to your normal federal return, while state returns and rules may vary by state.

- Liability. You're personally liable for all debts and legal actions against you.

- Risk and control. If you're a very small business, the risks are minimal, and you have a tremendous amount of control.

- Continuity of existence. This type of entity is you, so it cannot survive your death or be passed on to heirs.

- Transferability. Not as easy as other business structures.

- Expense and formality. The least expensive way to operate your business, with the least formality.

- Financial management. You can use your existing bank account, but a separate account is recommended.

As a sole proprietor, you will have more difficulty raising capital and seeking investors, because many will consider you "helping hands at home." But if you want to be small, this structure is ideal.

Limited Liability Company

This type of entity is a rather popular way for individuals or partners to start and maintain a business. The limited liability company is commonly referred to as the LLC. This type of organization is relatively easy and inexpensive to form and operate and has many of the benefits of a corporation, such as limited liability (as the name suggests) and the flexibility of a partnership (which I do not discuss at length here). This is a very common way for sole proprietors to protect personal assets and secure loans. It is not as economical as the sole proprietorship, because you may have to pay someone to form the organization and there will be additional tax returns. This business structure can be formed in any state. You can allocate the profits and losses of the LLC in flexible ways in different percentages from the ownership of the organization.

There is no double taxation issue, because the LLC is not treated as a separate taxable entity, and you do not need to be a U.S. citizen to own or invest in this type of organization. The LLC can also be owned by a combination of individuals or business entities. This might prove handy if one of your investors wants a piece of your business, perhaps taking part ownership through one of their own companies.

An LLC can be formed in one step, while an S corporation, though similar in its benefits, requires first the formation of your corporation and then election to the S corporation status. If you're not a U.S. citizen, an LLC will be your ideal structure as well, as only citizens and resident aliens may own an S corporation. With the universal adoption of the LLC by every state, it has become extremely popular.

If more than one person will own your company, the LLC can form an operating agreement that sets forth how the business will be managed. The members (owners) of the LLC typically contribute capital to the enterprise, and the profits are distributed at your discretion. Unlike corporations, no stock is issued when the LLC is formed, and no minutes of the board are required.

> Tip: Because of the highly flexible nature of the LLC, you can raise capital more easily, give investors a piece of the pie, and retain control via the operating agreement documents you prepare when forming the LLC

To review:

- Taxation. Profits flow directly to the members of the LLC in proportions designated by you with maximum flexibility. Each member is then responsible for paying taxes on their share of the profits.
- Liability. The LLC offers substantial protection from legal liabilities.
- Risk and control. LLCs hold moderate risk and offer excellent control over your taxes, ownership, and finances.
- Continuity of existence. The LLC can survive after one or more members dies, and it can add members with no limit.
- Transferability. Due to the flexible nature of the LLC, it can be transferred.
- Expense and formality. The LLC will require additional tax returns, and the formality is moderate, but it is a good trade-off if you want to protect assets and assure a fair and level playing field when doing business with multiple owners or a fairly good-sized company. It may be appropriate to create an LLC when you have grown your business somewhat.
- Financial management. A separate bank account is required.

C Corporation, S Corporation

When you hit the big time, it will be tempting for you to believe that forming a corporation is the next achievement required to prove your worth as a businessperson. The reality is that the LLC would still be the preferred way to go for most. In 1988, I formed my corporation, and I still operate it today, even though I have changed my line of business a few times. Because I have worked hard these many years to establish business credit and a reputation, it would not make sense for me to change my legal structure today; but frankly, were I to do it all over again, I would have formed an LLC.

A corporation (not an S corporation) is a fairly wild animal to tame. It is true that you can issue stock certificates and have an unlimited number of shareholders. Also, the corporation is its own entity and can live on well after its founders have passed away. This is why major companies are still in business today well over a century after they were formed. Shirley Plantation on the James River is the oldest company in America still in business today, celebrating four hundred years in business. A corporation can be bought and sold, and there are a lot of flexible benefits.

The downside is that the incorporation process requires a lot of paperwork, a burden that should not be undertaken by a small business owner. It also involves:

- articles of incorporation;
- bylaws;
- organizational board resolutions;
- stock certificates; and
- a stock ledger.

With a corporation, you can form a board of directors that has a general management duty to the business (kind of a steering committee). There are officers, such as the president, secretary, and treasurer, who handle the day-to-day responsibilities of the business. One person can act as the board and can also hold the position of multiple officers. Again, however, this type of organization will probably never serve your best interests unless you get really huge as a company, and at that point, you will want to refer the process of setting up your corporation to a professional. That process is beyond the scope of this book. If being an eBay consignment company is your only business, I'm not going to suggest setting up a corporation.

To review:

- Taxation. The corporation will be taxed separately, and you can pay yourself as an employee of the corporation. Dividends to stockholders are taxed separately as well.

- Liability. A corporation offers substantial protection from legal liabilities.

- Risk and control. Due to the higher administrative burden and higher cost of doing business, it is a higher-risk entity. However, for a large company, the corporation structure provides a great deal of control (financial and ownership), and stock can be easily transferred to others.

- Continuity of existence. The Corporation can have an unlimited number of stockholders (in essence, owners) and can survive indefinitely.

- Transferability. Ownership can be transferred quite easy via stock sales.

- Expense and formality. This is the highest-cost structure due to the administrative burdens, additional tax returns, and legal and professional fees for management of the company, as well as a high degree of formality in the formation documents, meetings, and minutes.

- Financial management. A separate bank account is required.

With the filing of form 2553 with the Internal Revenue Service, you can elect to have your corporation (typically called a C corporation) convert to what is referred to as an S corporation. An S corporation will allow you many of the same benefits of an LLC. You can allow all of the profits to flow directly to the shareholders. The S corporation may only have a total of 100 shareholders (more than you'll need) and has the same protection from personal liability as the C corporation. This designation with the IRS allows you to treat the income pretty much the same as you would if you were a sole proprietor. However, you get the benefits of having a distinct, separate organization. The formation and operational documents, as well as administrative requirements, are the same as with a C corporation. You will still have to file separate tax returns for your company, and the professional fees will also be similar. Fewer and fewer businesspeople opt for the corporation status, because the LLC brings all of the same benefits to the table without the high costs of operating a formal corporation. Aspirin anyone?

The upside to operating as a corporation (either type) is that the stock of the corporation can be transferred easily to other individuals and companies. This can make raising capital easier, as the investors can own a part of your company and also benefit from no liability in your operations. Single taxation is another benefit—because the profits flow directly to the shareholders of an S corporation, you do not pay the customary corporate tax in addition to the tax on your earnings.

It's worth noting as well that all of the legal structures, with the exception of sole proprietorship, require that you have a person or company designated and authorized to receive service of legal papers on your behalf (in the event of a lawsuit or other legal proceeding). Even though I seriously doubt that you will ever find yourself in court for any reason related to your business, you're required to maintain an Agent for Service of Process. If you don't know someone willing to do this for free, there are professional Agents who offer this service. You can check the phone book or contact your secretary of state for some names.

Taking It to the Next Level

If you want to form an LLC or a C or S corporation, you can contact an attorney in your area who specializes in setting up legal entities; or visit the websites I suggested earlier. A specialist will have the most knowledge and experience, and in the long run you will usually pay less for an expert's help than for the services of a general practice attorney. If you want to form the business entity yourself, SCORE can assist you in navigating the terrain.

When you operate an LLC or corporation in one state and you want to set up shop in other states, you do not need to create a new organization for each state. You do have to apply for and register a Certificate of Authority to do business in the new state(s). And you'll have to file a state tax return for each state in which you have a physical operation. Although this will probably never apply to you, it is something to consider if you're planning on opening multiple stores in the future.

There is a perception by the general public that a company with LLC or Inc. in the name is somehow better than a d/b/a. Although this may be very untrue, perception is so often reality, and thus this is a reality of business. Often as a sole proprietor, you will be treated as less serious, less credible, by prospective business associates, investors, banks, and clients. This is not to say that you should rush out and file for an LLC, but it is a reality that as you grow, your plans should include evaluating your legal structure at least once a year. Discuss the issue when you're working with your accountant at tax time. Closely related are the regular talks you should be having with your accountant about quarterly estimated taxes and tax planning throughout the year.

Reminder. Once you have decided which way to go in terms of your business structure, be sure to update your business plan with the new information.

On a personal note, as a small entrepreneur, I started out as a sole proprietor. When my income began to grow dramatically, I sought professional advice from my accountant, and when the time was right, I made the leap to a more formal business structure. When you're small, keep everything simple and grow into your new business a bit before you get too fancy. You will sense when the time is right to form an LLC or corporation, as no one knows your business better than you. If you're feeling a little confused about which business structure is right for you, I encourage you to contact me personally at borntodeal@gmail.com. Although I cannot give legal or accounting advice, I can certainly be a sounding board for your particular situation—and don't forget to seek help from a SCORE counselor!

4. Work from Home, or Open a Brick-and-Mortar Store?

I was an IBM executive working in Hong Kong and took an early retirement package in 1993 after 25 years of service. Upon returning to Florida, I wanted a steady addition to my retirement income but did not want to be locked into a storefront. I was looking for something I could do from my home. That's when I discovered eBay consignment selling. It also seemed like a great opportunity to help the older folks in our community who are downsizing and finding that their children don't always want many of their old items. I recently sold a client's Civil War photo album on eBay for $1,650. I charge a flat 40 percent commission, and I pick up all items from my clients' homes.
—Tom Murphy, Palm Beach Gardens, Florida; eBay user IDs "pga-auctions" and "tfmurphhk"; trading on eBay since September 1, 1998

Decisions, Decisions

The question that I'll pose before diving into this chapter is, "Do you have enough money—cash dollars—to open a brick-and-mortar store?" The question is simple enough, but there's another, closely related question: Just how fancy do you want to get with this new eBay consignment business? You can start a store with little more than a small, cheap space and a sign that says you're in business, or you can invest a considerable amount of money to create a high-profile, corporate-looking, professional image. The latter will require a considerable amount of planning and budgeting on your part before you sign a lease and start bidding out to construction contractors.

When I started selling on eBay for my friend Mike Richards, I had a completely unrelated career, and I was storing items before shipping them wherever I could find the space. Eventually my hobby had grown to the point where I graduated to a tiny, 444-square-foot office. There I stored the items and handled the day-to-day operations of my eBay business in a dedicated, distinctly separate space. Having a separate space from my home and regular business allowed me some sanity. I sought out part-time help on one of my favorite websites, Craig's List (www.craigslist.com), where I found individuals with a desire to work an occasional day here and there. Craig's List is a worldwide group of websites, each based in a different city, which offers a bit of something for everyone, including help wanted ads. As my client base grew, my tiny space was stacked to the ceiling with merchandise, and I wanted to expand. I quit my day job and began planning a retail storefront to run a full-time eBay drop-off enterprise.

I thought of the transition from occasional seller to full-time store as a natural one. The money I earned from my business more than paid for the cost of leasing, renovating, and advertising my new business. Mind you, this happened over the course of years. I started selling in 1998, and by 2003, I developed a retail store. I didn't take out any loans or have any investors. This business was something I wanted to build gradually, slowly, carefully. I am an extremely cautious investor, and I looked at my eBay business as an investment. I wanted to make certain that this investment would be profitable for many years to come. I wanted to learn the ropes thoroughly before expanding and to devise a system that would ensure me long-term profits. It took me just over five years to make the transition from being small potatoes to actually hanging up my shingle.

The decision to stay small or go big is something you'll have to grapple with yourself. Some possible scenarios for you might be:

- Work from home
- Work from your office
- Have an eBay consignment business within your existing retail store
- Create a simple drop-off store
- Create a high-profile, professional drop-off store

Your Cozy Cottage

This is your simplest and most inexpensive way to get started. As long as you can attract clients, working from home can be a great blessing, because you will have virtually zero startup costs. If you have a personal computer with an Internet connection and a digital camera or smart phone (or can borrow one, initially), then you're ready to start listing. You'll have to learn some basic accounting, because you will be collecting money for auctions, deducting your commission, and then paying your clients the balance. You will need an eBay account that is set up for selling as well as some basic office supplies. Because eBay provides an easy way to ship parcels via its integrated PayPal shipping system, and most shipping companies pick up packages (including the U.S. Postal Service), you can have a very efficient and streamlined business working from home. But there are drawbacks, and we'll cover them shortly.

Tip: If you are a super cautious person, working from home will be your best bet when starting out. You'll want to discover if this new career is the right fit for you before pouring lots of money into a larger, rented space.

Hang Your Shingle at Work

If you work for another company, working from "work" may be very difficult—impossible in most cases. It is hard to convince an employer that your eBay enterprise should take precedence over your duties as an employee. You might, however, be able to work out an arrangement with your boss by which you would do much, or all, of the eBay work over lunch or before/after your normal work schedule.

Why would any employer agree to allow this? Well, there are scenarios where this works. I have met individuals who offer to list their company's unwanted items on eBay for free in exchange for permission to spend breaks, lunchtime, etc., to list items for others. This arrangement is worthwhile for the company because it receives your services for free, and it's great for you because the company becomes a client. If you work for a business that sells a product, this might be a great fit. If you work at a job with any amount of idle time, you can make a fair argument that this is a logical fit to your job. If you work for a small, entrepreneurial company, you can earn the admiration and respect of your boss and make some extra money at the same time.

Piggyback on a Retail Shop

Do you own your own retail store? If so, then offering eBay listing services is a smooth and easy fit. Think of a hardware store with hundreds or even thousands of customers passing through the doors on a monthly basis. Typically, weekend warriors like to have nice, bright, shiny new tools. I am guilty of this myself, because I'll be the first to go out and buy a new electric screw gun when mine gets a scratch. I know, I'm spoiled, but so is the rest of America. How does a guy like me justify the expense of a new, air-powered nail gun? I sell my old one on eBay, of course. If a hardware store offered to help their customers sell their used tools and equipment on eBay, they would be stimulating the upgrade cycle

This can be applied to almost any retail product store. If you own a store that sells products to consumers, you can offer eBay consignment services within that store. It would be a simple matter of obtaining the necessary equipment and making up a flyer or other ad to get off and running. One clever way to present this service could also become a great marketing tool—offering to sell the items with no commission charged to the client/customer, so long as they spend the money that you obtain for them at your store. This could be in the form of a store credit or gift certificate. Offering a fee-free eBay listing service would generate quite a buzz for you, and the profits you made on the sale of new merchandise would make up for the free service. Perhaps throwing up a sign in your shop window will have your customers clamoring for this new eBay service.

The Simple Drop-Off Store

If working from home is out of the question and you do not have a day job, you might consider starting a cheap, small drop-off store. If you have savings, you may not need to borrow any money to get started, because you can probably find a small, suitable retail or office space to use for conducting business.

The idea here would be to keep your business and personal lives separate, while providing a reasonably professional environment to meet clients and handle the daily aspects of selling on behalf of others. You might work alone or hire full- or part-time help to keep up with the workload. In addition to possible one-time expenses such as buying a computer, camera, and lighting equipment, your recurring monthly expenses will include:

- Rent
- Utilities
- Telephone
- Internet
- Office supplies
- Salaries (if you hire anyone)

- Advertising expenses

Ideally, even in a low-cost office space, your landlord will provide some of the improvements, commonly referred to as leasehold improvements. If your landlord is providing a turnkey space, it will be painted, carpeted, and move-in ready. If you do not expect to depend upon foot traffic for attracting new customers, you can lease an office space or a retail space in a less than prime area. Commercial office parks can be quite inexpensive to begin with and less desirable for other types of businesses, so you may well be able to negotiate the rent down even further. You'll want to rent month-to-month or keep the lease as short as possible to give yourself maximum flexibility.

The High-Profile Drop-Off Store

So you have big bucks or a rich aunt, or you plan to borrow money from investors or a bank, and you want to set up a slick, professional looking eBay consignment store? A high-profile store requires a lot more planning. In addition to the requirements of creating a simple store, you will also need to think about leasing space in a high-traffic retail location. Along with a better location, you will not only pay a higher monthly rent, but you will also need to think about:

- Lease terms and conditions (a good location usually means a higher level of commitment to your landlord)
- Branding (the way your business looks)
- Store design and layout
- Renovation costs

If you have a tendency to think big, then this would be your strategy for making a splash. But with bigger overhead, your need for ideas to bring in new clients will also be much more intense and urgent. You will need to sell a lot more merchandise to cover your expenses. I'll be giving you a comprehensive education about the entire process of opening a store in Chapters 7 through 10. Opening a high-profile drop-off store is not nearly as expensive or complicated as opening most of the popular franchise businesses. Generally, a new McDonald's franchise requires a minimum of $750,000 in non-borrowed personal funds to start the process. Your total costs to open the doors will most likely exceed $700,000, forty percent of which must come from your non-borrowed funds. There's no doubt that setting up a very fancy drop-off store would cost significantly less than that, and if you're in a part of the country with a low cost of living, your monthly overhead will be relatively low, too. The biggest overhead expense in any business is usually labor, with rent typically second. But if you become quite large—listing hundreds or even thousands of items monthly—then your eBay bill will grow proportionately, perhaps even becoming your single greatest expense. The silver lining in all of this remains that people and businesses always have a never-ending supply of unwanted stuff.

Who Are Your Clients?

A considerable amount of thought needs to go into answering this question. In my early eBay selling years, my first and only client was my best friend. As word spread that I sold unwanted items for others, new clients came into my life from all directions. I was taking in substantially more things than I could list in a day, and I was working seven 12-hour days a week (Okay, I still work seven days a week, but I don't really have to.) Spending money on advertising never really crossed my mind, and until I opened my first storefront, I had never spent a dollar to place an ad to get new clients. I noticed immediately that the foot traffic walking by my store was not the upscale clientele that I was seeking; rather, it was mostly comprised of window shoppers and customers frequenting the various secondhand stores and antique shops near me. To attract a client base with the high-quality merchandise that would generate the profits to keep the doors open posed a real challenge. I had to advertise.

You might already have a list of eager people wanting your services, and if that is your situation, you can rent an office space or work from home. If you don't plan on being super busy, then you can open a simple store. The fancy store will require much more study—of the benefits of paying high rent for a good location. Quite a few of the successful drop-off stores I have seen are in the upscale strip malls common in Los Angeles. They are near other businesses that cater to the wealthy, such as dry cleaners, hair salons, or upscale supermarkets. The clients you want, as well as the level of activity you're seeking, will drive your location decision. Consider that the higher rent you pay for a fabulous location will reduce the amount of money you will have to shell out for advertising your store.

It would be a good idea to review your notes on how your competition is snagging their new clients. You should also consider the size of your town and cost of doing business. In Burbank, where I live and work, the cost of renting a prime retail space is a small treasure chest of money every month. And rent is just the beginning. You'll contend with salaries, insurance, utilities and an array of other expenses. How important will your location be to capturing the best clients?

Hunting or Farming?

Many eBay consignment shops survive with low rent because they provide high-touch customer service. Offering to pick up merchandise from your clients, instead of making them come to your place of business, accomplishes two things: you can get by without a fancy store, and you will be leaps and bounds ahead of any competitors who won't take the time or trouble to give this added level of client service. The catch here is that you simply cannot afford to make house (or office) calls unless the profit justifies the trip. You won't want to drive 15 miles to a client and spend time explaining your services—all for an item that ends up selling for $15. The value has to be there when making house calls. Some eBay sellers charge a flat pickup fee to cover this cost and others provide free pickup.

If you have clients who come to your place of business, you'll have to maintain a neat, organized, and professional appearance to attract picky clients. First impressions are important and perception is reality.

You also have to take into account that many wealthy individuals are busy. While high-income people always have unwanted things, it may be hard for them to find the time to come see you. You will have to be flexible to accommodate their busy schedules, and you may want to stay open evenings and weekends for their convenience. I have employees to help greet customers and accept items, but bear in mind that if you run a one-person shop, you may not last long with long hours and a strenuous schedule. If staffing is a concern, try staying open late once a week to meet individuals who work during the day.

Gradual Evolution

eBay has grown popular in great part because of the convenience of selling at will, and because, unlike most businesses, you can get started with little or no investment. When you sell from home, you can take a break or a vacation at any time, as long as your buyers and clients are being serviced. eBay is scalable, and there are no fees for using eBay unless you actually list and sell items.

But when you open a store, you no longer have the luxury of selling on eBay when and if it suits you. With the overhead associated with a drop-off store, you have to maintain a steady flow of merchandise. You can't simply lock the door and take a vacation without having someone to mind the store and take care of clients. Owning and running a store is like a marriage, with tremendous responsibility, and you should give this reality careful consideration before making the leap. If you have never operated a successful business before, I must discourage you from making the move to a high-profile drop-off store immediately. Consider selling part-time from home at first, learning the ropes of being an eBay seller. You can gradually evolve your business into an operation big enough to justify a full-time shop.

Having said all that, eBay is a dynamic marketplace, and as a seller you will have numerous options available for operating a successful business. You will quickly learn that keeping up with the latest changes and enhancements that eBay launches in the e-commerce universe is hard work. eBay's ProStores continues to provide new and innovative e-commerce solutions for your online storefront. Magento Go offers a shopping cart system that automatically synchronizes your inventory with eBay, helping you move more merchandise.

Part of doing your research is to be aware of the venues and services that are available to you as your client's expert representative. You should not try to digest too much at once. You will peel the layers of eBay knowledge and discovery over time!

Family Matters

Most everyone has a family life of one sort or another. If you live with other people, whether a spouse, significant other, or family members, others will be impacting and influencing your business. Positive or negative energy will have the expected effect on your attitude, on your very plan to become an entrepreneur.

Working from home in an unsupportive environment is a recipe for failure. You've got to have sugar to bake a delicious cake. Without positive emotional support, your business won't be fun. Lack of family support may even promote failure. This could actually be one of the reasons you might want to open a store—to separate your business from your personal life.

If you have the house to yourself during the day, then working at home will be much easier. But if others are around, it is only natural for the family magnet to drag you into this or that project and pull you away from your duties.

Jealousy and envy are part of human nature, and if you live with anyone who is not completely in favor of your work at home, you may find subtle or obvious efforts to undermine your success. Try your best to rally support for your plans to start and grow a business. If you're getting positive vibes, you can give it a try and see how things go. But when you start spending hours defending your use of the kitchen as a packing and shipping "department," and explaining why the hall closet is bursting with clients' merchandise, it's time to consider separating your business from your home life.

You will know what is right for you. My philosophy in business has always been to seek the path of least resistance. If something is too hard, it's probably not the right way to go. Do what comes naturally and easily. I don't mean that this venture of yours will be a cake walk—I'm simply suggesting that your decision to work from home or not be based on your natural instincts and feelings.

Cautious reminder. If you have a spouse or significant other in your life, they should be involved and committed to this new enterprise. As things grow, you don't want your better half to pitch a fit and cause the dominos to start falling over.

5. Start-up Costs, Capital Requirements, and Budgeting

My son was born prematurely and weighed less than five pounds. I had to quit working and stay home with him. One of my first items was an 1890s Nippon wall plaque, and my client had tried selling it at a local antique mall at $100 without success. After a year at the antique mall, my client wanted to try eBay, so I listed it with an opening bid of $99.99 and it ended up selling for $410! I have been so inspired by my eBay success that I now teach classes locally to help other people with eBay.
—Tricia Hanley, Keyport, Washington; Pacificquest Auction Services, LLC; eBay user ID "pacificquest"; trading on eBay since February 5, 1999

To Risk—or Not to Risk?

In the last chapter, I talked about the different ways to start an eBay consignment business. The start-up costs will depend on the direction you choose. If you're a risk taker with lots of ambition, are fairly savvy about borrowing money, and have a good personal credit score, you may well be considering the physical drop-off store. If you're not a risk taker and would like to take the more conservative route of working from home, your start-up costs will be the basics. Either way, you will still need to have some capital to start, and you'll want a budget to keep things moving along smoothly without the stress of a financial crisis due to poor planning. You will need to consider the source of your start-up capital before jumping into this new venture.

From Dreams to Reality

By now, your business plan has begun to take shape, and although it is a work in progress, you can use your plan as a guide for developing your financial projections. In the Finances section of your business plan, I asked you to formulate a break-even analysis, to make certain that your recurring expenses will be covered. You will now want to refine this section of the plan to ensure that you will have both enough start-up and working capital. The start-up capital is the money you need to open your doors, and the working capital will be the cash you need to stay in business, paying your day-to-day bills, while you grow your business into profitability.

With a home-based business, working capital is much less important, because most of your overhead is already covered. You may need funding for a computer, Internet account, a digital camera and lights for photography, and almost certainly for supplies. You might already have the first three or four items on the list, making your initial investment very, very small—perhaps $100 or less. If you will be working from your existing office or store, the start-up costs will also be nominal. You might want to add a few extra dollars to cover printing advertising materials and business cards, but for the most part, the budget is quite similar to that of a home-based enterprise. Before acquiring a new camera, check to see if your current smart phone will capture eBay-quality photos.

The brick-and-mortar drop-off store will be quite a financial leap in terms of both start-up and working capital. Here are sample budgets for opening both a simple and fancy drop-off store in a 1,000-square-foot space, with a rent of $1.50 per square foot per month. Remember, your actual costs will depend on your location, local market conditions, utility rates, etc. This is just a guide.

Item	Simple	Fancy
Security deposit and first month's rent ($1,500 rent plus $1,500 security deposit)	$3,000.00	$3,000.00
Computer, scanner, and printer	$1,000.00	$1,000.00
Telephone and Internet connections	$150.00	$150.00
Furniture	$500.00	$2,000.00
Leasehold improvements	$1,000.00	$20,000.00
Signage	$1,500.00	$5,000.00
Printing	$500.00	$2,500.00
Supplies	$250.00	$1,000.00
Camera (simple point-and-shoot type)	$200.00	$200.00
Lighting	$150.00	$600.00
File for a d/b/a	$100.00	$0.00
Set up LLC or corporation	$0.00	$1,000.00
Business license	$100.00	$100.00
Total	$8,450.00	$36,550.00

Contingency (25%)	*$2,112.50*	*$9,137.50*
Total projected start-up capital	**$10,562.50**	**$45,687.50**

Bear in mind that these figures are hypothetical, rounded-off examples. To keep things in perspective, a $1.50 per square foot retail space might be expensive in Geneva, Nebraska, but would be nearly impossible to find in Chicago, Los Angeles, New York, or San Francisco. You will have to survey rents in your city. The same will be true for many of the other expenses. It takes a bit of research and a few phone calls to fill in all of the actual expenses of opening your own store.

The majority of the expenses of opening your simple store are straightforward, and you won't have much trouble determining them. Usually more problematic are the leasehold improvements and signage. These costs can vary not only from location to location but also depend greatly upon your store design. With your simple store concept, you will act as the store designer, but with a fancy store, you will want the services of a store layout expert to help with the entire design and branding package. You will also want to talk in more detail with the owners of other eBay drop-off stores.

Chat With Your Neighbors

You may recall that I had asked you to immediately write down everything you observed when visiting your competitors. Take these notes out and review them carefully. Hopefully, you noted which shops were friendly, and if so, this would be a good time to confer with them in detail about your own store design plans. It is always better to use proven concepts than to try to reinvent the wheel. If you felt that you earned a new friend, you can invite them to come look at the space you've chosen before you sign a lease to hear their reactions.

If the drop-off site visits you made did not yield enough warm and fuzzy people, you can always expand your search beyond your immediate area. Try to set up appointments with the owners of at least three eBay consignment stores that you felt were well run and professional. Don't be shy or hesitant—it is very common in business to ask peers for their opinions and to solicit feedback. You could ask to have this meeting on your very first visit, but a good drop-off store is busy, and you don't want to impose on anyone while they are handling their daily routines. After you introduce yourself on your first visit—and if you feel the store is a model of elegance, professionalism, and efficiency—you could ask for an appointment at that time. But don't be discouraged if you're turned down. Not everyone is eager to help the competition, but if you're far enough away from this person's location, you can suggest that you will not be competing for the same clients. Polite, affable persistence will pay in the long run. Offer to drive them or pay their gas; and be sure you buy lunch.

Tip: Be armed with your questions about start-up capital and take notes. Ask about all of the expenses mentioned in the previous chart and add any additional items that might arise during your interview. As your knowledge and understanding of start-up requirements continues to expand, your business plan will also become more refined and clear

Pull Out the Piggy Bank

Working capital, the money you will need to stay afloat while you build your clientele base, the financial cushion to keep your lights on and your rent paid, will also vary greatly when you factor in the cost of paying employees.

Billionaire American business magnate, investor and philanthropist Mark Cuban believes that it's bad business to borrow money to start a new venture. He actually used some pretty strong words in his Bloomberg interview that I won't print here. His advice was sound and I'd encourage you to look this up on YouTube and listen to his advice on the subject.

If you have employees, their salaries may vary depending on the skills required. You may want to handle all your eBay listing and photography work yourself and add a part-time helper to assist with packing and shipping orders. If you have bigger plans for a high-volume operation, you will want to have employees handling nearly every aspect of your daily operations. To a great extent, your location will determine how much you will be expected to pay for good help.

Most of the tasks required for your business will be fairly repetitive and not really complicated. Launching eBay listings and taking photos of merchandise can be handled in a systematic and almost automated fashion. Even accounting will be a fairly simple task, because you're simply calculating your commission and determining how much is owed to your clients. You will be able to train good employees in the skills you require.

Tip: Reaching out to students and retirees can work well for you, because they can work part-time, affording flexibility and relieving you of any pressure to provide full-time employment

Some of the general tasks that will be part of your day-to-day operation will be:

- Greeting existing and prospective clients

- Receiving items for listing

- Creating listings

- Photography

- Packing and shipping

- Accounting

- Filing

If the cost of living where you reside is low, you can expect to pay anywhere from $7.80 to $10 per hour for any of the above jobs. If you live in a part of the country with a high cost of living, the wages may be in the $10 to $20 per hour range. It is important that you do as much of the work yourself as possible, especially when starting out, so that you can keep your budget lean and trim.

When determining how much you will need for working capital, you can project all of your costs, including salaries, into a time frame comfortable for you. But I would strongly suggest an amount sufficient to fully cover at the very least three, and ideally six, months of overall expenses. In my sample start-up budget, I said the rent would be $1,500 per month.

Here is a simple working capital projection:

Item	Monthly Cost
One full-time employee making $10/hour	$1,600.00
Rent	$1,500.00
Employment taxes	$200.00
Electric bill	$150.00
Office supplies	$100.00
Telephone	$45.00
High-speed Internet	$65.00
Bank fees	$15.00
Total	*$3,675.00*
Contingency (25%)	*$918.75*
Total monthly expenses	***$4,593.75***

This is a very simple monthly expense budget. Yours may be this basic, or you may have other expenses that pop up. You will notice that I did not add any line items to account for packing supplies or shipping costs. Those costs will be paid by the buyers of your clients' items, in addition to the cost of the items themselves. The shipping fees you charge may become a modest profit center if you're adding some extra handling charges to the actual shipping cost. (I suggest great moderation if you choose to do so, however. Most buyers expect or at least have no problem paying a minor handling fee, but you wouldn't want to be accused of "gouging.") Your detailed seller rating will be affected by high shipping charges and that will jeopardize your ability to achieve Top Rated Seller status.

Of course, you will be offsetting some of your monthly expenses with the commissions you charge for your services. Initially, however, you will be playing a game of catch-up, because in the very beginning, until your client base has grown enough to consistently provide a profit, your expenses will exceed the fees you collect.

As previously stated, I urge you to plan on having six months of working capital to cover all your expenses during the initial growth phase of your business—and definitely not less than three months' worth. Below is a simple chart that shows our $4,593.75 monthly expense bill as accrued over a period of three to six months.

Monthly	$4,593.75
x 3	$13,781.25
x 4	$18,375.00
x 5	$22,968.75
x 6	$27,562.50

Holy cow! That's a lot of money. Starting a brick-and-mortar business will require some cash. You may be having second thoughts at this point about starting big, but the real kicker is that you also have to add in the total start-up capital that I mentioned in our sample start-up budget. If we use the start-up capital we calculated earlier in the chapter and add in a six-month working capital allowance, you will need approximately $38,500 in cash to open a simple store with one employee and as much as $73,625 to open the fancy store. Your actual cash requirements can be anything in between—even more, if you find that you want to spend a lot on the store design and your tastes are expensive. Sounds like a lot of dough? Compare that to the franchise capital requirements of a Subway restaurant. The May 2013 Subway prospectus projects you will need between $116,200 and $262,850 to open one Subway location.

If you're going to become a high volume eBay seller, you will need the professional image you can only achieve with a physical drop-off store. Your business plan will need to demonstrate to investors or a bank that you have given due consideration to both the start-up and working capital requirements of your proposed store.

Rainy Day Money

Be sure to add the contingency allowance. A contingency is very similar to buying car insurance—you don't expect to need it, but when you do, you really appreciate having it. And don't be tempted to spend it. Keep your contingency allowance in a savings account so you won't be as easily tempted to use it for anything but a "rainy day."

A contingency allowance will allow you a comfort level, a cushion, enabling you to handle unexpected variances in your start-up costs. You will notice that in my example of start-up and working capital, I allowed for a 25 percent contingency. This provides for the possibility of error and will help to cover any unexpected and necessary additional expenses. Do not try to skimp here. If you're the type of person who spends their last dime just in time for the next paycheck, you will really have to be disciplined in budgeting your new business.

6. Licensing for Your Business

I have been selling items for others on eBay...with great success. I sold a Catholic priest's lifetime collection of miniatures from all over the world and got over $11,000 for the collection. I sold a catering trailer to a film production company in South America, several motor homes, and many other high-quality items of all types. We will sell anything if asked. We are committed to giving professional service and do whatever it takes to make clients happy. Our state has some licensing requirements, which we researched to make certain we were in compliance with the laws in Arkansas.
—Gary Puckett, North Little Rock, Arkansas; eBay user ID "puckettauction"; trading on eBay since September 4, 2002

Who Wants Your Business?

The government loves you. Usually they love you so much that they not only want to keep tabs on your daily business activities, but they also like to get paid to do so. Typically, this is done through a wonderful thing called a business license. There are all kinds of licenses out there for virtually every imaginable occupation, and it is important that you stay in compliance with local and state laws.

How does your local government classify the business of an eBay consignment seller? When you accept an item for listing on the eBay site, you're providing several services, including:

- Professional market value consulting
- Clerical work to prepare a listing
- Photography
- Storage
- Collecting the payment
- Packing
- Shipping
- Paying your client

In general, you're providing convenient assistance to anyone wanting to use eBay without committing the time and resources to create and manage their own listings.

Different states view business differently. Some states are quite aggressive about attracting business start-ups, and therefore are equally proactive in giving small businesses lots of breaks. Relaxed regulations and lower (or no) taxes are ways in which some states encourage business development. You're responsible for establishing your own fee structure and the range of services you offer, but some local authorities and states may have laws and/or regulations that affect the scope of the client services you provide. eBay does not check the laws for you; therefore, it is entirely your responsibility to determine not only the tax laws but also the licensing requirements for your business.

These laws may be very relaxed, or they may be quite strict. Either way, it's possible for you to operate a legal eBay consignment business. Get the whole story before you spend a lot of money opening a drop-off store. If you live in a city with restrictive licensing rules, it might be prudent to consider a nearby city in which to hang your shingle—the commute may be worth it. If you're near the border of another state that has more relaxed and business-friendly regulations, the same suggestion applies. Be tactful how you present your business to the government. Some agencies may try and lump you in with pawn shops and second hand dealers; therefore placing draconian restrictions on your business such as waiting periods before you can sell an item. Remember that you're extending a service to list clients' items and not buying them directly, nor taking title to the merchandise.

Keeping It Legal

It's completely natural for you to be apprehensive of anything even vaguely resembling a legal matter. But being in compliance with the laws of your city and state is just a routine matter. You don't have to pay a high-powered attorney to get the basic legal or tax advice that this relatively simple business requires. You will probably want an accountant's help if you operate a fairly good-sized business, but many sole proprietors choose to prepare and file their own taxes, and with today's robust tax software, doing so can be very straightforward if you have anything of a head for numbers.

Before you pay for legal help, you might want to reach out to SCORE again, this time for advice about licenses and taxes. And you will definitely want to give your state and local governments a chance to help you, too. In most cases, your local business license will be sufficient, but some states do require additional licenses.

The National Association of Secretaries of State (NASS) has a website (www.nass.org) that allows you to quickly locate the appropriate resources and contact information for your state. Here, you can learn more about your state's licensing requirements. Contact information is there, too, and a call to your secretary of state's office may be the best route to determining what state (not local) licenses may be required.

Talking with a government representative may be important, because the industry is constantly evolving, as is selling on the Internet in general; and frankly, in some state governments, there seems to be some confusion as to the exact nature of an eBay consignment shop. This is important, because some state governments want to classify you as an auctioneering business, or secondhand dealer. Such licenses may be more restrictive and/or expensive than those more appropriate for what you actually do. You should clarify this distinction when speaking with your state's representative. We'll go into more depth on this subject later in this chapter.

If you have a little anxiety about all of this and don't mind paying for the help, you can engage the services of an attorney. Most attorneys are specialists, and you will want an expert in the field of business licensing. Try to obtain a referral from a colleague in business or by contacting your state's bar association, which handles the licensing of attorneys. You can locate the appropriate bar association on the website www.findlegalhelp.org.

But it is very rare for an entrepreneur to hire an attorney simply to handle a routine matter such as obtaining a license. I would suggest this only as a last resort. Generally you will want to work directly with your state and ask them for help understanding their requirements. If you're friendly and professional, you will no doubt succeed here and save yourself a bundle by doing it yourself.

Do You Need Permission?

All states have special permits for businesses that buy products wholesale and sell them retail at a profit. When buying this way, most companies don't pay sales tax on the wholesale purchase, but they do charge their retail customers sales tax on the final sale. The sales tax is collected by the businesses, to be paid to a state agency that will then distribute these taxes to the state treasury and possibly the treasuries of the county and local governments. A permit is required if you're doing business this way. You may not need to acquire such a permit, but many eBay sellers find that they can make additional profits by selling boxes, offering packing and shipping services, and selling supplies or other merchandise from their store. If you own a drop-off store, you really will want to add packing and shipping services to your list of services—the increased shipping volume will allow you to negotiate discounts with the shipping companies you use. If you sell products, in this case packing materials, boxes, tape, etc., you will be collecting sales tax and then paying it to the state's coffers. You will need to get a permit to do so.

> Tip: A response in writing will be a good thing to have in your files as
> proof of your due diligence when communicating with regulators

If your state does not have a sales tax, this is a moot point and you can move on to the next section. States call these permits by various names, but they all allow the collection and payment of sales taxes. Some of the names used for such permits are:

- Resale permit
- Resale license
- Resale certificate
- Sellers permit
- Certificate of authority
- Use and sales tax license
- Use and sales tax permit
- Application to collect and report tax
- Transaction privilege tax

These permits are also known by other names, depending on your state. And states may have different rules regarding the collection and payment of sales tax as well as other taxes. It would be a good idea to give your state officials a call and ask for details about the rules of the road where you live. You can use the conventional URL for your state as in this example: www.state.ny.us, where **ny** is the postal abbreviation for the state in question. This will take you to their website, where you can obtain contact information and information about state-specific regulations.

NOTE: Collecting sales tax on Internet sales/purchases is currently a hot topic across the United States. Most expect it will become a reality in the very near future. Be sure to find out what your obligations, if any, might be regarding collecting sales tax on Internet sales/purchases with state and local authorities. And be sure to check periodically, as your obligations may change.

The Locals May Want a Slice of Your Pie

Your city may or may not have a licensing requirement if you work from home, but most will if you work from a drop-off store. Again, it's important to contact your local city licensing office and discuss your business, whether home based or office/store based. As discussed above (and below in more detail) with regard to state licenses, because eBay consignment work is a rapidly changing industry, your city may not have a business classification which exactly fits.

These issues should be settled early on with your local government through good communication. I suggest calling for an appointment with the appropriate city employee and speaking to them in person about your proposed enterprise. Don't be afraid to deal with these folks. They are usually quite willing to help any new enterprise and want to assist in making your new business a successful one. Remember that you will be generating new sources of tax revenue for your local community with your payment of a business license and sale taxes and the creation of new jobs for any employees you need.

I like to think of myself as a global enterprise. With a significant percentage of my sales being made to individuals in cross-border trading, I'm making my small contribution to bringing new money into the United States from abroad.

Even if you're planning on working from home, a business license may be required. Be sure to get one and stay in compliance. You might be able to stay under the radar for a while, but as you become successful, you will be getting daily visits from UPS or the postman, and the volume of packages exiting your home will be a telltale sign of a home-based business. A nosy neighbor might turn you in, and you don't want to deal with the stress of possible fines for operating an unlicensed business. If you're a previous business owner or have worked in a small business, this will all seem routine and quite simple. If you're new to the business world, the mere thought of dealing with government types might cause you to break out into a cold sweat. Don't stress yourself out. It really is a routine matter, and you will take great pride—and be able to sleep well at night—in knowing you're running a completely legit business enterprise.

What You Are . . . and Aren't

Many lawmakers and regulators nationwide are trying to place eBay consignment sellers in the same category as auctioneers, pawnbrokers, or secondhand dealers. Because you will deal in both new and secondhand goods, for licensing purposes, you may be pegged as a secondhand dealer, a business designation that may require additional licensing and regulatory red tape. Secondhand dealer permits or pawnbroker licenses usually require that you send a daily report of items received to the police or sheriff's department as well as hold the items for up to 30 days before you can sell them. You must avoid this at all costs. A key difference is that you never take title (ownership) of the goods. You're merely providing a service...listing these items on eBay for a fee.

In some states, secondhand tangible personal property that bears a serial number, owner-applied number, or personalized inscriptions or initials or property such as jewelry and sterling silver utensils may be of concern to regulators. Contact your local police or sheriff's department for details on what is required to be reported to them.

Varying from state to state, some lawmakers are looking into the possibility of requiring eBay sellers to fingerprint their customers who drop off items for listing on eBay and to record transactions for possible inspection by police. Some state governments are proposing special registries and tracking databases to curtail trafficking in stolen merchandise. On a personal note, I have never seen a study from a reliable source that provides evidence that trafficking of stolen merchandise is a problem on eBay. In fact, as I write these words, I have never been required to return a single item to any law enforcement agency as the result of allegedly stolen goods.

eBay's government relations folks oppose these concepts and reject the notion that eBay consignment sellers are analogous to secondhand dealers, auctioneers, pawnbrokers, or consignment stores. You're not the actual seller of the goods; rather you're providing listing services for clients. And because eBay is an open and transparent marketplace, there is no good argument for creating a separate registry or additional regulations, because anyone can find an item quickly and easily on eBay by searching for it.

When dealing with government offices, avoid using the terms consignment or auction when talking about your business. Your basic argument sounds like this:

A person who operates an eBay consignment business provides listing assistance on eBay and cannot "recognize" bids made in an online auction. The auction-style listings on eBay receive bids through proprietary software owned by eBay, and you neither solicit bids nor do you gather bidders together to allow bids to be placed. You list items on behalf of the seller, who is your client. You provide them with what can be considered overblown secretarial work. Your client is the seller and at all times retains complete ownership and control of their merchandise. Title of the goods is *never* conveyed to you at any time, rather, it is transferred from the actual seller to the buyer and you're merely acting as a facilitator.

Whatever the regulations in your community, be in compliance at all times to avoid getting tangled in a web of legal troubles. Just as you pay your taxes and renew your driver's license, operate your business in a 100 percent legal way so that things will run smoothly.

7. Selecting a Suitable Location and Negotiating and Signing a Lease

One of my clients gave me a box of various Native American items. At the bottom of the box was a small, squished basket. I steamed the basket over a pot of boiling water, and it looked like new again. It ended up being a baleen basket from a Northwest Indian tribe, and we sold it on eBay for $950.

—Mark Floersheim, Albuquerque, New Mexico; The Platinum Store, eBay user ID "frostypaws$$$$"; trading on eBay since July 5, 2000

A Brave, New World

I trust that by this chapter, you're feeling clear and confident about your new venture. Now that financial issues such as start-up and working capital requirements have been reviewed, you may feel comfortable presenting your plan to potential investors. But many banks will require further explanation of your location selection, and you need a solid grasp of how to proceed with inspecting and analyzing prospective locations, selecting a space, and consummating a deal to rent or lease it. Many factors will affect your choice of location; for instance, you will need to decide if you want a more pricey retail location with strong walk-by traffic, to generate potential clients, or if you think your primary sources of merchandise will allow you the luxury of cheaper and possibly larger digs. You need to consider these questions very carefully, because not only will you spend a lot of time and money opening the store you will spend a lot of time working there, too. Your space needs to be a comfortable, pleasant, and productive environment for you.

Contact three or more licensed real estate brokers who specialize in leasing small- to medium-sized retail (or office) space. Brokers not only sell buildings but they also manage and lease them for clients. Explain your business and give them your budget. It's okay to work with more than one broker simultaneously, and try to maximize your appointments with them by asking to see at least three locations. Customarily brokers are paid by the property owner, and you will probably not have to pay anything more than your first month's rent, some form of security deposit, and possibly the last month's rent.

You should cast a large net when looking and scan the classified advertising section of your local newspapers. And use the Internet—localized websites such as Craig's List (www.craigslist.com) are good sources, and your local newspaper probably has a website for classified ads, too.

I found my store by driving around. I love the Magnolia Park neighborhood of Burbank, and when I was looking to grow into a larger place, I would look for stores that had "For Lease" signs on them. You should spend at least one afternoon each weekend looking, armed with a notepad and pen. Call on your cell phone whenever you see a promising sign and see if the broker is available. Good locations in nice neighborhoods will lease rather quickly, so the sooner you call the better. If you see a sign that has been up for a long time, you can bet it's either a bad location or the price and/or terms are unattractive. Call anyway and see what you can learn about the property. You will get a quick education by speaking to as many people as possible and looking at as many locations as you can. Patience is the key.

Consider Your Clientele

You can run a successful business by selling excess inventory from companies, in which case a commercial space, such as a small warehouse in an office park or retail space off the beaten track, would be fine.

But if your primary clients will come to you with their merchandise, it's important to have a clean, safe place to conduct business, ideally near other upscale retail businesses.

Your location needs available parking unless, of course, you live in a city like Manhattan. In virtually all other cases, allowing clients easy access via a dedicated parking lot or nearby public parking will be critical.

Is Heavy Traffic a Good Thing?

Most probably yes. A location with constant foot traffic will be extremely beneficial to you—it's a great form of advertising. Your store will need good signage that grabs the eye and shouts the message, "I sell on eBay for you!" You can't survive without customers, and the less foot traffic passing your shop, the harder you will have to work to attract new business. Renting a cheap office with access from an alley will look like a great cost savings, but it will hurt your business and actually cost you more in the long run because of increased marketing costs. If you pay less in rent, you will ultimately have to pay more for necessary advertising. Your store should be easy to find, and being on a major street or near a major intersection is always a plus.

Location, Location, Location
Strip Malls

Many of the eBay consignment stores I have visited are located in strip malls (also called strip shopping centers). These stores depend heavily on the luxury shops and upscale supermarkets in their malls to draw in foot traffic, especially the well-heeled clients who likely have high-quality merchandise. The key is to find a location that will draw the right people to you. Look for busy strip malls with upscale stores, boutiques, and dry cleaners. But if you specialize in antiques, you may want to avoid placing yourself right next to an antiques shop, because it will be in direct competition for your client's attention, pulling at their inclination to sell their merchandise outright.

One benefit of a strip mall is shared common area maintenance and a sense of safety. Clients like to visit clean, secure businesses, and professionally managed shopping centers and strip malls usually have good maintenance.

The downside of these locations is the cost. Typically, you will pay not only your own rent but also a customary additional charge for common area maintenance and possibly some of the owner's property taxes as well. And it's not unusual at very busy and successful locations for the mall to even charge you a percentage of your sales. You have to weigh the benefits of the foot traffic against these costs. But again, spending more money on the right location might save you thousands a year in advertising.

Business Park

A business park is typically located off the beaten track. The businesses in these mixed-use locations don't depend heavily on foot traffic and need larger, less expensive spaces. A business park may have offices, offices with attached warehouses, or just storefront warehouse space. If you already have a steady flow of merchandise and anticipate doing most of your deals by phone or by picking up the clients' items, you can locate in a business park and save a lot on rent. Ideally, your space would have an office with a warehouse attached, and this configuration is very common. You can conduct your daily business in the comfort of your office and receive, store, pack, and ship items in the warehouse. Keep an eye out for a warehouse with shelving already installed. Always check that high-speed Internet is available in the location before considering a lease. Some office parks are so far off the main drag that they have older telephone infrastructures, and it may be difficult and/or more expensive to get the fast Internet you will definitely need. This is less and less a problem as phone and cable companies improve and expand their Internet service—but be sure to check.

Look for clean, well-maintained locations. Because office parks are cheaper, their owners often have lower maintenance standards. Attractive and well-groomed landscaping is a sign that the owner cares for the property.

Security is also an issue. Because fewer people will be around the office park at night, you want to make sure that your space is safe and can be secured with an alarm and good locks. Check for any security weaknesses, such as older, vulnerable windows and doors, and ensure that there is no easy roof access for burglars. Office parks are often like a ghost town at night and can be easy targets for thieves. Most strip mall spaces have bathrooms in the units, but in a business park, you need to make sure that a restroom is included in your space or that common restrooms are close by. You may also wish to consider what eateries are nearby for lunchtime meals unless you're a brown bag lunch type of person.

Free-Standing Building

In areas with a lower cost of living, you may that find a free-standing building is the ideal location for your drop-off store. A clean, attractive free-standing building will be inviting to your clients, especially if it has big windows (look for tempered glass windows for maximum security). Such buildings are usually equipped with bathrooms, but don't forget to check. Because your business will need lots of different work areas, look for a building that can easily be configured for your use. Although you may be able to negotiate improvements with your landlord as part of the lease, you'll always get a better rate if you take the space as-is and do the work yourself. But keep a sharp eye out for anything that might become a money pit. Avoid former restaurants and buildings that would require a major renovation. Try to focus on spaces that are modern and up-to-date. A wide-open space would be more productive and configurable than one that's been configured with a bunch of different rooms.

If you find a perfect spot that just needs a little cleaning and paint, grab it. A dirty location can be brightened up relatively inexpensively, but keep in mind that with a freestanding building, you will most likely have to maintain the landscaping and curb appeal yourself. Unlike with shopping centers and some business parks, maintenance is rarely included in a freestanding building lease.

Buy Your Pants a Few Sizes Bigger

With eBay, your business' growth can be explosive, and you might actually become the victim of your own success. Outgrowing your space can be very frustrating and costly. If you become flooded with items for listing on eBay, you may find yourself bursting at the seams. It's critical that you carefully consider your growth potential and be very realistic about the room you will need to process and store items. Areas you will need include:

- A waiting area for clients, ideally with seating
- A work counter for evaluating and receiving items
- A staging area for cleaning items
- A comfortable area for listing items
- A photography area

- An item storage area

- A staging area for pulling, preparing, and packing shipments

- A temporary storage area for placing parcels that are awaiting pickup by your shipping companies

- A filing area for keeping important records

- An area for storing office supplies, packing materials, and cleaning products

Don't try to squeeze everything into a tiny space. Be practical and allow plenty of room to work comfortably. I keep lots of folding tables around to use as quick staging areas and as temporary storage for items I'm evaluating or listing.

Creature Comforts

In a mall, you will usually be leasing in a modern building with central heating and air conditioning. Be sure to ask the leasing agent or owner if the property has separate temperature controls. My first office space didn't have its own control, and I would alternately be freezing or sweating. Having to constantly ask the neighbor with the controls to make an adjustment was a huge hassle. Separate controls are a must—don't compromise on this detail. Comfort is important in any business where you're performing physical activity all day long.

In older buildings, you may find that the space is heated or cooled with through-the-wall or window units. These units are often not large enough to heat and cool the space properly, and you will want to check their BTU (don't ask me why, but it stands for British Thermal Units) rating. I try to make sure that the units put out at least 25 BTUs of cooling and heating for each square foot of office or warehouse space. This means that a 1,000-square-foot location will need air conditioning and heating units rated to put out at least 25,000 BTUs of cooling and heating. The ceiling height is a factor here, and if the location has very high ceilings and you pay for the utilities, you can find that your monthly overhead just took a big jump. I would avoid older buildings, high ceilings, and these types of wall or window units.

In office parks, it's not uncommon for the office portion of the space to be the only area with heat and air-conditioning, while the warehouse is neither heated nor cooled. Clearly this can cause very uncomfortable conditions for you and your employees. The comfort of your work environment will have a remarkable effect on your productivity—it's important that you feel good. Not to mention, some collectible items can be affected if not stored properly.

If your lease does not include utilities and you have to pay for them separately, check with the different utility providers (gas, electric, and water) to see if they will provide you with some historical utility bill amounts for the property you're considering. I have found that many utility companies will provide this information by phone. Don't be shy— just be professional and ask. Add the projected utilities cost as a line item to your budget and update your business plan accordingly. Don't forget to ask if a deposit is required, if you don't already have a business account with them.

Security and Safety

You will be handling other people's possessions, and some of the things you take in may be very valuable. The security of your space will be critical. When touring office or retail space, be sure to inspect the building's security features. As with a business park, look for strong, solid doors and modern, secure, tempered glass windows. Be sure no points of entry can be easily breached, such as access through the roof, and that all the locks and latches appear to be in good working order. Look for a location which is well lit at night. Consider an alarm system with live monitoring that will notify the police if the alarm is tripped. It is also possible to find old bank or jewelry store locations that might have an operating vault or at least the original vault room that can be made into a strong room. I purchased my electronic floor safe from Harbor Freight Tools for less than $200. They have a store in my town, but they also ship to any address in the country.

Because you're an online business, you will have little or no concern about shoplifting. Employee theft is a reality to consider. It's important that you store client items in a part of your space that is not easily accessible to unauthorized persons coming to your location. Keep the merchandise stored far away from the public. If you have a public restroom, be sure that merchandise is not accessible to anyone who uses it. Escort any vendors delivering supplies beyond public areas. I prefer to have my own employees handle deliveries beyond the front-of-store. This minimizes the possibility of curious and prying eyes. I also do not permit clients to view other clients' items. This is for their own security and comfort as well. And I never discuss clients' names with others—I feel that confidentiality is a key part of my service.

Employee theft is retailers' number-one source of "shrinkage"—their term for loss of merchandise. But shrinkage comes in other forms, too, so when considering a location, look for configurations that allow you maximum control over your space. During office hours, we use only one entry and exit door. We keep our back door locked at all times, and if an employee is working alone, they are required to lock the store if they step out, even if only for a moment (putting up the good old "Back in 15 Minutes" sign). Security is a top priority when choosing a location.

Lastly, walk the neighborhood. Take in the environment. What do you see? Are there classy people and nice businesses nearby? Are the sidewalks clean? Speak with neighboring businesses, tell them you're considering starting a business nearby, a key part of my service. You should meet your future neighbors and learn about the area that you will call your second home for months or years to come. Ask questions about neighborhood safety.

You may also want to pay a visit to the local police department and find out about any burglaries or other crime in the area. The newspapers often compile and publish crime statistics as well.

Working with the Landlord

Leasing your new store can be a nerve-racking experience if you're a first-timer. Be calm. Even though you may think that the location you have found is the most fantastic deal or the perfect spot to hang your shingle, don't let the owner or leasing agent sense desperation. If you're working through a leasing agent hired by the property owner, you will be in a good position, because agents are paid on commission and will work hard to earn your business. If you lease in a large office complex or mall, you will most likely be dealing with an agent and not the owners.

My business philosophy is based largely on the concept of following the path of least resistance. I prefer to do business with people who want to do business with me. If I find interacting with someone an uncomfortable experience, then I tend to move on and work with someone else. If a building owner is "drama" in the beginning, you'll be likely to experience the same during your tenancy. Brokers and leasing agents also tend to mirror the behavior of their clients.

When working out the terms of a lease, I am confident, relaxed, and comfortable. If the owner or agent makes me feel uncomfortable, as though I'm being rushed or patronized, or conjures up some complex set of rules or hoops to jump through, I simply walk away. There are always other spaces you can lease. Be professional and courteous at all times but ask for clarification of anything you don't understand.

Dealing directly with property owners has both pros and cons. Because the leasing agent acts as a buffer between you and the owner, you'll find that tempers rarely flare. But sometimes the owner of a property can be so personally (and emotionally) involved in their investment that they view you almost as an adversary, and you may find yourself being grilled about things such as your credit, your references, and the type of business you will be operating. Be extremely patient if this happens. Often owners soften up once they get to know you better. If the owner shows you the property personally, be affable, genuine, up-front, and candid and try to build a rapport. You're proud of your business plan, and this is a golden opportunity to use it. A compelling business plan will speak volumes about your professionalism and ability to think through the requirements of your business.

Both the landlord and tenant have responsibilities. Normally, the landlord simply provides a space with a secure roof overhead. Unlike when renting an apartment, you won't find many commercial property owners plunging clogged toilets or fixing broken air-conditioning units, unless these services are specified in the lease. The landlord will probably want to get some or all of the following from you:

- An application
- A credit report (and possibly a fee to pull it)
- Business references
- An explanation of your business and a written assurance of your exact business use (but try to avoid getting too specific, or it may prevent you from providing other services down the road as your business grows)
- Their lease agreement signed by you

Curb Your Enthusiasm

You should ask the agent or owner if you can review a copy of their lease agreement, even if you will continue to view other properties. If you think you have found your perfect location, I strongly urge you to continue your search until a lease has actually been signed. So many factors can play into the lease negotiation process that it's always best to have options. Curb your enthusiasm about any particular location and carefully review your requirements before proceeding with the negotiation phase of the leasing process. When reading through the lease, be certain you fully understand all the terms and conditions as well as the security deposit and initial payment requirements (first month's and possibly last month's rent, etc.).

Owners want to see that you're qualified to lease their property. Being prepared will improve your chances and put you ahead of others who may be interested in the same site. Credit reporting agencies will provide you with one free copy of your credit report each year. Besides a copy of your credit report, I suggest providing your prospective landlord with proof of your financial stability in the form of bank statements. Your business plan will also have your financial statement. I use www.myfico.com to obtain regular updates on the status of my credit reports from the major credit bureaus. The cost is nominal and includes notification when your report changes and tips on ways to improve your credit.

Negotiations: The Floor Was Gross, but the Price Was Right

Negotiating a good lease can save you money. Establish what concessions your landlord is willing to make for you. When I leased my store in Burbank, the property owner would not agree to a lease term longer than three years. The location was fantastic for me, just walking distance from my home and next door to a busy bank and many retail shops. The rent was low, but the place was a wreck. Outside, it looked like any other retail store, but inside, the floor was gross, the paint was peeling, and junk and old furniture were everywhere. It was also dark and depressing. Because the price was extremely low, I didn't drive a hard bargain. It was very clear to me that I would be putting some elbow grease into the store to get it into good shape. But I did try to get a one-year term with the option to lease for up to five years with one-year renewal options. I really loved the location.

The landlord would not budge on the length of the lease so I ended up having to settle for the three years. I knew that I would be putting a lot of time and effort into marketing my business, and I wanted to make sure I had a secure and stable location. Because my rent was going to be very low, I paid to remove the trash and excess furniture. I then painted and carpeted. The results were dramatic. The landlord was nice and fair. As I expected, with the low rent came no assistance with renovations and absolutely no maintenance except that I was promised a leak-free roof over my head.

Keeping Your Options Open

The terms of a lease almost always favor the landlord, so be sure to keep this in mind when you review your lease agreement. With a little effort, you will probably be able to negotiate better terms—leases are, by the very nature of any business deal, negotiable. Your ability to gain concessions in any lease negotiation will depend greatly on the local rental market. In hot markets, you will be granted few concessions, because the landlord will have no problem leasing the property. In slower markets, however, you will be in a great position to seek concessions.

When you depend on walk-in traffic for your business, it's helpful to have long lease terms, which accomplish through renewal options. But at the same time, you will want to have the shortest possible initial term, such as 6 to 12 months. In case the location doesn't work out, the last thing you want is to be trapped in a $3,000-per-month, three-year lease. Ask for renewal options that will extend your lease for additional years. If you're renting in a business park, on the other hand, you may want to seek a month-to-month lease. When you're not depending on a prime location for attracting clients, you can have a short lease.

Nowhere to Go but Up

Never assume the asking rent is firm. Looking at comparable properties will give you a good sense of the prices for similar space in your market. Keep good notes on the cost per square foot that each landlord is asking. Most landlords will ask for a moderate rent increase each year, so it's important to try to put a cap on the percentage or dollar amount that your rent can go up. Some landlords will tie this number to a cost-of-living increase, but I always prefer to stick with a fixed percentage. Paying an increase of 3 to 5 percent is fair. If the location is very desirable, the landlord may ask for more, or they may simply try to avoid specifying the increase method altogether. Try hard to get this locked in.

With Leases, Gross Is Good

There are several types of customary leases. Here are the most common:

- Gross lease. A property lease where the landlord pays all expenses normally associated with the ownership of the property, such as utilities, repairs, insurance, and taxes

- Modified gross lease. A property lease where the landlord pays the property taxes and building insurance and the lessee (you) agrees to pay for utilities, repairs, and maintenance

- Net lease (also known as a triple-net lease or closed-end lease). A property lease in which the lessee agrees to pay all expenses normally associated with ownership, such as utilities, repairs, insurance, and taxes

- Double-net lease. A property lease in which the lessee pays rent to the landlord as well as all utilities, taxes, and insurance, while the landlord pays maintenance expenses

It would be in your best interest to try to obtain a gross lease. Though the rent will no doubt be higher with a gross lease, often it's better to pay a higher monthly rent that's fixed and predictable. Winter heating bills and summer cooling costs can really add up. With net leases and multiple tenants in a mall or building complex, each tenant pays a prorated share of the costs based on their unit's square footage. This can get complicated, and if this is your first lease, I advise sticking to simple lease agreements. I pay my own utilities and maintenance, but my landlord pays for maintaining the roof. It's pretty simple, and it's essentially a modified gross lease.

Renting It Again

Request a subletting clause in your contract. This means you have the right to rent the space to someone else in the event that you have too much space or if you want to move on to another location, business, or job. Subletting to someone else does not relieve you of the financial obligation to pay, it simply permits you to move out and let someone else move in who is qualified to pay the rent to you, while you continue to pay the landlord according to the original lease terms. In theory, you can charge any amount you want and even make a profit on a sublet agreement.

Ask for a Hand

If the property needs a lot of improvements, you should ask the landlord what improvements they would be willing to handle before you move in. For shorter leases, the owner may not be willing to do much, but if you're planning on staying for a long time, it will be a good opportunity to save a few bucks. Maybe you can ask for carpet or paint. These are basics, and many landlords will throw them in. Be fair with your requests—if you appear too demanding, you may alienate the owner and the deal could fall apart.

When to Walk and When to Jump

When a landlord is completely inflexible on terms and you know that their price is not the lowest around, it's time to walk. You want to rent from someone who is professional, and a professional person is willing to negotiate. Working out a lease is a give-and-take process, and if you aren't getting anywhere, don't worry—this isn't the right deal for you. Give yourself permission to move on. It's not a defeat to pass on a deal. It would be reasonable to look at five to ten different locations and make offers on three or more of them to see which landlords are willing to work with you.

Once in a blue moon, you will be presented with an unreal opportunity—that perfect store location near the right mix of busy retailers. If the price is fantastic and you know you're getting a great deal, you need to move fast. Thinking too hard about a good deal may let someone else lease it instead of you. Landlords make killer deals for a variety of reasons. A smart landlord wants long-term tenants and no vacancies. A good tenant means few calls and little maintenance. A superior tenant keeps the property in as good condition as if it were their own. When you meet up with a once-in-a-lifetime deal, rent it. Don't bargain too hard, or don't bargain at all.

Check Your List Twice

Here's a checklist to help you when reviewing your lease agreement. Never sign a lease on the spot when it is presented to you. Take the time to consider each clause carefully and ask questions if you don't understand something. This is a big decision, so you may want to discuss the lease with friends and family, or possibly an attorney if you can afford it. In other words, take a copy home and review it. Areas to review are:

- Rental amount.
- Duration (lease term)
- Options to extend the lease
- Escalation amounts (rent increases) and how they will be calculated
- Any required security deposit and whether or not you will earn interest on it
- Any restrictions or conditions on your advertising signage
- Who will pay utilities, insurance, and taxes
- Any restrictions on the use of the space (can you change your line of business?)
- Any concessions such as paint, carpet, or other improvements that may be needed
- How the maintenance of the building, roof, and plumbing will be handled and who is responsible for paying these costs
- Who will be responsible for maintaining the heating and air-conditioning systems
- The amount of notice you're required to give before you terminate your lease and if it automatically renews if you do not
- Any rules and regulations you're required to follow
- Possible restrictions on your hours of operation

> Tip: Check with other merchants in the area and ask if they would be willing to share a copy of their lease agreement with you. If they are willing, you can gain valuable insights (and experience) from them about the dos and don'ts when signing a lease of your own.

8. Buying a Commercial Building Space

We own a restaurant in Dubuque, Iowa, and we have a spare room in the back that we use for trading on eBay. A client had a vintage coffee pot that we listed with a starting bid of $2.99, and when the auction ended seven days later, it had a new owner who bid $380 for one of the very first mass-produced electric coffee pots from Silex. The client's wife had originally wanted to throw the pot in the trash, so he was really shocked by the final sales price we obtained for him.

—Paul H. Connor, Dubuque, Iowa; eBay user ID "ezsellusa"; trading on eBay since January 17, 2005

Playing Monopoly

eBay has been good to me. And so has real estate. My eBay earnings have allowed me to purchase a lot of it. I can honestly say without exaggeration that my eBay business has made me a millionaire.

Why then do I lease a retail office space? Well, that's really a function of where I live. When I offered to buy the building from my landlord, and he has politely said no. There is very good reason why you rarely see a "For Sale" sign on commercial property in my neighborhood—values keep going up, and landlords keep collecting rents. Unlike homes, commercial properties don't sell frequently here.

If I lived in an area where buying a building like mine didn't cost a million bucks (literally), I would have owned my own building long ago. When I was first starting out, it would have been easy and affordable to buy a building in my area, and with the larger number of available properties at that time, my landlord might have sold to me.

If you own your own home and understand property ownership responsibilities, buying might be the right decision for you. You have to consider the possibility that you will own your business for a very long time, and you may prefer to be the master of your own destiny.

Unlike single-family homes, you can expect to put up a pretty hefty down payment for a commercial property. Because a failed business can be abandoned rather easily, whereas a home is where you live, most lenders have a much higher down payment requirement on commercial properties. You can expect to put down between 10–45 percent of the total purchase price of a commercial property. But if commercial property is affordable where you live, and you have the cash, owning is better than renting. Mortgage interest rates on commercial buildings are also higher than residential property rates.

My favorite book on real estate investing is "The Weekend Millionaire's Secrets to Investing in Real Estate: How to Become Wealthy in Your Spare Time" by Mike Summey and Roger Dawson. This book is a quick read and will be very helpful in making you an astute real estate negotiator and buyer.

To Buy or Not to Buy

The benefits of owning:

- Your rent will not go up based upon someone else's arbitrary decision.
- As you pay down your mortgage, eventually you will own the property completely.
- You can take advantage of tax breaks for renovations.
- You can lease the property to someone else if you decide to close your business.
  The disadvantages of ownership:
- Your mortgage will most likely be of the adjustable rate type, and you may pay more or less each year based upon the current market interest rates.
- You have to pay for all taxes, insurance, repairs, and maintenance costs.
- If you do not keep up with your payments, your credit will be affected.
- If you want to sell the property, it may be hard to do so quickly in a stale real estate market.

The Brokers

Just as with commercial leasing agents (many of whom also sell commercial property), you want to find a real estate broker who is professional, patient, and courteous. Buying a building is a very big commitment, and it is imperative that your broker fully understands your business needs.

Start the process by showing your business plan to your broker. Engaging them in the nuances of your planned business operations will help them to weed out inappropriate properties, instead showing you just those most suitable for your needs. Use the same considerations discussed in the previous chapter on leasing. While working with real estate professionals, have a detailed checklist of your requirements on hand and have a budget in mind.

You will find that most real estate people will be aggressive in helping you to find property, if they believe that you're capable of meeting the financial requirements necessary to make the purchase. Meeting with a bank representative at this stage, with your credit report and in hand, will give you an idea of your qualifications and how much you can afford. A prequalification letter from a bank will show the realtor and the property owner, both of whom will want to make certain that you can actually qualify for the purchase, that you're serious.

Many realtors will ask you to sign an exclusive representation agreement with them. I caution you to avoid doing this until you get a good feel for the realtor's qualifications. Most real estate is listed in the Multiple Listing Service, also known as MLS. Any realtor can show you property listed with the service, even if the property is not represented by them. Any realtor can submit offers to the listing's real estate broker, who in turn can present such offers to their client, the owner of the property. Therefore, if you're dealing directly with the listing broker, you will be eliminating a middleman from the process. And if your realtor is the listing broker on many commercial properties, it's fine to sign an exclusive representation agreement with them, provided that it has a reasonable term (not more than a month or perhaps two) and the broker has inventory that is suitable for your use.

With or without an agreement, when dealing with a realtor, it is important that your conduct be thoroughly professional. It is never appropriate to try to sidestep your broker by attempting to deal directly with the seller's broker when you have been shown the property by your realtor. The two realtors typically split commissions on sales when a seller and buyer are represented separately.

If and when you make a make an offer to purchase a property, your realtor will submit the offer through a formal process as mandated by your state's regulatory agency for realtors. Although there is a little latitude on how this process is handled, the initial offer will normally be prepared on a set of forms.

I encourage you to ask your realtor to show you at least three properties with the features you need in your price range. Your realtor will make a hefty commission on the sale, so don't be shy about asking to see many properties, as long as your expectations are reasonable and you're respectful of their time. Most real estate investors look at dozens of properties and make a lot of offers before they finally get the deal they want. This is a process that you should never rush.

You should work with a realtor who is both patient and aggressive. They should be aggressive in trying to find suitable properties for you, but you should never feel pressured to make an immediate decision. There are certain tactics that seller's realtors may use to try to close a sale, but remember that many properties are usually for sale at any given time—make sure the one you buy is as close to ideal for your needs as possible. You most likely will be working in this space for a very long time, and you want to make sure it fits your personal tastes as well as business needs.

When reviewing properties, keep a written checklist of all the same basic requirements discussed in Chapter 7 on leasing and consider the following additional points:

- Age of the building
- Condition
- Method of construction (wood, brick, etc.)
- Location (you want your property to appreciate in value, and a better neighborhood will help to ensure this)
- Tax and utility costs
- Adjacent uses

"Location, location, location"—it's so important in valuing property, and the old saying holds true for you, too. The location and quality of the neighborhood where you buy should be conducive not only to your business needs but also to appreciation—you want a property that will increase in value over time. Your local chamber of commerce may have economic studies and statistics that could be valuable in location decision making.

When going out with a realtor, ask them to line up as many properties as possible for you to see. Carry a notepad and jot down anything that may jump out at you, especially problems. There's no need to share any of this information with your realtor, until it comes time to assess the value of the property. Then you'll discuss any deductions you may want to make for problems. You should also sketch a floor plan of each property, indicating any problem areas. The floor plan will help you later in your evaluation of the space and its suitability for your eBay drop-off store needs. If the list of issues is substantial, try to imagine at what point, looking at other properties, you would simply rule this building out.

> Tip: Never buy any property with your emotions in high gear. It is easy to overpay when you are in love with something. In both slow and overheated markets, it is always possible to make an excellent decision when purchasing real estate, if you take your time to study the market and learn as much as possible about the neighborhood, comparable properties, and prevailing prices.

Take Your Time, but Don't Be a "Tire Kicker"

Your realtor may ask you to consider making an offer right away, but I caution you to look at many properties and review your notes before making any offers. Take photos of the exterior and interior of each building, and pay attention to details. During and after viewing properties, don't show your realtor much emotion. Avoid selling yourself on any one property and take time to digest the pros and cons of each building while reviewing your notes and photos. Talk to other business property owners before making any decisions so you benefit from other people's experience.

You may want to have a building with a loading dock and a big warehouse area if you foresee listing a lot of large items. If you will handle expensive items such as jewelry, you want a building that is secure and can be protected with an alarm. There are too many possible variables to list—you'll have to try carefully to project all your possible business scenarios and needs.

Be sure to thank your realtor after they have shown you each property, and let them know you will get back to them if you're interested in making an offer. Be relaxed—you'ren't in any rush—and let the realtor know that you're considering all possible options before making your final decision. Be respectful of the realtor's time—if they sense you're a "tire kicker" or a window shopper, they may well stop returning your calls or simply be too "busy" to meet with you again.

Put Your Money Where Your Mouth Is

If you look at a building that seems absolutely perfect for you in every possible way, you will still want to make certain that it's in good condition. A building that appears to be in great condition may have problems lurking behind drywall or under a subfloor. There may be dry rot that you can't see, or an army of termites munching away.

Most offers are contingent upon later inspection. It is illogical to pay someone to inspect a property before you make an offer to purchase it, because if your offer is not accepted, you have wasted your money. Prior to submitting your first offer, you will want to have a professional, licensed property inspector, and probably a termite extermination company, lined up for inspections of the building if your offer is accepted. These inspectors should be in place prior to your offer, because if your offer is accepted, the time window for the contingent inspections is typically only one to two weeks.

The property inspector will look at every single nook and cranny of the building; check the roof, plumbing, structural aspects etc.; and submit a comprehensive written condition report, including, of course, any problems they found. Professional inspectors are experts in evaluating the condition of equipment as well. Most termite companies will conduct an inspection for free in the hope that eventually it will result in some extermination work. If you have any trouble finding a good termite company and/or property inspector, you should contact the chamber of commerce in your city for referrals.

Once you have made a decision on the suitability of a property, it's time to make an offer for purchase. Normally making the offer will require a good faith deposit that you pledge towards the deal if the offer is accepted. This shows you're serious, and most sellers will not consider an offer without this deposit, called earnest money. The earnest money can be $500, $1,000, or a percentage of the property's value. I have seen it all over the map, and I have given up to 3 percent of the property's value when making an offer. Customarily, your check is not cashed until your offer is accepted.

The Offer

The offer will be a rather long document and may have some terms or concepts that are new to you. As part of the offer process, this document states whether you're asking the seller to pay the costs of handling certain aspects of the transaction. Below are some of the costs that are often associated with the sale of a property:

Escrow fees. In some states, a separate, third-party company holds all funds during the transaction and manages all of the paperwork in conjunction with a sale. Although an escrow company is not required for cash purchases of real property, lenders will require an escrow company or, alternatively, a property title company to handle the money; file legal documents with the county to confirm the transfer of the property from the seller to you; pay all fees to various parties, such as the appraiser, etc.; and to make sure in general that the sale process runs smoothly. A "title" is the property ownership, in effect proof that you're the owner of the property, which can be evidenced by a deed. Don't worry about all these terms—your realtor and your lender will ensure that all documents are filed properly. The escrow fees are often split equally between buyer and seller. You can ask the seller to pay all of them, but that would be very unusual. The escrow company or title company will ensure that you have secure title at the end of the "close" of escrow.

Appraisal fees. Most commercial lenders will require that a licensed property appraiser assess the property's value. This will involve a physical inspection of the property and research to determine what other similar properties have fetched recently. The recent sales of similar properties are called "comps." The lender will usually bill you, the buyer, for the appraisal. If the property has had a recent appraisal, you should let your lender know, and asking about this detail may save you a large sum of money. I suggest that you don't allow the property to be appraised until you have a formal approval letter from your lender. Your offer's time frame should allow enough time for you to accomplish this task, and if you were able to get prequalified by your lender, this process should all move very quickly and smoothly.

Survey. A property survey is essentially a formal statement from a licensed surveyor that shows the property boundaries. The survey is important in making certain that everyone (especially you) knows the actual physical boundaries of the property you're buying. If the seller has a survey on the property already, this is a moot point, and you can use their survey. If the seller doesn't, it's not unusual to ask them to pay for the survey.

Termite work. Virtually all lenders will want to have a termite inspection of the property. This is crucial. You may want to have your own company do this, because often sellers or their realtors have close relationships with their own companies. I am not saying that your seller or their realtor will assert undue influence on this inspection either way, but in the past, I have found extensive infestations of termites after I'd purchased property, even though the seller's termite inspection had come back with no evidence of infestation. It's appropriate to have a truly neutral person handle this. It is also normal for a seller to provide a property that is free of infestations, and the seller should, and typically will, pay for any termite eradication or termite-related repairs. Because the building you're buying is probably 100 percent commercial use, it is practical to "tent" the building to exterminate any infestations. In tenting, the termite company will cover the entire building with a special tent and then pump gas into the property to kill all of the termites or any other existing pests. This is the only truly reliable way to kill all the termites, and you should try to negotiate with the seller to pay for this type of treatment if infestations are found. Remember that the day after the tent is removed and the gas dissipates into the air, termites will come back to make themselves at home again. Pest control is an ongoing process for as long as you own a building.

Loan costs. The lender you select to finance this property will normally charge some fees. These fees are completely at the lender's discretion and vary greatly. Some lenders will charge no up-front fees, but the interest rate they charge may be a bit higher to compensate. Almost all lenders pay their loan agents some form of incentive or commission, typically paid for through "points." The points are a percentage of the total loan and are charged to you in return for the loan's origination. These fees can be negotiated, and if you shop your loan around to various lenders, you may be able to avoid paying points and still obtain a favorable interest rate. Remember that an appraisal fee is paid to an appraiser, but the loan origination fees are paid to the lender itself, so the lender may have a lot of discretion with these fees. If you're dealing with a direct lender, these fees are typically very low. If you deal with a loan broker (i.e., someone who sends your loan package out to a number of lenders), you will most certainly pay points to compensate this broker for their commissions. Many lenders may charge a loan application fee as well, and this fee is usually nonrefundable. With a loan broker, you may be able to avoid this application fee, but you will probably end up paying a bit more in the long run. An aggressive loan broker will increase your chances of obtaining financing, but you will most likely pay more for the money. You need to weigh these factors. For first-time borrowers, I suggest you work with a loan broker.

Title insurance. The property's title (ownership records) can be guaranteed by an insurance company through what is normally called title insurance. Lenders will require title insurance to assure that there are no liens against the property or other problems. Normally, the seller pays for title insurance. If you plan on adding a second (or even a third) loan to the property at some later date, you can pay an additional fee to obtain a buyer's title insurance policy, which will save you money on future title insurance for these additional loans. If interest rates are relatively high at the time you secure financing, I'd ask the title company for their guidelines on fees they charge when you go back and refinance your property.

Property insurance. Lenders will also require that the property have hazard insurance in place at the time of closing. You should shop around for this insurance to get a favorable rate. However, you should always get a policy from a highly rated company—you will be glad you did if you ever have the need to file a claim. Include the cost of hazard insurance when estimating your total costs for acquiring the property. It would be a good idea to obtain estimates from this same insurer for the policy you will need to cover your business operations as well as worker's compensation insurance (if you intend to have employees). An insurer will give discounts for multiple policies, including your auto and homeowners' insurance. I have saved a lot of money by carrying all my insurance policies with one company.

Property taxes. The county where you reside will charge you an annual assessment for property taxes. You may pay taxes to your city for municipal services as well. These taxes will be paid twice a year. I suggest you ask your lender to impound or escrow both your property taxes and hazard insurance. The lender can spread the tax bill over your monthly mortgage payments and make it more digestible. You need to consider your tax bill as part of your overall overhead when buying a building, and at the time your real estate purchase is consummated, you may see an adjustment for prorated taxes.

Miscellaneous fees. Other fees associated with the purchase of real property include government fees for the filing of the deed as well as fees charged to you by the escrow or title company for preparing various documents and mailing or sending them via express courier. You will incur an additional fee if you live in a state which requires an attorney to prepare your deed. These fees are usually rather nominal, but they can add up.

Before you make an offer, you should ask your lender to review your credit and your income to estimate both what you can afford to buy and also the total cost of making the purchase, including the down payment. Make sure you have the cash necessary before you start making any offers.

Study your floor plans. Does the building have enough space for you to handle listings, photography, storage, packing, shipping, and future growth? Once you have compiled a list of which properties will work well for your new eBay drop-off store, it's time to start writing offers. I would never offer full price for any property. There is no need to make offensively low offers, but all sellers expect to receive offers below their asking price. The exception would be if you're in a very hot real estate market, when it is normal for offers even to exceed the asking price, especially if there are multiple offers. But if a realtor tells you there are multiple offers on a property, it's not necessarily an indication that you should make an offer above the asking price. Your realtor must submit any offer you present, whether or not they believe it will be accepted. You should expect to make many offers, on numerous properties, before getting a great deal on one you want. You can pay full price for any property and get it fast—or, with a little patience, you can wait until you find a great deal. This simply depends upon how quickly you need to start your business. When I am investing in property, I am always patient, and I never overpay.

When writing your offer, remember to determine who will pay for each of the above anticipated costs, and remember that all this is totally negotiable. There is no right or wrong way to make your offer. You can ask the seller to pay for all the closing costs, or you can agree to split them. Remember that your real estate broker works for you. If your broker scoffs at your ideas and how you wish to structure an offer, you may wish to secure a second opinion. Brokers should be flexible and ready to work with you. In your offer, indicate who pays for:

- Property inspection
- Termite work (if any)
- Repairs to the property (if you found problems after a property inspection)
- Title insurance
- Escrow fees
- Survey
- Any other costs for closing

Your realtor will have forms to use for making the offer. Read these over carefully and be sure to indicate in every instance whether you or the seller will pay for a particular cost. You will also want to allow ample time for the property inspection, termite work, and loan approvals. These items should be written into your offer in the form of contingencies, which will state that the offer is subject to inspection of the property, a clean termite report, and approval from your lender with terms that are acceptable to you. All of this will protect you from losing your earnest money deposit in the event you cannot secure financing or if you discover something drastically wrong with the building after the inspections have been completed.

Haggling

Once you submit your offer, the seller will have a period of time specified in the offer in which to respond. If the seller fails to respond within that time, your earnest money check will not be cashed. If the seller agrees to your offer as-is, the earnest money will go to the title or escrow company mutually agreed upon by the buyer and seller. Many realtors have in-house escrow services, which can speed up the closing process.

If the seller comes back to you with a counteroffer, review the counteroffer with your realtor to understand the terms that have been modified and/or added by the seller. It's not uncommon to go back and forth a few times before settling on final terms and conditions that are acceptable to both parties. Rarely will a seller accept the initial offer.

Remember at all times that your realtor and the realtor representing the seller are paid on a commission basis. They have a strong financial incentive to sell the property to you. And it is important that your mind is clear and that you very carefully think through the terms of the sale before making a final agreement.

Be prepared to walk away from an unfavorable deal. Keep your emotions under control and understand that you're making a business decision. Often, a seller will come back to the bargaining table when a buyer walks away from a deal. Being prepared to say no is a powerful negotiating tool for you, because it shows that you're not desperate. Play it cool and relax. No deal is ever a once-in-a-lifetime opportunity.

If you plan to make offers on more than one property, you should bear in mind that more than one offer may be accepted. Unless you've written in some clever contingencies, you'll be required to complete the transaction or risk losing your earnest money deposit.

Tip: You can hold title of real property with any legal business entity or under your personal name. You can take title of a property as an individual, jointly with another individual (or individuals), through an LLC, a partnership, a corporation, or one of various other legal entities. It may be a logical decision for you to hold title as an individual and then lease the property back to your new company for a nominal sum (such as $1 a year). This will help to create a layer of protection for your property against potential liabilities such as lawsuits or liens in the event your business fails (but we don't think it will!)

Other People's Money

As previously stated, your down payment requirements can be as low as 10 percent and as high as 45 percent, depending upon the loan program. The Small Business Administration (SBA) has loan guarantee programs that allow making a lower down payment. The SBA also offers programs that will guarantee your financing for the entire business, including your leasehold improvements, so it's smart to ask your lender if you qualify for one of these programs. And you may want to show your lender your business plan and determine if you can obtain financing for your new building and your eBay business at the same time.

Each lender will have their own loan application guidelines, and they will look at your financial strength and the feasibility of your project before agreeing to lend you money. They will also want to see that you have sufficient working capital to keep the business operating during your initial start-up and growth.

Work closely with your lender and establish a strong rapport with them. If they feel very positive about your proposed business, they will go above and beyond the call of duty to make certain you have every possible chance of obtaining financing.

Many sellers have owned their buildings for a long time and often have a very small mortgage or own the property free and clear. Because of this, on several occasions, I have been able to purchase property with seller financing. This means that the seller, instead of a commercial lender, carried the note on the property. These deals are rare, but they do come up. And when they do, it's a wonderful thing, because the seller won't charge you fees and points as a bank will, and typically their guidelines for lending you the money will be much more relaxed than a bank's. If the seller is highly motivated to sell, they may be willing to help you with some or even all of the financing.

You should ask the realtor if the seller would consider financing the mortgage. If you're short on cash, you can also structure offers in which the seller carries a second mortgage as part of the purchase agreement.

The terms of the financing will vary from lender to lender, and your payment terms could range from 5 to 30 years. Your payment will be determined by the amortization period: if the loan is fully amortized for 30 years, the payment will be lower than if the same loan amount were amortized over 15 years. It is important for your financial projections to know what terms the bank can offer you. Many seller-financed properties will have a long amortization period, but the seller will want a balloon payment in a shorter period of time, such as three to five years.

Closing the deal on your new building may take as little as a few weeks (with seller financing) to as much as a couple of months. You will end up with a deed to your new property, and you will be the proud owner of your own building. Then the real work begins—now you have to get your doors open and your new eBay venture off the ground.

I haven't attempted to make you a real estate expert in one chapter. However, this chapter is a good primer for understanding the mechanics of purchasing your own building to start your eBay drop-off store.

You're the Landlord Now

When you're just starting out in a new business, having cash coming in is very helpful. If you have decided to purchase a building with lots of extra space, you might be able to sublet parts of your space to help pay your bills. You can rent office or storage space, or you might offer to handle warehousing for other companies. When you're in downtown Los Angeles and gazing up at the skyscrapers with big-company logos on them, you can rest assured that these firms rent office space to help cover the cost of owning these buildings.

If you have extra space with secure and separate entries, you can attract other businesspeople who are seeking temporary places within which to conduct their small businesses. In my store, we offer parcel shipping services to increase our revenues. Be creative and think of ways to benefit from being the landlord.

You can put out the word to leasing agents and offer them a commission to help you sublet parts of your new building. You can attract tenants with ads in local newspapers or on the Internet. You might even rent meeting space or conference rooms by the hour. You own the building now, so if you're trying to stretch your dollar, find creative ways to bring in the extra revenue.

9. Insurance

Someone we knew told us that his 1993 Mazda MX6 had a seized engine and was heading for the junkyard. He had been offered $250 for scrapping it. We talked him into letting us sell it on eBay, and it ended up going for $2,550. The winning bidders were a couple in Oklahoma. The husband was a former mechanic, and his wife needed a reliable car to attend college classes. They towed the car away and, even though it needed a new engine, they were pleased with the bargain price they paid—and my client got more than ten times what he was offered by the junkyard.

—Andy and Deb Mowery, Fort Collins, Colorado; eBay user ID "debnroo"; trading on eBay since October 1, 1999

The Reasons for Insurance and Why You Cannot Operate without It

If you're working from home and don't handle a lot of expensive items, buying extra insurance may not be necessary. You will probably already have theft coverage with your homeowner's policy, and if you don't own your own home, you should have a renter's policy that serves the same purpose. Be sure to check your policy to see if it provides sufficient coverage, and ask your insurance company if a work-at-home business will be covered. Bear in mind that most items will be in and out the door in a period of less than two weeks; so you're financial risk exposure isn't going to be huge.

If you operate a drop-off store, you will need to plan your insurance coverage carefully to make certain you and your clients will be protected in the event of loss due to theft, fire, or acts of God (referred to as force majeure). In Los Angeles, we're also prone to earthquakes.

Unless you have very deep pockets, you can get into a lot of financial trouble if you don't have insurance to cover a loss. Don't take excessive risks by running your new business without insurance. If you hire employees, you will also need to have worker's compensation insurance to cover them in the event of an on-the-job injury.

Brokers—Part Deux

Most insurance companies sell their policies through authorized agents or brokers. Some sell insurance directly by telephone without using brokers. With so many insurance companies providing all types of business insurance, it may be confusing, so it's helpful to shop around to learn about the various companies and their offerings.

You can talk to your auto, homeowners', or renters' insurance company and see if they also offer business insurance. You will get better service (and often a better price) from a company when you have multiple policies with them. You can also reach out to friends, family, and your chamber of commerce for referrals to a great insurance broker.

Explain to the broker that you will be operating a business where you handle and store items on behalf of others, and that because you will probably rarely handle cash, most of the liability will concern your equipment and business records and the clients' items. Also, if you own your business' building, you may have to buy separate coverage for it. Because your insurance rates will be determined by the amounts of coverage, your location, and the policies of the insurance company, it is important for you to be classified as the correct business type. Insurance companies' rates are based on the severity of the risk they are insuring. Being an eBay consignment seller does not normally involve a lot of dangerous activities or unusual risks. I celebrate your rights under the Second Amendment to the United States Constitution, however I don't recommend keeping firearms at your place of business. It may raise further implications with regard to insurance rates. Using a firearm against a robber can also raise liability issues. It's best to deal with security and safety in other ways.

Ask the insurance broker if they specialize in insuring businesses, and if they have a variety of carriers to choose from. You may do better working with a broker who is an independent agent and can shop your policy to more than one company. Ask the broker to shop your policy only to companies with a strong financial rating. You want an insurance company with a solid financial base that can make prompt payment on claims. You also want to avoid any companies that may have government regulatory actions pending.

Report Cards

AM Best (www.ambest.com) provides ratings of insurance companies' abilities to meet their obligations to their policyholders. Below is their rating system:

- A++ or A+ (superior)
- A or A- (excellent)
- B++ or B+ (very good)
- B or B- (fair)
- C++ or C+ (marginal)
- C or C- (weak)
- D (poor)
- E (under regulatory supervision)
- F (in liquidation)
- S (rating suspended)

This is Standard and Poor's (www.standardandpoors.com) rating system for insurers:

- AAA (extremely strong)
- AA (very strong)
- A (strong)
- BBB (good)
- BB (marginal)
- B (weak)
- CCC (very weak)
- CC (extremely weak)
- R (under regulatory supervision)
- NR (rating suspended)

Moody's (www.moodys.com) is another company that rates insurance companies:

- Aaa (exceptional financial security)
- Aa (excellent financial security)
- A (good financial security)
- Baa (adequate financial security)

- Ba (questionable financial security)

- B (poor financial security)

- Caa (very poor financial security)

- Ca (extremely poor financial security)

- C (lowest financial security)

Ask your broker to look at companies with a great or superior rating from one of the above companies. Stick to insurance companies that have a rating from any of the above three ratings firms that starts with an A. Don't be seduced by the lowest price quote—it may be from a financially unstable insurance carrier, and you need to be sure that your claim will be paid, promptly, in the event you need to use your insurance policy.

Raise That Deductible

Your insurance broker, just like a real estate broker, is paid by incentives (commissions), and they will want you to be a customer for a very long time. It is in their interest to sell you good insurance and offer you coverage that will protect you both personally and in business—not just sell you cut-rate insurance.

The price of your insurance depends upon a variety of factors, including:

- Your deductible (the amount you have to pay on each claim before your insurance kicks in and starts paying)

- The number of policies that you have with the insurance company

- The insurance company's financial strength (rating)

- The amounts and types of coverage

- Your location

- The type of building and its construction

- Your security system

- Your claims history

Insurance is really designed to cover you in a catastrophic situation. If you break a client's $50 lamp, you will pay for it out of your own pocket; not file a claim against your insurance. Most likely, the deductible would be higher than the value of that item, and the insurance company wouldn't pay anyway. You will want your insurance to cover something big, like a runaway truck smashing into your store, a tornado moving the building to a new zip code, or an earthquake leveling the shop—this is what insurance is for.

You will find that the rate you pay will drop substantially as your deductible goes up. I suggest you go for a high deductible, such as $1,000 (or more if possible). You want your business insurance to be affordable, so in the event of a loss, you want your deductible to be the largest amount you can reasonably pay out of your own pocket without putting a strain on your finances. Ask your broker to give you a variety of quotes based on different deductible amounts so that you can compare the rates and see what makes sense for you.

Tip: If you cannot find a single insurance company to handle all your insurance needs, be sure to read each of your policies carefully to make certain you do not duplicate coverage.

People, Property, and Umbrellas

Your insurance should cover both people and property. Here are the different types of insurance and what they cover.

General Liability

- Bodily injury. This covers your liability when someone else is injured at your business location. Examples would be slip-and-fall injuries or injury as a result of a box falling on a customer.

- Property damage. For damage claims to the property of others, such as damage caused by force majeure. If something happens to your clients' items while in your custody, you will be covered.

- Personal injury. Coverage for things such as libel, slander, false arrest, or wrongful entry. These situations will probably not occur in your type of business, but this coverage is often automatically included in a general liability policy.

- Advertising injury. This covers your legal liability for damage to others caused by your wrongful advertising of your business' goods and services. In the unlikely event that you misrepresent yourself, such as making exaggerated claims about prices you can obtain on eBay, you will be able to get legal defense from your insurance company.

Commercial Automobile Protection

- Liability. This will cover you in the event you or an employee are sued as a result of an auto accident while using a vehicle in connection with your business, such as when picking up items from a client's home or running errands.
- Collision. Pays for physical damage caused to your business' vehicle as a result of an automobile accident.
- Comprehensive. Covers damage to your business' vehicle as a result of fire, theft, or glass breakage.
- Rental reimbursement. Special coverage to pay for a rental vehicle for a specific length of time while your vehicle is disabled due to a covered loss (such as while it is being repaired after an accident).

Business Property Protection

- Protects your building and its contents in the event of physical damage or loss

Umbrella Excess Liability Coverage

- An umbrella policy will provide very high limits in excess of your other coverage. Individuals with a high net worth should invest in this type of additional coverage to protect their primary residence and assets in the event of a major lawsuit or personal injury claim arising out of the business' activities.

Worker's Compensation Insurance

- This coverage is legally required in most states and covers employees and their medical expenses in the event of an on-the-job injury. The rate you pay is normally a percentage of your estimated payroll. Some business insurance packages will also include worker's compensation insurance.

Be sure to discuss all of the above coverage options with your insurance broker. Don't skimp on insurance—you want to be sure you have sufficient coverage to meet the conditions of your business activities. To help take the bite out of the insurance bill, virtually any insurance company will give you a payment plan if requested, so that your payments are spread out in monthly installments.

But you also don't want to be over-insured, paying for policy limits far beyond anything you'll need. Because the average eBay listing duration is seven days, you won't have a lot of items lying around, so your exposure for other people's property will generally be limited, unless you get behind on your listings or have very expensive items in your care.

You will want to get a policy in place before starting any property renovations so your protection is in force right away, even while you're getting ready to open your doors.

Tip: Frame a copy of your insurance policy and hang it in the lobby of your
business along with your business licenses. Clients will appreciate
knowing and that you are an insured business.

10. Store Design and Construction

I deal mostly with corporate clients, because corporations are much less attached to their goods and have little time for handling their own sales on eBay. I have a major account who asked me to move a bulk lot of over 2,000 pairs of shoes. I'm using eBay's Reseller Marketplace, with the client assuming all of the fees, to move larger lots through eBay's wholesale marketplace. My daughter is getting married soon, and I'm using eBay to help pay for a spare-no-expense wedding!
—Robert O. Sachs, Memphis, Tennessee; eBay user ID "rosachs"; trading on eBay since September 21, 1997

> If advertisers spent the same amount of money on improving their
> products as they do on advertising then they wouldn't have to advertise
> them. — WILL ROGERS

Let's assume that you have made the decision to open a drop-off store. (If you're planning to work from home or from within an existing business, you won't need to design and build a store as we'll discuss here.) Though you have secured your location and are eager to get going, it would be very unusual if you could simply open your doors. There is work to be done, including laying out your work space—your daily working environment must be comfortable and functional. I like to have lots of staging areas where I can place merchandise while I work on it. Perhaps you'll have a work counter for greeting customers that doubles as a shipping center. You can even offer to ship packages for local residents as a way to draw in more people. Photography and listings can be conducted at the front of the store for all to see, and from the street you can see bright photography lights—a beacon that will draw potential customers into your store out of sheer curiosity.

Your plan at this point calls for either a simple or a fancy drop-off store, and either way, you will need to have a plan—a design—to organize the store to make it work. You will need about 30 to 45 days to get your doors open if you plan to have a fancy store. A simple store may take less time to get started, but you should be realistic about your timeline, which will also depend upon the existing condition of your space. Also, don't forget that many municipalities will require a final "sign-off" from the fire department or possibility some other agency. Be sure to have your local business license secured before opening.

Building Blocks

A good store design includes some basic elements:

- Functionality
- Atmospherics
- Visual merchandising

Functional Elements

These are the basic tools of the trade—desks, staging areas, work and photography tables, storage, etc. Don't underestimate the value and necessity of these elements in your design. You will need elbow room and lots of it, because a successful drop-off store will be receiving tons of items to list, and you will need to be able to manage them easily without working around piles of clutter. Be generous with the square footage you allocate for working space.

Store Atmospherics

The interior decoration of your store is critical for "environmentalization." This helps you, your employees, and clients feel welcome and comfortable. The lobby of your store should have a place to sit down, some warm, attractive artwork on the walls, and possibly plants. It's really up to your personal sense of style. Overly sanitized, cold, or sterile atmospherics will turn off clients, consciously or unconsciously, while a pleasant environment will enhance your mental well-being as well as that of your employees.

Visual Merchandising

Any successful business has to attract customers, and your store is no exception. Having a great exterior sign is a must. If you have a retail storefront, you will also want to put something in the windows to draw the eye. Why not set up a visual merchandising display in the windows of your store presenting items that you have listed on eBay, with a sign that says "Presently on eBay"? Inside your store, you might have a menu of your services similar to those found in fast food restaurants. Even your listing and photography areas should be in plain view to serve as visual merchandising for your business. The point of visual merchandising is to appeal to potential clients and spark their curiosity, drawing them in and motivating them to buy your service. Selling your service involves not only excellent customer service but also the entire visual and emotional experience created by your functional, elegant store design. Your store's appeal to clients starts with the exterior façade and window displays and continues with the interior merchandising.

Peer Group Treasure

By now, you have already made a visit to one or more other drop-off stores. In this more advanced stage in developing your new operation, it is important to go to the well again—by reaching out to your peers. Don't be shy—no doubt you have already made some friends among your colleagues in the industry, and it's time to confer with them on the subject of store layout. To avoid repeating others' mistakes, and you will need all the help you can get. Study your notes and carefully consider the other stores you visited. Did any particular store strike your fancy? What was your initial reaction when you walked in? Did something appear particularly clever or interesting to you? Another visit to your favorite stores might help you formulate your final plans for your own layout. Call for an appointment with your peers and ask if you can seek their advice about store layout. Make several copies of your store's floor plan so that you can try different ideas while you talk with others.

Remember that the shortest path to success will come with the help of others. Most people have a good heart, and you will usually get the help you need.

Someone Has to Design It

Your store layout and design will be based on your planned operations, as discussed in the previous chapters.

You will also want to consider your potential customers so as to create an ambience that will attract the right type of people for your business. If you're seeking high-quality items from an upscale clientele, you will need to develop upscale, professional and attractive visuals.

If you're comfortable with computer software, you may want to try your own hand at designing the store. I recommend a program called SmartDraw (www.smartdraw.com). This software has tons of templates and wizards to help you design your office (including a home office) or virtually any other sort of floor plan. It comes with a free trial so you can give it a test drive before buying it. The program includes graphics for desks, computers, and just about anything else you may need to lay out your new store. But software is no substitute for a creative eye and experience, so use it only if you feel comfortable doing it yourself or if you're planning a simple store.

Basics you will need to think about include:

- Materials (wood, Formica, tile, etc.)
- Access for electrical and Internet wiring
- Cost
- Time for construction
- Permits from your local city to complete the work legally

The physical areas of your store should include the following:

- A customer counter for meeting and consulting with clients
- A temporary staging area for placing items before they are listed
- An area for cleaning items before photographing and listing them; perhaps near a sink
- A desk or work bench with plenty of elbow room so that you can research and evaluate the items prior to listing them
- A photography booth or table where the photos are taken
- A storage area for placing items while they are listed
- A storage area for boxes, tape, sheeted newsprint, foam packing peanuts, bubble wrap, and other shipping supplies
- A storage area for keeping office supplies such as printer/copier paper, pens, cleaning supplies, and anything else you may need for your daily operations
- A shipping counter with a computer for handling shipping tasks

- A storage area for placing packed, outgoing boxes awaiting pickup by the respective shipping companies

- A comfy table and chairs for eating lunch and relaxing at break times (optional, but important if you have employees)

- A bulletin board for reminders, staff schedules, and anything else you may need out in plain view

- A place to hold unsold items that require pickup by clients

If you're not a naturally creative person, and especially if you're opening an upscale store, it may be time to engage the services of a professional store designer. If you're opening a fancy store, this will be money well spent, because you will be investing quite a bit of cash into the store construction and a designer doesn't have to be expensive. Ask owners of other drop-off stores for a referral if you like their store design and layout. And if you're buying off-the-shelf furniture and fixtures, many of these retailers now have in-house design services to help you put together a floor plan. Reach out again to your chamber of commerce for referrals.

Interview at least three designers and ask to see their portfolios of other store designs, with photos. Insist on this. Any designer will have a portfolio, and they should be happy to share it with you—this is their visual resume. You should hire someone who has actually designed stores similar to the look and feel you're seeking. If you're having difficulty finding the right person who shares your creative vision, walk through upscale retail shopping districts, and when you see a store design you like, simply ask who designed that store. This is an outstanding way to get the look and feel you want.

You may also want to pick up a copy of "The Budget Guide to Retail Store Planning and Design" by Jeff Grant to get some additional information on the entire store design process, including how to clarify your expectations with design firms, sample contracts, and much more.

When you seek the services of an outside professional, be sure to share with them your business plan and budgetary expectations regarding the entire renovations project. You may also want to have an installment payment agreement with the designer to ensure timely delivery of their work. Paying in full upfront for design services is not within my vision for you.

You should ask them to allow some time for revisions of their initial design, so that you can make minor modifications as you see fit. And before you ask them to show you any designs, you will want to find a contractor. Your designer and contractor will need to work hand-in-hand to establish the look and feel of your store, the materials used, and the overall cost of making it happen. Get the contractor on board before the designer puts anything to paper, and I suggest holding off on paying out any money until you have had a chance to meet with both of them.

Who Will Build It?

Your designer will most likely know qualified contractors. Consider using them, because the designer will be familiar with their work, reliability, and ability to adhere to a budget. Meet with the designer's contractors and get a feel for your comfort level with them.

As with finding store designers, use other businesses in your area whose look you admire and your chamber of commerce as potential sources for contractor referrals.

A few questions to ask when interviewing contractors:

- Are they licensed and bonded contractors? Surprisingly, many are not, and you can check with the state to confirm their licensing status.

- Do they carry workers' compensation insurance for their employees? Liability insurance? Ask to see copies before work commences.

- How much money will they require up front, and how much more money will they require during the construction of your store? Paying upfront and in full for these services is not recommended.

- Do they guarantee their work against defects? For what period of time?

- Do they guarantee that they will complete the job in a specified period of time?

- Would they provide at least three references? Visit these people and see the contractor's work in person.

Don't feel pressured to go with any particular contractor. You should have two or three to choose from, and each will have their own particular style and way of doing business.

Wheeling and Dealing Again

My user ID on eBay is "borntodeal," and I like to think that I was born to deal (perhaps a completely misguided thought, but my own thinking nonetheless!). I like to negotiate the best deal possible when I hire a contractor. There is a different between negotiation and being unrealistic. It's never a problem to ask for a discount, but asking for the moon and the stars; and not expecting to pay fair market pricing will have the contractor heading out the front door.

You must establish a firm budget. Custom construction, flooring, lights, fixtures, and everything else you will need for your new store can add up quickly. You may spend a lot or a little, but either way you must have a firm financial plan—you don't want a runaway budget.

Get estimates. Set up meetings with your store designer and prospective contractors. Be diplomatic, because busy contractors may dislike competing for your business. Specify your budget and determine what elements of your store are critical and which are flexible (or optional). You may be able to reduce the cost of your project by using off-the-shelf furniture and fixtures rather than asking the contractor to build everything to order.

The curb appeal of your store will have the most impact on your ability to attract clients, so focus on such things as the exterior paint colors, signage, and the lobby. The rest of the store will be functional, and you may want to have the open space beyond the front counter set up in such a way that you can reconfigure it at will. Perhaps you want the ability to move your photography table from one end of the store to another, or maybe you want to option of adding or removing storage shelves.

Having a flexible floor plan will reduce the amount of work that your contractor will do, because these areas can be set up with movable furniture instead of fixed counter and work space. You can set up your own shelving units using inexpensive, readily available boltless systems. We chose these systems because they can be dismantled in a matter of minutes. We also use inexpensive plastic folding tables for instant staging areas and work spaces. Although this may sound a bit cheap, actually these tables are actually rather attractive—and they allow us the luxury of flexibility.

Here are some tips on what to talk about during the meetings with the designer and contractors:

- Establish whether the contractor will be installing your signage and who will create the graphics for that sign. Do you need a separate sign contractor to bid this job and install it?

- Does the contractor handle every aspect of the job, or will they require you to get separate bids for such things as electrical work and plumbing?

- Is the contractor familiar with the permit process in your town? Will the contractor obtain all the necessary permits from the city, and will their bid include these permit costs?

- Does the contractor offer financing of the project? If so, at what interest rate and repayment terms?

Find out from the contractors you interview about their current workload and schedule, and get some idea of the speed of their work. You want to avoid hiring a contractor who has poor planning and scheduling skills. I prefer to deal with people who are highly confident about their ability to complete a job in a specified amount of time. That alone may be worth paying a bit more for, because a job that takes too long can cost you a tremendous amount of extra money in the form of lost business, additional rent, or loan payments—and the domino effect of everything else falling out of place while you anxiously attempt to get this business off the ground.

> Tip: Always ask to be able to see the completed work of any subcontractors. If you are hiring a tile installer to tile your front lobby, ask if you can see other projects this installer has completed. When you hire a sign company, ask to see two or three of their signs at actual installed locations. Visit the locations at night and be sure the sign is bright, crisp, and easy to read. Be picky—it is your money, and you want quality work for your store.

A Million Dollars a Day

I also like to discuss early completion bonuses with contractors. I would never work on a time-and-materials payment arrangement with anyone doing a job this big. I prefer to get a flat rate for completing the agreed-on work, and I would suggest offering a completion bonus for each day the job is finished early. After the 1994 earthquake in Los Angeles, the contractor who was repairing the freeways was paid a bonus of one million dollars a day for each day the completed project was ahead of schedule. This is an extreme example (also quite controversial), but it seems perfectly reasonable to me, considering the immense expense the city was racking up due to police overtime for diverting traffic and the general inconvenience to the public due to the traffic congestion. If your mortgage (with interest and taxes) is $1,000 a month, you could offer the contractor $30 to $40 a day for each day the project comes in early, because that approximately matches your daily cost for the building. If your mortgage is $3,000 a month, paying an extra $100 a day for early completion would be a savings to you. A contractor may work night and day until your project is finished, knowing this extra money is on the table. It is always in your best interest to pay more (within reason of course) for a faster job, as late work is no bargain.

Pen to Paper

It will come as no surprise to you that I suggest you take notes during your meeting with each contractor, and that you be sure to write down your thoughts about each one after the meeting is concluded. Gather the ideas from each one and see what strikes your fancy. Use these notes in formulating your final plan for the store layout, before you write a check to start the process with your designer. And again, please seriously consider making your work space flexible and configurable, thus avoiding a marriage to one specific floor plan.

Give your store designer some final guidance and work out their final fee for the design with the contractor budget as a top priority. Create a written agreement with your designer that specifies your expectations, their fee, and your contractor budget. Establish a deadline with your designer for the first draft of their design plans.

Remember to put in writing how many revisions you can expect to request before being charged an additional fee. When agreement in writing has been reached, both you and your designer should sign off on the design fees. As a rule of thumb, I would pay the store designer no more than 10 to 15 percent of the total contractor budget. I am not saying you should offer them a percentage; I am suggesting you limit their fees to what you can afford to pay on the overall project.

Although it may be fine to operate with verbal agreements, I suggest you always get everything in writing the first time you hire someone. I rarely leave this to chance. Unless you have the luxury of an unlimited budget or time frame, you should establish all expectations in writing. This does not have to be a complex or fancy contract—just something to establish a meeting of the minds.

With your first design plan in hand, review it carefully and talk it over with friends and family. Did the designer execute on paper what was originally in your mind? Does it faithfully resemble what you and the designer discussed at your meetings? Take the initial plan to other, experienced retailers, and especially to your colleagues who own drop-off stores, and discuss it with them, too. As always, take notes.

If you want changes, go back to your designer and ask for the revisions you feel are needed. Be respectful of their time, and don't expect more than is reasonable for what you're paying them. You establish a successful business relationship when everyone involved feels they are getting what is just, and creative people can have a higher sensitivity to what is fair or unfair than a hardcore businessperson.

Once you have settled on your initial plans, submit them to all of the contractors for written bids. Ask them to review the required materials and to identify in their bids any aspects of the design plan that they are not qualified to complete. Often this may be the exterior sign. Sign design and construction is a specialized field, and I have seen more than a few bad ones. A great sign will not be cheap, but it is a high priority—be prepared to pay in proportion to its importance. If the contractor gives you a list of items on your plan that will require additional contractors, ask for referrals and bid those jobs out separately. Be sure to account for these separate bids in your final budget.

Ask for confirmation as to whether the cost of permits will be included in the bid or if they will be charged separately. And don't forget sales tax! Materials, and sometimes labor, may be taxable items, depending on your state. Ask if the tax is included in the bid or if that will be charged separately. This can be a huge additional cost, so don't forget to mention it. Finally, be sure to ask the contractor for their first available date to begin the work and an exact number of days required to complete it (weather permitting, etc.).

A Match Made in Heaven

First and foremost, don't take the lowest bid automatically. This may be tempting, but consider all available information, including your gut feeling about the contractor. Check their references and ask each reference if the contractor was clean, professional, and timely in the completion of their project. I once hired a roofing contractor who was the highest of three bids, because he provided me with over two dozen references, and each of them spoke very highly of the quality, timeliness, and professionalism of his work.

Consider your feelings about the contractor from your initial meeting. Did they arrive at the appointment on time? Did you feel they were professional and attentive to you during the meeting? Did they make you feel completely comfortable? What were their payment terms? Did they require a lot of money up front, or were they willing to defer the majority of your payments until the project was finished?

My most trusted and faithful painting contractor's name is Ernesto. I recently hired him to do some work for me that involved well over $2,000 in materials alone. He is so confident in the quality and satisfaction he provides to his clients that he agreed to wait until the job was 100 percent completed before he received one dime! His work for me has always been even higher quality than I expected. He is punctual and highly professional and always asks questions about how I want the completed project to look and about the small details. Every job he touches turns out perfectly.

Most contractors will require a deposit, often 25 percent (or possibly more) of their total fee before the work starts. For large jobs, a contractor will require progress payments, to cover their materials and labor costs, as they complete various stages of the work. These payment arrangements are negotiable and may help in determining who you hire.

Once you make up your mind, agree on a start date (in writing), sign off on the estimate to indicate your approval, and pay the contractor's advance.

Nosy is Natural

When working with someone unfamiliar, it is critical to be present for the start of the construction. Do a walk-through on the first day of the work to discuss any minor details and to show your new contractor that you're "hands-on"—available to confer and answer questions.

Develop a friendly rapport with your contractor, and make certain that your plans are being followed. Make an appointment to return at the end of each working day, if possible, to review the work in progress. Make a note of any issues and report them immediately to the contractor to avoid costly delays or major changes later. Being hands-on will pay off for your vision and expectations. Being obsessive won't be welcome, but being present, polite and present will move your project forward in a powerful way.

Be mindful of the relationship between your design and construction contract. Be aware that changes to your design plans may translate into extra costs in your final bill. Be fair about this, and if you do want to make on-the-fly changes to your plan, establish in advance the amount of any additional charges so that you can budget for them. Perhaps you realize that your store's bathroom has a small sink and you really need a larger one for washing and cleaning items, such as china. Maybe you notice that the front counter is too low and you need it a couple inches higher. These kinds of things should be relatively easy to fix along the way, but be prepared to foot the bill for the modifications.

If you have established a payment schedule, be prompt in meeting your deadlines as well. You will obtain the best service when you're prompt in paying for it as agreed.

Giving Your Stamp of Approval

When dealing with people in general, it's best to trust but verify. As with supervising the work in progress, you should also make a final inspection of all work completed before you sign off on the construction of your new store and make your final contractor payment.

If you're using money from a third party such as a bank, you may be required to provide them with photographs of the work or even arrange for them to make their own inspection of your project.

Be sure to review your written agreement with the contractor carefully and walk through and inspect each and every item on your agreed-upon list. If the city is required to approve any of the work that has been completed, it is important to have these inspections finalized before you make your final payment to the contractor. If for any reason the city disapproves the work, it is the contractor's responsibility to make certain that the work meets local codes and regulations.

Tip: You may be able to get creative and cut some corners if you are on a limited budget. An upscale look for your store, without the high cost, may be possible by checking the newspapers for auction sales of businesses that are closing. If you want to go for an antique look, you can visit the weekly auctions in your area and look for fancy old wood counters to use in your shop. If you want a modern look, drive around and look for signs that a business is closing its doors and see if you can pick up any of their furniture, fixtures, or storage racks. You may be able to get lots of great equipment cheap this way, saving yourself a bundle. Having a flexible floor plan will also allow you to use secondhand furnishings and equipment easily in your new business.

11. Setting Fees for Your Services

I listed and sold a wonderful cowboy Western oil painting by a local artist, J.A. Kirkpatrick. He has exhibited artwork at prestigious galleries nationally, and his paintings hang in the Smithsonian Institute and the U.S. Senate building. My client was selling it to help pay for his daughter's special schooling needs. The minimum bid was $300, and 10 days later it sold for $2,705 with 27 bids. I collected a $20 listing fee and a 20 percent commission on the final selling price.

—Michael J. Ellingson, Fargo, North Dakota; eBay user ID "phonomike"; trading on eBay since October 18, 1998

Who Am I?

Let's do a quick reality check—what type of business will you be operating? Yes, it's an eBay consignment business, but ask yourself—what is it, exactly, that you do? Think of yourself as being in the unwanted item liquidation business. Your clients have things—unwanted things—that they want out of their lives. Therefore, when setting your fees, you have to realize that you're providing an extremely valuable service. You're offering "lightening in a bottle". If you seek out clients who want new channels to sell brand new merchandise or want to maximize recovery of their original investment in their unwanted items, you're bound to have trouble justifying your fees. Your ideal client is someone who has things for which they have no further emotional or financial attachment, things that can be sold for whatever price the market will bear.

Keep this concept in mind at all times when discussing your fees—fees that reflect the high value of your service.

Time is Money

What is your time worth? How much were you making on an hourly basis at your last job? If you owned or presently own a business, how much money do you keep at the end of each week, month, or year? Many new business owners fail, because their businesses do not collect a sufficient amount of revenue to pay expenses and leave a tidy profit. A common pitfall for many new business owners is a failure to realize and value the importance of their time. I'd be bold enough to say that you cannot and should not offer both cut rate pricing while delivering exemplary service. They are in conflict with each other.

Not only will you have to evaluate each item you might list, to determine if it can make you a reasonable profit given the time you spend handling it; you will also have to confront the true costs of doing business and create a schedule of fees that will return the profits you need.

I have set a standard for myself. I decided that I want to make no less than $80 per hour while I am working at my office. I know this may seem high, but my services are worth this much. So I have had to reverse engineer the revenue at my business, establishing fee rates for my clients that will provide this value for my time.

When you advertise your business, you will receive many inquiries from people interested in your services. Such inquiries will flow in from having a retail store as well. If you accept items worth $5 each for listing on eBay, you will find yourself quickly losing money regardless of what percentage you charge your clients. The reality will quickly become apparent—it takes the same amount of time to list an item worth $5 as it does to list one that is worth $100, $500, or even $5,000.

When you set your rates, you should also remember that your client is paying not only for your time, but for your staff, rent (or mortgage), insurance, office expenses, and any other costs associated with operating your business. You have also made substantial investments in equipment and in developing your business and your reputation.

Let the Market Set the Price

At my store, we charge no up-front fee for listing items on eBay, but we also rarely accept items for which a minimum price is required by our clients. There is a good reason for this: we are in the unwanted item liquidation business. We are neither profit maximizers nor distributors for manufacturers or dealers of new products. The fees that eBay charges are dependent on both the final selling price and on the starting price of any item—the lower the starting price, the lower the fees eBay charges us for the listing. We have learned the hard way that, for the most part, when you agree to take an item at a minimum starting price or reserve price, the likelihood of your selling that item decreases dramatically. A reserve is a secret "hold back" number that you establish to ensure that an item will not sell below this pre-established figure.

The eBay site used to be predominantly an auction-style listing venue. Now though, fixed prices dominate. However, for many people there is a certain excitement in bidding. Items that start at low opening bids generate this excitement, and some bids bring in more bids. We have seen this phenomenon literally thousands of times in our own listings. We want to sell every item we accept for listing, and taking items with minimum prices or reserves means that we might spend our valuable time creating a listing with no guarantee of profit, because the item may not sell.

Although you can charge an up-front listing fee for taking any item, in practice you may find a tremendous amount of resistance from clients when asking them to pay more money on an already depreciating asset with no assurance that they will get a return. Most clients feel this is throwing good money after bad. Though up-front fees are common in the eBay consignment business, it is my strong belief that having such a fee will reduce your chances of getting an item submission.

You want every item to sell, and at my shop, we encourage a lot more business by having no up-front fees for listing items (except in extremely rare cases). It is also my general policy that we do not accept items for which the client demands a minimum selling price. We use auction-style listings and start most of them at $9.99 with no reserve. The eBay marketplace sets the price by competitive bidding, and the items end up selling for what they are worth to the highest bidder. I have listed items starting at $0.99 that sold for thousands!

Don't Second That Emotion

I want you to contemplate very carefully the type of items you want to attract and the type of people you want coming through your doors. How you present, and how you price, your service will determine both of these.

I prefer the upscale client with quality, brand-name items that they no longer need or want and to which they have no emotional of financial attachment whatsoever. These well-to-do folks don't really care how much they will recover from their sale, but at the same time, they realize that with a yard sale, they will end up giving their things away for virtually nothing. When they receive their checks, most of my upscale clients are amazed at the prices I have realized for them on eBay.

What the Others Are Charging

Your name may not be Bill Gates, but it is possible to run a monopoly. eBay consignment businesses are still a rather novel concept, and you may find very little competition in your area. If no other shops exist near you, then you can pretty much call the shots as to how you charge for your services.

If you live in a bigger town, as I do, you will find eBay consigners and eBay drop-off stores all over the place. It is important to know how they run their businesses and charge for their services. You're already armed with quite a bit of knowledge about their operations because of your previous fact-finding visits to them, including, hopefully, their rates.

As I write this book, my company charges 50 percent commission. Holy cow! You may be thinking "That's a huge piece of the pie!" Not really--when you consider that the industry standard commission for consignment shops is also 50 percent. There's quite a bit of overhead to cover, the high cost of labor for my staff; and my customers receive the benefit of my years of positive feedback ratings to help lift the sales price skyward. Is that figure negotiable? Never say "never" because businesses should always be flexible and entrepreneurs should always prepare to adjust with changing times. Geography, overhead, competition, your work volume, area of specialty and many other factors may affect how you set rates for your time and services. I once sold a triple-black Porsche 911 turbo Carrera for a close friend and charged him $500 flat. I made a great rate for my time and he was very happy.

Some consignment shops might charge a much lower commission, but they will also charge you rent for any space you use in their shop. I have a client who routinely brings in high-end collectibles and antiques for us to list on eBay. He has been paying $150 a month to rent a small display case in an antique mall. He sells a lot of items there and pays only a 15 percent commission, but the antique mall clears a guaranteed $150 a month from him, regardless of his sales.

In the rare event that we do list a client's item at a minimum price, my store charges the client an up-front fee of $9.99 per eBay listing. This nonrefundable listing fee helps us defray the cost of the eBay fees and the handling of the item if it doesn't sell. For Reserve Auctions we charge a $24.99 Listing Fee plus a 2% Fee based upon the reserve price. I have seen other stores charging up-front fees ranging from $2.99 for a basic auction all the way up to $500 for listing a piece of real estate on eBay. But of course, these fees don't guarantee the client a successful outcome.

Nickels and Dimes

Having the lowest percentage commission of all your competition is not your goal. You should always remember that you're a highly skilled and specialized consultant. You bring additional value to the transaction, and if you can net your client more money because of your expertise, the quality of your photos, and your excellent service, the percentage you charge becomes quite irrelevant. Having a good sense of your competition's practices and routinely checking the other shops' rates will empower you with the knowledge you need to be in the ballpark with them. Also, being the lowest-cost in your market will tend to attract a lower grade of clients. Someone who chooses to go with the cheapest company will be a picky, thrifty individual who will likely also try to nickel-and-dime you to death—asking for even further reductions of your fees.

Clever but Flawed

Take your survey of the other eBay consignment businesses and review it. Do you find their fees confusing or easy to understand? I have found that many stores appear to have low fees, but in the fine print, they charge the client all the eBay and PayPal fees in addition to their commission. This may appear to be a clever sales practice. A client will believe they are getting a low commission, until they receive their check and realize that the eBay and PayPal fees add up to a rather large bite out of their net proceeds. In the long run, this is probably not the best way to keep good clients coming back.

In considering your commission percentage, you should realize, too, that your average item will be of bread-and-butter quality. Unless you have great luck or tremendous connections, the average person bringing you merchandise will have items valued at between about $50 and $500. We sell a few items here and there for more money, but the high-ticket items are fewer and further between.

> Tip: Many eBay consignment sellers offer their services to the competition. If you have an area of specialty that your competitor does not, you can help them write a winning description for their auctions and take a fee, either a fixed amount or a percentage of the sale, for helping them evaluate something they aren't familiar with.

"How Much Will You Charge Me?"

In general, you should charge as much for your services as the market will bear. But rates can be adjusted depending upon the amount of business coming in the door. You may have noticed that popular hotels will charge more for busy weekends, holidays, and special events than they normally charge the rest of the year. Your fees can vary depending upon the final price of the sale, whether or not it's a "regular customer" who brings you a lot of business, your level of expertise in a particular field, and other factors such as your current workload. If you find yourself constantly backed up with weeks of work, as is often the case at my store, you can either raise rates or become more selective about the value of the items you accept for listing.

Nothing should be set in stone, but you do not want to change rates too frequently. I suggest giving your fees much thought, coming up with fair rates that the market can bear, and sticking to them.

Here are some questions to ask yourself:

- Are you offering to sell items for which a special skill or knowledge is required? If so, you can command a higher fee.

- Do you plan to sell vehicles or real estate? Doing so may also require special licenses, and the eBay fees are higher for these types of items. Before establishing your fees, be sure you understand eBay's fees for listing items and PayPal's fees for receiving payments. (Be sure to check their fees regularly and update your fees accordingly.)

- Will you charge an up-front listing fee for each item you accept? Will that fee be charged only if the client wants to start off the item with a minimum listing price or reserve? Will you refund this fee if the item sells or apply it to the commission?

- Will your commission include eBay and PayPal fees, or will you charge your clients those fees in addition to your commission?

- Will you accept virtually any item, or will you require a minimum item value or other criteria for acceptance?

Because the fees charged by eBay and PayPal may change over time, you should always be sure to keep up-to-date on any changes, to be able to change your rates accordingly.

To view my fees, go to www.borntodeal.com , then click on FAQs. Next click on "How much does this service cost?" Then, at the end of the paragraph, after "to see our list of fees," click here.

Flat Fee Finito

I have seen some people charge only a flat fee for each item they list, with no commission at all if it sells. One such company, not far from my store, couldn't make a profit this way and discontinued their operations. I firmly believe that you must share in your clients' success by charging a percentage-based fee. This will give you the incentive to give the time and care appropriate for each item, and hopefully it will also keep your business in the black.

eBay's Side of the Coin

Now let's get some perspective on the costs you will incur when you list an item on eBay. First, for each eBay listing, you will pay eBay a nonrefundable fee called an Insertion Fee, whether or not the item sells (but you will not be billed until after the auction ends). Insertion fees are flat fees and are calculated differently depending on the category of the item, selling format you choose, and if you're a Stores subscriber. For all sellers, the insertion fee is free for the first 50 items per calendar month. If you're a Basic Store monthly subscriber, your first 150 listings per calendar month are free. However, your subscription will cost $19.95 per month. If you buy a yearly subscription, the cost works out to $15.95 per month. Depending on the volume of your listings, you'll find it beneficial to subscribe to a

Basic, Premium or Anchor Store. (Anchor Store subscribers get 2,500 free listings per calendar month.)

Certain categories of items are not eligible for free fees. These include real estate, boats, cars, trucks, motorcycles, some heavy equipment, imaging and aesthetics equipment, etc. Be sure to check eBay Insertion Fees to get the latest information. eBay provides a Fee Calculator to help you determine what your actual fee will be.

After a buyer commits to purchase an item, you're charged a Final Value Fee. If a listing ends without a sale (not including any successful Second Chance Offers), you don't pay a final value fee. Final value fees are calculated based on the total amount of the sale and are charged per item. Currently, sellers who do not subscribe to an eBay store pay a final value fee of 10% of the total amount of the sale, with a maximum of $250. Subscribers to eBay stores pay category-based rates from 4% to 9%.

In addition to Insertion Fees, eBay charges an additional fee for using a reserve, a value you can place on an item to prevent it from selling below a desired price. For example, say your client is unwilling to accept anything less than $150 for a particular item. You might list his rare sterling pitcher with a $150 reserve but with a $9.99 opening bid, or starting price. Even though the starting price is $9.99, no bidder can have the item until bids reach at least $150. Up to that point, the listing will show "Reserve not met"; when the bidding reaches $150, the listing will read "Reserve met" for the bidders' information. As of this writing, if the reserve price is less than $199.99, the fee is $2.00. If the reserve price is $200 or more, the Reserve Fee is 1% of the reserve price, with a maximum of $50. The Reserve Fee is charged only if an item does not sell. This is important to keep in mind when dealing with clients who may want to set unrealistic reserve prices. Remember that, with rare exceptions, your business should be liquidating unwanted items, those to which your clients have no emotional or financial attachment.

Candidly, eBay fees have become a bit more complex over the years. When I first started selling on eBay, they were pretty simple. Review and understand these fees. It's key to earning a profit in this industry.

Enhancing Your Listing

You can also add enhancements to your eBay listings to provide more visibility on the eBay site. These enhancements are designed to stimulate more bids and higher sale prices. With a standard listing, you can add up to 12 pictures. The first "thumbnail" picture appears in the top left of your listing and next to your item's title in search results. It's called the Gallery picture. You should always include at least a Gallery picture. Why? The Gallery photo allows buyers to see your item and determine immediately if it's what they're looking for, before even going to your listing itself.

Other Upgrades are available for your listing, at additional cost. Typically, the advanced listing tools help you create listings with more impact and better results. Gallery Plus provides an enlarged version of your photo when a buyer rolls their curser over it. Other tools include: Scheduled listings, Listing Designer, Subtitle, Value pack, Bold, List in 2 categories, and International site visibility. Check the eBay site for descriptions and current fees.

Once you've had a bit a success on eBay and feel comfortable with the process, there are other Selling Tools offered by eBay that you'll want to check out. All help you list, manage and track your items more efficiently. While advanced listing tools enhance individual listings, selling tools enable you to automate the process of running your entire business. Selling tools currently available include: Turbo Lister, Selling Manager, Selling Manager Pro and File Exchange. Supplemental services offered are the Global Shipping Program and Managed Returns. Check the eBay site for descriptions and current fees.

Fee Recap

As I mentioned, if your listing sells successfully and you do not subscribe to an eBay Store, eBay will take an additional fee, called the Final Value Fee, which is currently 10% of the total amount of the sale, with a maximum of $250. Subscribers to eBay stores pay category-based rates from 4% to 9%.

Now that your listing has "sold," there's still another fee to be aware of. This is the fee charged to process the buyer's payment. If you use PayPal as a method of payment for your listings in the United States, you'll pay 2.9% of your item's final selling price for the service plus $0.30 per transaction. A Discounted Merchant Rate of 2.2% is available for high-volume and nonprofit sellers. A rate of 3.9% plus a fixed fee based upon the currency used will be charged for international sales using the PayPal service.

To recap the fees you can expect from eBay and PayPal:

- Insertion Fee. The cost you pay eBay for your listing, based on the starting or reserve price of your merchandise

- Listing Upgrade Fees. The cost you pay for enhancing your listing with special features such as Gallery Plus.

- Final Value Fee. The percentage of the final sale price or fixed fee you pay to eBay when an item successfully sells. With some types of merchandise, this fee may be a fixed amount or have a cap (e.g., motors, real estate, and capital equipment).

- PayPal Fee. The amount you pay to PayPal for receiving money from buyers (buyers do not pay a fee to send money).

Here are the eBay and PayPal sites with their fee information:

- For eBay: pages.ebay.com/help/sell/fees.html

- For PayPal: www.paypal.com/us/fees

Adding Your Overhead and Profit

Within the fees you charge your clients, you not only have to recover all of the fees mentioned above but you also have to pay your overhead. And you need to make a profit for yourself. Be sure that your rates are sufficient for you to realize the profit margins you deserve—you're providing a valuable service.

I believe you can reasonably charge your clients whatever the market will bear. I have seen other eBay consignment sellers charge fees of up to 50 percent of the final sales price, and clients who gladly pay this rate to get rid of unwanted items. But of course, markets vary, and yours may not bear this rate. In general, though, I think you will find it hard to charge this price for higher-ticket merchandise. Common sense will prevail in those cases and I have found that charging lower percentages for higher-value items is a mandate. Be flexible and prepared to negotiate.

Ultimately, setting rates is a rather cryptic mix of math, market research, and gut instinct. You want your clients to feel that they are getting their money's worth for your work. At the same time, I want you to go home every day feeling that you have been paid very well for what you do. You deserve it and you should be able to enjoy the fruits of your hard work, expertise, and high-quality services.

Setting Your Fees—Recap

To reiterate key points about how you set and structure your fees:

- If you do not charge an up-front listing fee for your services, you will attract more clients, but you will also need to be extremely diligent about accepting only items that will sell successfully—at a price that will make you a profit.

- When charging an up-front fee for minimum or reserve price listings, be certain you recover not only your eBay Insertion Fees but at least enough in addition to justify your time spent on unsuccessful listings. Items that don't sell are time bandits, taking you away from other clients for whom you can make successful sales, with a profit for everyone.

- The simpler and easier to understand your fee structure is, the fewer fee-related questions clients will ask. Charging eBay and PayPal fees separately may be logical, but it can easily confuse clients who don't understand these fees.

- If you include all eBay and PayPal fees in your commission, use this as a selling point. On the surface, you may appear to be charging more than the competition, but in reality, you're charging less once you account for the eBay and PayPal fees you're paying out-of-pocket. Be sure you explain this to your clients.

- Try using a graduated commission scale. As the total cost of an item goes up, the commission rate comes down. I'm commanding 50% commission on my consignment sales. But this doesn't work for every situation.

- Type up your fee structure in a simple, easy-to-understand, single-page format. You can then provide not only a detailed explanation of your services but also of your fees when a client asks about them.

- Remember to publish your current fees on your website.

- If you're going to sell vehicles, real estate, or capital equipment, be sure to check your local and state laws first regarding any regulations for sales of these items. You may also want to charge an up-front fee, because the eBay Insertion Fees are substantially higher. Study the fee structure for these items carefully.

Your fees may spark a debate with some clients who feel every business transaction is a negotiation. You may find yourself being questioned or even chided about your fee structure by those who don't understand the work involved in selling for others on eBay. Many will attempt to negotiate down your fees. I can't say that we never negotiate our fees, but rarely do we make concessions. The item in question would have to be a very, very rare piece indeed and/or something of extreme value. In general, stick to your guns and don't cave in. I have found that, if you set a fair fee structure and stick to it, regardless of whom you may lose along the way, you will attract the quality, upscale clients you need. And their referrals will bring you even more fine merchandise.

12. Contracts and Other Paperwork

One of my clients asked me to sell a 1950s Italian Gamma camera. After doing some research, I knew it was rare and of great value. I listed it at a minimum bid of $0.99 with no reserve. It received several bids immediately but hovered at just over $200 for most of the week. Within the last 30 seconds of the auction, the price escalated rapidly, and it sold for $1,425! I earned $427.50 on the sale, which was my 30 percent commission. After my sixth child was born, and with my sales growing by leaps and bounds, my husband decided to quit his full-time job and spend more time with the kids. I love the fact that my children have so much more time with their daddy. If I can be a successful eBay seller with six kids running around the house, then anyone can do this.
—Teresa D. Bankston, Madison, Mississippi; eBay user ID "teresab_foundvalue"; trading on eBay since March 24, 2005

The Meaning of It All

Frankly, in my life I've had my fair share of legal disputes with people. I've been to court a few times to collect personal and private debts, among other things. But I've been very fortunate with my eBay business—I have never had a legal dispute with a client. I attribute this good fortune to the use of consistent contractual practices.

I feel it is very important, in any business, to formalize agreements between people. There is solid logic here—we all tend to forget things over time, and you will want to avoid the possibility of miscommunication or a misunderstanding at some future date. Because you're a professional eBay seller, you fully understand your services and how they work. But your business may be completely novel to someone else, who, even with your clear verbal explanation, may not fully understand all of the obligations of both parties within the transaction. Selling items for others on eBay is a fairly simple process, but it helps to get a formal, written agreement to avoid misunderstandings between people.

I once had a client who brought us a collection of Star Trek memorabilia to sell. We listed all of her items, and virtually all of them sold. Some of the merchandise that had sold was still sitting on our shelves awaiting buyer payment. And one day while I was away, she barreled into the store and frantically demanded of John, my photographer, that he turn over all of the remaining items because she had an important job interview and the prospective employer was a huge Star Trek fan. She wanted the items as gifts, to help persuade the employer to hire her. John was so caught off guard by her urgency that he actually did give her the items. And no sooner was she out the door with a box of Star Trek collectibles, than John realized to his dismay what he had done. Those items were now the property of a new owner, the eBay buyer, and the client had no right to the memorabilia. We did have a written agreement with the client, which would have legally entitled us to damages for her actions, but our staff was partly to blame. Fortunately, the eBay buyer took the situation in stride and agreed to release us from our obligations. We sent a token payment to the buyer as compensation for their time and trouble.

It's not good enough simply to get someone's signature on a contract; you also have to explain the essence of that agreement and make certain your client fully understands it. A contract is a formalization of an agreement, not just a piece of paper that you hastily sign simply to have a written document.

> Tip: Contracts should be simple and easy to understand. Avoid complicated language. A contract in plain English is just as binding as a contract with complex and obscure wording—possibly even more so, because the client will have a harder time arguing that they misunderstood the agreement when it is articulated in nonlegalistic language.

Details, Details, Details

There are a couple of ways to go about the process of handling client contracts:

1. Develop a single document that serves as an individual item listing agreement
2. Develop a master agreement for each client and a separate item submission form for each of their items

If you routinely receive a small number of individual items from one person or company, having an all-in-one document would create the least amount of paperwork for you in the long run. To save more time, you can use no-carbon-required (NCR) paper for your agreements, so that you can quickly hand your client a copy of the contract without having to make a photocopy. If you use a separate item submission form, triplicate works: one copy for your files, one copy for the client, and a copy that can sit on the storage shelf with the item itself until it ships out.

For each client, you could prepare a folder to be filed alphabetically by last name or company name. If you use separate item submission forms, you can file the master contract in this folder along with one copy each of that client's item submission forms. You should be able to access the master contract and/or an item submission form for any particular client in a matter of seconds if you need to refer to it.

By having the additional copy of the item submission form with the item itself, you can quickly pay your client from this form when the item actually sells and ships.

Making It Rock Solid

Contracts are the basis upon which business is conducted, and well-drafted contracts can help avoid unnecessary problems. A contract exists when two or more parties (people or entities, such as a corporation) mutually agree to exchange property (including money) or the promise of future performance. Contracts can be verbal or written, but a verbal agreement is risky, because one or both of the parties may later fail to remember the terms and conditions of the agreement. And a verbal contract may be unenforceable if its terms aren't executed within a specified time (such as one year) or if the agreement involves more than a specified amount of money. In many cases where disputes arise, proving your version of a verbal agreement can be difficult.

Having a good written contract is so important that you will want to hire an attorney to review your contract. I urge you to author the initial draft of your contract yourself, but some legal nuances may require professional "wordsmithery" by an attorney.

I am deliberately avoiding giving you sample contract language because every state has different laws, and the contract should be reviewed by a competent attorney anyway. The good news is that, if you perform your responsibilities diligently and honestly, there is only a remote chance that legal issues with clients will arise.

Here is an overview of the basic elements of a good contract:

Names. The contract should include the names of each party signing the agreement. Give full names for individuals and proper legal names for organizations (such as an LLC or corporation), for which you should also specify the state within which the organization was formed.

Competence. A contract should only exist between competent parties, and your client should be at least 18 years of age, or the contract may become unenforceable. Your contract should have a space to write down their identification information, which you will verify. You may want to provide a check box on your contract that indicates you verified that your client is at least 18 years of age.

Definition of Terminology. In this section of your agreement, it would be prudent to define any terms that might not be used in everyday language.

Obligations. This section of the contract must clearly outline the obligations and expectations of both parties. It should include details such as what services you will perform as the seller, the costs of your services if the item sells (and if it does not), and your rights as well as those of the client. You should also specify the time frame within which the obligations are to be performed. Some time frame items can include:

- How long you will be permitted, from the day you receive the item(s), until you must list it on eBay

- How long the item should be listed on eBay (there are one-, three-, five-, seven-, and ten-day listings, as well as longer ones for eBay Stores listings)

- Whether or not you're required or permitted to relist unsold items

- How soon a client must pick up unsold items

- What you will charge for storage if the unsold items are not picked up promptly (you do not want to offer unlimited and indefinite free storage)

- If items are not picked up after a specified period, how you can dispose of them (donate to nonprofit, etc.)

Try to think through every possible scenario. Much of what is important in your agreement will become clearer as you actually start to list. Even having read this book, no doubt you will learn something from trial and error. My foremost problem when starting out was the issue of unclaimed unsold items. Most unwanted merchandise really is unwanted. Paying for actual storage is expensive, and some clients will have no problem using your store as a free, secure storage facility if they can. In my agreement, I give my clients seven days from the date their listing ends on eBay until I have the right to donate the unsold item to nonprofit. Before I added this clause to my agreement, there were items remaining in my store for months on end despite phone calls and reminder letters.

Force Majeure. This section of your contract provides you with partial or total excuse from performance of your obligations as a result of acts of God (earthquake, hurricane, etc.). Such clauses are common in contacts and referred to as force majeure.

Liquidated Damages. In the event that either party fails to perform their responsibilities in the agreement, this section will serve to define the consequences for that nonperformance. The amount of damages can be defined in advance when actual losses may be hard to determine. For example, if you have sold an item that was not stored on your premises, and the client is unable or unwilling to deliver the item to you for shipping, your contract can call for liquidated damages equal to three times the current market value of the highest-priced eBay sale for the same item. This is just a hypothetical example to give you an idea, not necessarily the actual language you will use.

Jurisdiction. When you're doing business with clients who may not be located in the same state as you, or if they are on the other end of the state and your state is a big one, you will want to determine where disputes will be settled. The jurisdiction clause should specify which state's laws will govern the dispute and the location in which the dispute will be settled (where the parties are to appear in the event of a dispute, such as Los Angeles County, etc.).

Legality and Severability. Naturally, for your contract to be enforceable, it must be legal. If any portion of your contract is found to be illegal, the entire contract may be null and void, unless you provide language that states that any such provisions will become severable. This means that a clause in your contract would specify that any portion of the contract deemed to be unenforceable would not affect the validity of the rest of the contract.

Arbitration Clause. Arbitration is a less formal way to resolve legal disputes than using the courts, and arbitration does not necessarily require attorneys' involvement. Arbitration procedures are much less formal than those in court, and the costs are far less. Because eBay consignment work is fairly simple, a clause making arbitration an option would be advisable. However, more complex disputes are more difficult to arbitrate.

Attorney's Fees. If you wish to recover your attorney's fees and costs as the prevailing party in a dispute, your contract will most likely need a provision for this. In most states, you cannot recover these fees unless your contract specifies it. The provision for attorney's fees will also act as a deterrent to disputes or litigation. Should a party prevail, they would be entitled to recover these fees, which can be substantial.

Personal Guarantee. If any party to your agreement is not an individual person, you may wish to indicate whether you want the individual officer(s) of the organization(s) (corporation, LLC, etc.) to be personally responsible as well. If so, you will require that all parties sign both in their capacity for the organization and personally. Normally, however, this is to be avoided, because one of the purposes of most organizations is to shield the principles from personal liability.

I suggest that you take a first crack at your contract by typing up the above sections yourself. If you're planning to use a separate item submission form, be sure that this document states that it is a master agreement that will govern the submission of items using these individual forms. Once you have a first draft of your agreement, you can run it by an attorney, who can then make any necessary modifications. Generating the first draft of the contract yourself will make the attorney's task much faster and less expensive. I caution you not to simply write up a contract and start using it without first having it reviewed by a legal professional. There is never a substitute for qualified legal advice. If you can't presently afford an attorney, you may have to start off with verbal agreements backed up by a simple written item submission form that defines your terms as clearly and completely as possible. If you're opening a drop-off store, however, you really should budget for an attorney, because the stakes will be much higher than if you work from home or do this type of work part-time.

Item Submission Form

As noted earlier, your item submission form and contract can be one document. This would work best if you normally receive a small number of items from each client. If you expect to be handling lots of items from individual clients, a separate form for each item may be helpful. If you have huge numbers of items being listed for individual clients, you may also want to have an item submission form that covers multiple item submissions.

The item submission form should contain this basic information:

- The date that the item was submitted
- The client's full legal name or company name
- The client's address (for correspondence and payments)
- The client's telephone number

- The client's identification information (such as driver's license or state identification card number)

- A check box that indicates you have verified your client's age (as being 18 or over)

- A space to describe briefly the item that you're accepting

- The minimum agreed-upon starting price (or reserve price) for the item

- The type of listing you will be creating (auction-style or buy-it-now)

- The fee you're charging for accepting the item (if you charge a fee up front)

- The fee you will charge if the item sells successfully

- Some brief terms and conditions (how soon the item must be picked up if not sold, etc.)

You can create your item submission form using a word processor or spreadsheet program. It doesn't need to be fancy. You can also try one of the many form creation software packages on the market. You can find plenty of them by searching the keyword forms at www.download.com. You can use your own printer to create copies of the form, or your local commercial printer can print them in triplicate with NCR paper, as discussed earlier.

Because the submission form contains everything you need to know to pay your client, it's also a quick way to handle your accounting at the end of the sale. You can lay out the form in such a way that the client's name and address will show through a standard window envelope when folded into thirds like a letter. This way, you can stuff that extra copy of your submission form into an envelope along with a check, speeding payment to your client.

Testimonials—High-Octane Fuel

Testimonials are a powerful way to convince prospective clients to use your services. Initially there will be few, but as your business grows, so will the potential for gathering compelling client testimonials about your high-quality work and services—and the compelling financial rewards they bring.

To solicit glowing client testimonials, you can prepare a simple letter:

Dear [client],

Thank you very much for your business. We truly appreciate your giving us the opportunity to serve you, and we would be very grateful for your help in spreading the word about what we do. We would like to get your comments about our company's services. Please tell us what you think by writing your comments in the blank space at the bottom of this letter. Can we also have your permission to quote your comments and use them as part of our testimonials? If so, please simply say so at the end of your comments. As a token of our appreciation for providing us with your feedback, we would be delighted to give you one free listing just for responding.

Warmest personal regards,

Christopher Matthew Spencer

A form letter similar to this could be included with every client payment. Over time, you will build a library of testimonials that you can use for your website, printed literature, and even when asking banks for additional loans. Be sure to include a self-addressed, stamped envelope if you expect to get a response.

Testimonials are one of the most compelling and effective forms of advertising. Very few satisfied clients will turn you down when you ask to print their words on your marketing messages. Most individuals will feel honored to be included. Your testimonials will have much more credibility if the client will grant permission to use their full name as well as their city; they no doubt would be pleased to have their website address included if they, too, run a business. You can see the mutual benefits of a testimonial such as this:

I was astonished! I turned my entire excess inventory over to the folks at XYZ Company, and they turned it all into cash in less than two weeks! I received a check for more than two times the amount I was offered for the same items by a local liquidator.

—John Doe, Sioux Falls, South Dakota (www.johndoeautoparts.com)

You can correct any spelling or grammatical errors, but don't polish or edit the testimonials you receive. Let them speak for themselves.

> Tip: When you are new in business, until you build your list of clients, you can seek out testimonials from friends and colleagues who can speak about your honesty and integrity.

Putting the Cards on the Table

One of the most common questions you will be asked from day to day will be, "How much do you charge?"

Having a simple printed rate sheet that quickly explains what you do and how much you charge for doing it will help:

Thank you for your interest in our services. We are professional eBay sellers, and we help you sell your high-quality, unwanted items on eBay. We specialize in selling antiques, cameras, car parts, and electronics, but we can help you sell anything of value on eBay. We will handle all of the work, including photography, listing, storage, shipping, and accounting. All you have to do is drop off your items, and we'll do the rest! Our fees are based on the final selling price of your item. Here is a chart of how much we charge for our services . . .

Most people have rather short attention spans. You're catering to busy, upscale people, and you want to get your information across quickly, so keep the text of your rate sheet nice and lean—don't overdo it. Include your name, address, telephone number, website address, and hours of operation on the document. Don't forget to specify whether you include all eBay and PayPal fees in your fee or charge them separately. You might also want to include a few of your strongest testimonials on your rate sheet—but keep it trim!

To the Letter

I have already suggested a form letter for soliciting testimonials. No doubt there will be other times when you will communicate with clients, and it's a good idea to save this correspondence in a folder on your personal computer, for reference and repurposing.

Some of my clients don't have e-mail, and many are slow to respond to phone calls. The latter is natural: they are busy people—that's why they called on me to handle their eBay sales in the first place. Communication with such clients can be challenging, but nevertheless you will need a quick way to get additional information from your clients, update them, and inform them of your actions or decisions.

Letters you may want to develop immediately include:

- Request for additional information on an item (provenance, original cost, certificate of authenticity, chain of title or ownership, etc.)

- Request to your client for a lower minimum bid price or reserve (when you feel, after further research, that their original price is unrealistic)

- Notice of delay in listing their item (if the item requires additional research or for some other reason)

- Request that a client pick up their unsold items, with a deadline and a reminder of your company's policy regarding unsold merchandise unclaimed after the deadline (donate to nonprofit, discard, etc.)

- Notification of delay in making a payment (due to a customer service problem, buyer return of merchandise, or other reason)

- Notice to a client that their item is prohibited for sale on eBay and therefore cannot be listed

Incorporate your letterhead into the document so that your company's logo and contact information appears. For information on business correspondence formatting, go to www.writing-business-letters.com.

Personalize your form letters by typing in your clients' names and addresses in the proper business letter format and by adding a few personalized words pertinent to the specific client. You want to connect with each client, making sure they feel like a person, not a number.

13. Technology

A client brought us an advertising handbill for a 1967 concert featuring Jefferson Airplane and the Grateful Dead, which was held in Toronto. It measured a mere 4¾ by 7 inches. We received 13 bids and ended up selling it for $4,057.53—for one little piece of paper! We typically ship FedEx because it is extremely reliable and, with our volume, they provided us with a free computer shipping system in addition to a substantial discount. When we pay with our American Express card, we receive an additional 5 percent off our volume discounted rates.

—Kevin McGinnis, Berkeley, California; eBay user ID "pictureitsold"; trading on eBay since July 19, 2003

Can I Get an Upgrade?

It might seem a contradiction, because eBay itself is so technology rich, but I think of an eBay consignment sales business as a fairly low-tech proposition. A plethora of software, services, and equipment are available to operate an eBay-related business. But though much of it could indeed make your life easier, be cautious—many of these products and services are designed primarily to make their inventors wealthier. This business can be operated entirely without any additional software. For instance, if you use the item submission forms discussed in the last chapter, you can easily track hundreds of items a month manually without complex or expensive software programs.

I have been a seller for many years now, and have never used a third-party software application other than that offered directly by eBay. In 2004, I was granted the honor of developing all the official eBay online training videos for their seller tools.

The temptation to keep changing and upgrading software is a time bandit, eventually leading to your being in the software learning business instead of the eBay selling business. Your goal is to spend your entire time acquiring new clients and selling their items, and if you can stay organized, you will be able to keep your technology requirements simple.

You should determine your technology needs carefully, before spending money on them. This is particularly true of software. I never buy any software program until I have fully tested it. Most software manufacturers offer a free trial, and I maintain that if you can't try it, don't buy it! And I never implement any new technology into my actual business until it has been tested in a nonoperational environment. We call this our beta testing process. If you have employees, any technology changes you make will cost you even more money because of the additional training required to get the staff up to speed.

Your Technology Toolbox

Basic equipment you may need:

- Modern computer system (with an Internet connection)
- Digital camera or a smart phone with a great camera built-in
- Photographic lighting equipment
- Credit Card Machine (may be provided free from your credit card processor)
- Printer – These last four items may be combined into an all-in-one device
- Copier
- Fax
- Scanner

Things you may want:

- Shipping software for each shipping company you use (United Parcel Service, U.S. Postal Service, etc.)
- A shipping scale that "speaks" to the above software, automatically entering the weight of your parcels
- A label printer for printing shipping labels (oh so handy!)
- More advanced lighting equipment
- Internet telephone service (Voice over IP or VoIP such as Skype, Vonage or something similar)

I could devote an entire book to technology and equipment, but what really matters is that you're comfortable using it. And equipment for your business doesn't need to be expensive. I have purchased a lot of my office equipment used on eBay, but be wary of buying personal computers or printers used—both of these become obsolete fairly quickly, and purchasing them used is really false economy with the vast array of low-cost new options available. I have found both eBay and Wal-Mart (via www.walmart.com) are great sources of equipment and supplies for my company.

Computer Analysis

Hopefully, you already have a computer and don't need to invest in a new one. You can use an older computer to run your business. Most of the computers we use for listing items on eBay are not new. In selecting a computer for use on eBay, whether it's new or used, you may want to determine first if you will be listing items directly on eBay without the aid of additional software. If so, any Internet-ready computer should be fine for your purposes. A more powerful computer will probably only benefit you if you want to use high-powered software, such as certain of the photo-editing programs. We do virtually no editing at our company, because we shoot eBay-ready photos and do not retouch our images. And the reality is that, for listing on eBay, the speed of a computer is really moot. You won't benefit greatly from a superfast computer, simply because the speed of your Internet connection will be far more important in terms of your efficiency.

There is no reason to buy a new computer if you have a perfectly good one that does everything you need. Lots of non-techie people are duped into thinking that they have to spend thousands to get a computer that will do basic tasks such as browsing the Internet or authoring documents. I suggest making do with what you have until it no longer serves your purposes. Don't feel pressured to constantly upgrade.

But if you do need to buy a new computer, I would strongly suggest that it be Windows-based. I know that Apple makes fine computers that are aesthetically pleasing and work wonderfully—but the reality is that most business software applications are written for computers that use a Windows operating system. And if you're planning to use any of the software that eBay provides for listing items, it only works with Windows. (I am just the messenger—don't shoot me!) However, if you already own a Mac, there are workarounds available on the Internet.

With every passing day, computers become more powerful and cheaper. Recently, I saw an ad for an HP All-in-One (tower-free) Desktop with a 20" monitor for $420. It had an AMD E2 processor, 4G memory and a 500 GB hard drive. This is certainly sufficient for your business. The last two computers I purchased for my business both cost under $500, with a monitor. Because we really don't need tremendous computing power, these machines served our purposes well.

Anyone who uses their computer to play video games will have different requirements. I don't think it's wise to use the same computer for your business and your gaming.

Another option might be a laptop instead of a desktop. Many computer users are buying widescreen laptops instead of desktops because they are extremely powerful and portable. Most laptops will work splendidly in your office environment and can be taken with you when you're traveling. I caution you to frequently backup your important files if you do go laptop, because a stolen or dropped laptop can mean the end of all your precious data if no copy is stored securely somewhere else. Laptops with a 17" screen, 6GB of memory and a 750GB hard drive currently cost just under $600.

> Tip: Set a budget and determine what you must have outside of your eBay business—this will help you define what you want and need for your system. If you will need Quickbooks or Quicken accounting software, for instance, you might look for a system with this software already installed. Most systems do not include the pricy Microsoft Office programs, and you will want to have word processing and spreadsheet functionality on your machine.

Tips on Buying

Your computer's processor, the part that does the work, is important. You'll want to buy a computer with an Intel I3, Intel I5, Intel I7 or AMD Processing. Here's a quick check list of things to look for when comparing computer brands and features. Most are industry standards (or minimums) so they should be readily available:

- Processor. Intel I3, Intel I5, Intel I7 or AMD Processing
- Processor speed. 2GHz or higher
- Front-side bus. 800MHz or higher
- Memory. 4gigabyte (GB) or higher
- Hard drive space. 350GB or higher (the bigger the better if you plan to have a lot of images stored on your computer)

- Networking. 10/100 or 10/100/1000 base (using category 5 cable)

- Modem. Only if you live in an area (typically rural) where high-speed Internet is not yet available and you're forced to use a dial-up connection

- Speakers. Optional but nice to have and very cheap

- Monitor. Flat panel with high definition (HD)

- Media readers. Depending on your camera, you will find it helpful to have a computer with a built-in media card reader that will accept the type of media card your camera uses—saving your camera batteries and allowing you to work with picture files while still using your camera for other things. Most computers sold today include this feature. If you're using a smart phone to take photos, you can use the supplied cable to transfer pictures.

- Sound card. The built-in sound cards for most computers are perfectly fine, unless you're a serious audiophile and plan to use this computer for multimedia and games—but you need a business computer, right?

- DVD/CD Slot. This can be internal or a relatively inexpensive external add-on. More and more computers these days are sold without them.

- Ports. You will want the fast Universal Serial Bus (USB) version 2.0, because most up-to-date external peripherals use it. This is standard.

- Mouse. An optical mouse is the industry standard.

- Keyboard. Your computer's keyboard is important because you'll be using it a lot. If you're a fast typist as I am, you will want a keyboard that has a great tactile feel. The keyboards sold bundled with most computers are not very good, and I suggest looking at spending an additional (small) amount on a better one. Test drive a lot of keyboards before you decide—pamper your fingers with the best one you can find. If you decide to run your business with a large tablet, be sure to get one with a detachable keyboard.

Regarding computer brands, I always prefer to buy preconfigured systems from major manufacturers. They are nearly always cheaper than building your own computer, and many of the bigger companies offer customization when you're ordering a system anyway. Avoid buying a lot of unnecessary software and hardware add-ons that you'ren't sure you will need. I won't recommend specific brands because everyone has their preferences, but a major company will stand by its products, and most computers will perform reliably for a long time.

When pondering an extended warranty or service plan, consider the added cost carefully. In all my years of owning computers, nothing has gone wrong except for a couple of faulty power supplies and one bad hard drive. Largely because they have moving parts, power supplies and hard drives can fail, but only rarely. For the most part, unless you have a lot of power surges in your area, you should never have a problem. Getting a good surge suppressor would be smart if you expect lots of lightning storms or inconsistent power. If you back up your data regularly, you can consider extended service plans a luxury and avoid them. They are pricy, and if anything goes wrong with a computer, it will usually present itself within the manufacturer's warranty period.

Surfing the World Wide Web

You will be spending much of your time online, and you always need to have the absolute fastest Internet connection that you can reasonably afford. The cliché "time is money" is incredibly relevant to the use of the Internet as a business tool. Each minute you waste waiting for a slow Internet connection is time you could be spending on other profit-making tasks. Even if fast Internet is costly, it's worth it! When I first started selling on eBay in the late 1990s, broadband Internet was just becoming available in my area. The fastest Internet connection I could obtain from my phone company was $179 a month—and I gladly paid it! Today, you can get blazing Internet speeds for prices ranging from $30 to $60 a month, with the higher end of the price range providing speeds that were once available only to big corporations spending hundreds or even thousands a month.

Getting Connected

Most people connect to the Internet through their cable TV, telephone or satellite service provider. In very rural areas, you may have to use dialup, which provides contact to the Internet via your phone line. Compared to everything else, dialup is incredibly slow.

Most likely you've already got some type of Internet access or can bundle it (along with your phone) with your TV. Bundling can save a substantial amount of money, especially if you're running your business from your home.

One thing to remember about all Internet connections is that they make your computer vulnerable to attacks from hackers. It will be necessary to make sure that you have an Internet firewall (see below) on at all times to prevent unwanted people from accessing your computer.

Internet Telephone Service

This chapter is pretty darn long, but I want to mention the value of Internet telephone services. These services are known by different names such as IP telephony, voice over IP or the abbreviated term VoIP.

Vonage (www.vonage.com) is a cool service I use to make telephone calls via the Internet. Vonage sends you a special router that integrates your Internet connection and a standard telephone. For a monthly cost ($25.99 plus taxes and fees) you can make unlimited calls anywhere in the United States and Canada with no additional charges. International calls are cheap too. The call quality is outstanding, but if you have poor Internet connectivity, you may experience some erratic quality, and you will really need a broadband Internet connection to get the most from this service. Check with Vonage to see if it is available in your area code. With all of these services, sharing the Internet with your computer, gaming system or entertainment system will affect sound quality when you're streaming a movie, downloading files, or if many people are using the connection.

There are lots of other Internet telephone providers on the market, including Skype (www.skype.com). Skype enables you to talk to and see customers (on your computer monitor) as you speak. Your customer must also have downloaded the Skype software to their computer. The software and service are free. You must know your customers' email address or Skype User ID to make contact. Calls to other Skype members are 100% free, and calls to conventional mobile or landline telephone numbers are very economical. I love Skype for talking to customers across the globe. For the totally free calls the person you're calling does have to be online and signed into their Skype. The price of a call depends on where you want to call and whether you choose to pay as you go, using Skype Credit, or buy a calling subscription. Skype is a hugely popular way to communicate.

Google+ (pronounced Google plus) Hangouts (www.google.com/hangouts) are gaining popularity. The White House uses the free Google service to bring multiple people together into a video or voice conversation. If you have a Gmail or Google Apps account, you already have Hangouts. You can make free voice and video calls with Hangouts. Hangouts permit up to 10 people to join the call with you. You may purchase an optional telephone number to receive incoming calls as well. Text messaging is supported, allowing you multiple ways to communicate with others. Notifications can also be sent to your inbox or wireless phone. The service works on both Android and Apple devices.

Navigation Tools

Microsoft's Internet Explorer ("IE") is used by just about everyone on the Internet. The reason is simple—IE is embedded in the Windows operating system. IE does the job of surfing the Internet quite well. Some eBay features behave differently with IE than they do with other browsers. I hesitate to suggest that these features work better with IE because it's all a matter of opinion. Google Chrome is the most popular Internet browser even though it's not installed on most computers out of the box.

Here's a list of the most popular Internet browsers that are available today and all of them are free to install:

- Google Chrome (46.02%)
- Internet Explorer (20.47%)
- Firefox (17.71%)
- Opera (5.45%)
- Safari (3.10%)

Wikipedia's server logs have provided us with some valuable insights into Internet browser popularity and I provided the desktop computer usage share percentages above based on their June 2013 report.

I use Chrome. It's fast and easy. I recommend it without hesitation.

Slamming the Door on Nosey People

A firewall protects your computer from Internet outlaws who may be trying to ruin your day. Some of these pesky hackers roam the Internet committing wrongdoing for fun, but many will try to steal your passwords so they can hijack your eBay, PayPal or other secure accounts. Having a firewall installed on your computer will help prevent unauthorized access.

I have used my laptop computer, using a shared network, on planes and in hotels countless times, and I am always amused when I can "see" the contents of other people's computers—they aren't using a firewall. When you're online without the protection of a firewall, you're allowing the entire world to peer inside your computer's hard drive.

There are almost as many firewall programs on the market as there are fish in the sea, but before you spend any money, be aware that Windows XP, Vista, 7 and 8 have a handy firewall utility built into the operating system—all you have to do it turn it on. So if you're using Windows, you're married—to Windows. It's best to love the one you're with!

Internet Exterminators

In the early days of Windows and the Internet, most folks purchased anti-virus software to help protect computers from infiltration by malicious scripts and programs. These programs, often called malware, are written by hackers, jokers, and fraudsters, who develop them to do harm, but usually with no apparent motive other than to piss us all off.

These days, it is typical to install a complete Internet security suite which contains many tools to help prevent these programs from finding their unwelcome way onto your computer. I used to recommend specific software but these days, there are so many good programs on the market to ensure your safety.

I'm currently using AVG and I've been satisfied with the results. It's not a good idea to have multiple Internet security programs running at the same time. They can generate conflicts with each other and cause problems for your computer.

I use LogMeIn to access my computer remotely and I have found that some antivirus programs detect it as a vulnerability and attempt to remove it. Don't automatically remove every program that's suspected as malicious. Review each one and selectively remove those you don't recognize. All programs should allow you to restore any files that are removed in the event their removal caused problems with your computer.

Your local computer retailer or repair shop will recommend their favorite.

Goodbye Spies

Spyware is software that secretly mines user information through an Internet connection, usually for advertising purposes and sometimes for identity theft. Spyware applications are often bundled with freeware or shareware applications that you may have downloaded. Once spyware makes its way onto your computer, it can secretly monitor your activity and transmit your personal information, such as email addresses, login information, credit card numbers, or bank accounts, to someone else.

Spyware can be introduced into your computer through email, or when you're browsing websites. Sometimes these programs reside on removable media when you share files with someone else; and therefore it is important to have anti-spyware software installed on your computer.

Your Internet security program should perform well in locating and removing spyware in real time.

Everybody Loves Freebies

I love free stuff. Maybe it's genetics, because my mother grew up during the Great Depression, but I am by nature an enthusiastic cheapo. And there is a vast community of software programmers who love to develop fantastic software and give it away for free. I won't ask why. Many of these individuals and companies make their money by providing support for their free products, but a lot of them just design software because of their passion for their art.

Google Drive (drive.google.com) is a wonderful free service that permits storage and access to any computer file. Google Drive stores files safely and securely. Files can be viewed and shared online. Documents, presentations, spreadsheets, forms and drawings may be developed within the program directly. These may then be exported into PDFs,

Microsoft Office-compatible files and other useful file formats. Free basic storage for Google Drive is included with a Gmail or Google Apps inbox. You can purchase a license for additional storage into the terabytes. Multimedia files can be watched directly from the interface without downloading. Dozens of file types can be viewed right in your browser— even if you don't have the program installed on your computer. Documents, spreadsheets and presentations store revision history indefinitely. The biggest bonus is that a crashed computer won't tsunami everything away.

Apache OpenOffice.org (www.openoffice.org) is a free multiplatform office suite program that's compatible with other major software such as Microsoft Office. This is useful because with OpenOffice.org you can author and view all of the same files that are prepared in Microsoft Office without paying Microsoft's hefty price tag. OpenOffice.org prepares and edits documents, spreadsheets, presentations, web documents and graphics. If you plan to purchase a new computer, try to avoid paying for an office suite and download OpenOffice.org instead.

IrfanView (www.irfanview.com) is a small freeware graphic viewer and editing program. Although it's not a full substitute for the expensive and feature-loaded Photoshop program, it accomplishes all the picture manipulation tasks you'll probably need as an eBay user. Working with pictures in IrfanView, you can rotate, crop, resize, adjust color and brightness/contrast and more. My favorite IrfanView feature is the batch conversion function. The program will allow you to change a large group of files at once (be sure you make copies first!). I find this very helpful because, for instance, I can quickly resize hundreds of image files with a few mouse clicks. IrfanView also plays movies, enables scanning and printing, and converts files from a large number of supported formats. It's a very handy tool to have on your computer.

Pixlr (www.pixlr.com) is a free online photo editor. I love that it will allow you to open Photoshop files directly. Pixlr allows you to fix and play with your images. There's no registration required and completed files can be saved to your local computer when done. It's a very handy tool if you're not sporting a copy of Photoshop.

LogMeIn Free (www.logmein.com) allows you to securely register your computers and remotely access them from anywhere in the world on virtually any computer device. The program uses a fancy bank-quality 256-bit SSL encryption for security. LogMeIn offers the free service for a total of ten computers per account.

Supercharge Your Business

Listing tools are designed to help you put items on eBay faster. eBay provides some great free and subscription tools, and there are numerous commercial listing tools available from third parties. Software can be a great ally or a tremendous burden. If you struggle when learning new software, and are listing only a few items at a time, then a manual system may be the best solution for you. Before eBay (or anyone else) had auction and listing tools, I managed my business for the first couple of years with no extra software and I was able to pay clients accurately and efficiently by using a manual system. If you're running a big business (I mean really big), a software solution will be necessary because of the large volume of data you will be processing.

eBay's tools are described below, and can be found at http://pages.ebay.com/sellerinformation/sellingresources/sellingtools.html

Selling Manager

Free for all sellers and located in My eBay, this online program provided by eBay allows sellers to organize and track their listings more effectively. The program shows the status of your sales so that you can manage payments, shipping and feedback more efficiently. It provides email and feedback templates, bulk re-listing, invoices and shipping labels, downloadable sales history reports and allows you to process unpaid items and feedback in bulk. There is no software to download and you can access this program from any Internet computer.

Selling Manager Pro

This program has all of the same great features as Selling Manager and adds inventory management, listing statistics, additional reporting, and free listing designer templates for dressing up your listings. With this program you can fully automate emails and feedback, and it allows you to set automatic re-listing rules for your item inventory. Entirely web-based like Selling Manager, it also has a free 30-day trial, and costs $15.99 per month thereafter. The program is free when you have a Featured or Anchor eBay Store subscription. Because both Selling Manager products work entirely online, they work well with older computer systems.

Turbo Lister

This is eBay's free bulk listing tool, and is an application you download and install on your computer. It is not a listing management program; rather it is designed to help you prepare listing templates and bulk load items, and is ideal for anyone wanting to sell quantities of the same product. With the templates it lets you design, Turbo Lister stores information so that you can avoid repetitive data entry tasks. It won't handle consignment equations, but if you sell media in quantity (books, videos etc.) Turbo Lister allows you to quickly enter thousands of items by author, title, ISBN number or UPC code, using eBay's pre-filled item catalogs. For media sellers this program is an extreme time saver, and if you add a bar code scanner, listing these items will be incredibly fast because you can scan the bar code on the book, video or other supported item directly into the program. This program's templates can be handy for sellers listing many products for the same person or for lower-volume consignment sellers. It can be used effectively in conjunction with eBay's online Selling Manager programs to both list and manage your sales. Turbo Lister works very well on older computers because it doesn't require a lot of processor speed or memory, and works well with dial-up Internet connections because you can work offline.

If you want to consider third-party products or services to help with your sales on eBay, visit solutions.ebay.com to browse the offerings of Certified Providers on eBay's Solutions Directory. These companies' products are designed to help high-volume sellers with listing and post-sales management, and you should browse this rapidly-changing directory for software designed specifically for consignment sellers just like you. Always request a trial version of any software or a trial password for any online solution before you sign a contract or make a commitment. Third parties charge for their services in a variety of ways, including subscription fees, percentages, per-transaction fees, and these fees are additional to your eBay and PayPal fees. If you decide on a third-party tool, you will need to do some math, add these fees to your profit projections, and update your business plan accordingly.

There is a plethora of other software on the market designed to help you with your eBay business. eBay publishes a directory that contains many of these solutions. Because the universe of software designed to help consignment sellers is rapidly expanding, it would be a good idea to evaluate solutions from the directory, and perhaps post questions on eBay's Community Boards (hub.ebay.com/community) to solicit feedback from other eBay members before you buy anything.

Tip: There is a really cool do-it-yourself application called Contribute 3 for eBay that can be purchased from Macromedia (pages.ebay.com/contribute3/). This software has helped many novice computer users design award-winning eBay Stores and it only costs $99. If you prefer, you can delegate your Store design to a third-party company which charges fees based on your specifications and needs.

A Shipper's Best Friends

If you're a low volume seller, you can use eBay's shipping system, which is integrated with PayPal. When your item sells successfully on eBay, a link on the listing will appear that enables you to print a shipping label for either FedEx or the US Postal Service. The label will print directly on plain paper and you can then apply it to your parcel. If you do not have a daily FedEx pickup, you can drop your parcels off at any nearby FedEx location or authorized shipping outlet. You can save a tremendous amount of time with your US Postal Service parcels by arranging a free Carrier Pickup on their website—your regular postal carrier will pick up all of your mail without additional cost. Both services will deduct the shipping fees directly from your PayPal account.

UPS can be seamlessly integrated into other software programs to improve productivity. UPS WorldShip software can accomplish this. Your UPS representative can set this up for you. This handy program will print shipping labels on a variety of printers and works in real-time with a lot of different shipping scales. I bought my label printer on eBay for under $50, and found a great-quality surplus scale for under $30. The UPS customer service representatives can help you with a list of supported label printers and scales, and then you can hunt for them on eBay. I use an Eltron printer (now owned by Zebra) and a Fairbanks scale. Even though they're old, they work perfectly well. Be sure to check model numbers on the compatible list of supported devices before buying a printer or scale. For the supported printers UPS also provides free labels that you can order on their website (registration is required).

For my shipments through the US Postal Service, I use DAZzle software by Endicia (www.endicia.com). DAZzle makes preparing your US Postal Service shipments so much easier, and it supports the same printers used by the UPS WorldShip, so you can print labels for both services on the same label stock. Since parcels insured by the Postal Service require a visit to the long lines at the post office, and preclude Carrier pickups, their insurance is not a cost-effective option for us; DAZzle also has its own insurance, so that you can insure your parcels at your place of business, even with US Postal Service Carrier pickups.

Image is Everything

A digital camera is a must, and ultimately may be your single most expensive purchase (assuming you already own a computer.) Keep in mind that digital cameras come in all sorts of flavors, sizes, resolutions, and prices. We have been in business selling on the Internet since 1998, and we have always used a standard point-and-shoot consumer-grade digital camera. We have tried digital SLR (Single Lens Reflex—professional grade) cameras and we found them heavy and difficult to use. You're not shooting for the cover of Vogue—you simply need clear, well-lit, and in-focus pictures of your items. If you browse eBay for a few minutes and study the listings, you will see that the vast majority of sellers have pictures that are not professional-looking or particularly excellent.

This doesn't mean that your pictures can't be excellent. Many sellers get by with pictures that are just adequate. You must be better.

I would not suggest buying used camera equipment even if you can save a little of money. Your camera has to work all the time, and a camera with a warranty will allow you to sleep soundly. Stick to major brand names. You may save a little money buying an off-brand camera but in the long run you will be unhappy. The major companies have invested millions of dollars in research and development and they know imaging. Their cameras are going to work best.

You don't need to have a fancy camera with lots of bells and whistles. Here's what to look for:

- Light-weight
- Simple features
- At least 2.0 megapixels
- Built-in macro feature (avoid digital macros, make sure the macro function is optical)
- Manual white balance
- Has a removable battery so that you can have one battery charging while you take pictures and do a quick swap-out when the battery runs out

The key to buying a camera is trying it first. You might want to speak to friends and family and if possible borrow several cameras to try out, before purchasing a new one. I have tried many different brands and models, including expensive ones with high ratings from various consumer reporting organizations. Cheap cameras do a fine job. The lighting is generally more important than the cost of the camera.

Starting July 1, 2013, eBay requires at least one photo per listing that is at least 500 pixels on the longest side. I recommend at least 1,600 pixels on the longest side for best results. eBay supports photos in many formats which are JPEG, PNG, TIFF, BMP and GIF.

Fight the urge to buy the most expensive camera you can afford. Digital cameras get cheaper and more powerful by the day and you won't really benefit from a fancy camera in the long run. The pictures you use on eBay will be relatively very small file sizes normally shot on the lower settings of your camera. Shooting at the camera's full resolution is going to be overkill when using it for eBay listings. A brief online search for point-and-shoot cameras displayed many brand name models under $100.

I've mentioned that a smart phone will do nicely as an eBay camera. If you're doing this as a full-time business then I'd suggest you buy a separate camera.

Let There Be Light

You will need to light your items for photography and lighting is more important in taking excellent photos than the camera itself.

I use professional lights these days—a Novatron lighting kit that contains strobes with photo umbrellas. I bought the Novatron V240 Fun Kit, and it requires a camera with a hot-shoe for synchronization with the strobes, but most consumer-grade digital cameras don't have a hot-shoe. The Novatron allows me to take photos quickly. There's less thought that goes into preparing the item and lighting it. In light of my volume, I'm buying new cameras frequently and you'll find some higher-end point-and-shoot cameras have a hot-shoe. I've avoided recommending camera models because I'll probably be using something newer by the time you read this book.

I'm also opposed to your spending a mint on equipment. I had the money and I splurged. If I had to do this over again, I would have gone the cheap route.

Dane Howard is a fellow author who has developed a video course entitled *Product Photography for E-Commerce*. You can search this and many other titles at www.christopherspencer.com. Dane demonstrates how to build a do-it-yourself photo lighting studio for as little as $10. He offers powerful advice on lighting in this course. I recommend it.

Avoid being seduced into buying a lot of expensive equipment. Make due with cheaper solutions. Initially, you can construct a simple and inexpensive lighting setup yourself with items you can find at a local hardware store or camera shop. Dane explains how. Indirect natural light can provide fabulous results too.

There is a bit of trial and error in using lighting equipment. You should learn how to white balance your camera. And you can pick up quite a few tips on photography and lighting on the eBay Discussion Boards. Post questions and get answers from other eBay members. You'll find the Boards at community.ebay.com.

All-in-One Machines

I bought a Canon MF4350d multi-function machine that is a combination of printer, copier, fax and scanner. This is much cheaper to operate than separate devices, because the all-in-one machine uses the same print cartridge for both faxes and printouts. I use the fax a lot more than I ever imagined, and having a fax handy is a good idea. These machines are typically cheap, with manufacturers selling them below cost, because they make their profits selling the ink and paper supplies.

If you foresee a lot of printing, it will be cheaper to use a black and white laser printer than a color ink printer. Stick to the major brands—the supplies will be easier to find and cheaper in the long run. Brand new aftermarket toner cartridges are available for my machine on eBay and some of my favorite online retailers for a fraction of the cost to buy the original equipment brand. In the past, I would buy remanufactured toners and they didn't print well. The aftermarket toners are brand new generic product that's just as good as the brand name. I buy from retailers that offer a returns policy if I'm not fully satisfied. I've never had to return any toners.

Although my all-in-one has a black and white laser printer, it scans in high-resolution full color which I use to scan magazines, photos, coins and flat items for listing.

Most new all-in-ones provide high-quality color printing and color scans. However, you should see a sample of these before purchasing to make sure you're satisfied with the quality or save the receipt.

14. Building Your Name Online

An elderly Swedish man asked me to list 11 decks of old playing cards for him. One deck was quite nice—over a hundred years old with hand-colored illustrations of Swedish royalty from that time. We could find very little information about them, but we decided to start the bidding at $19.99. Several bidders asked for additional close-up photos, and by the end of the auction, the deck of cards sold for $2,575 for my client. The buyer was a man in the Netherlands who indicated that he had not seen this particular deck offered anywhere in over 27 years!

—Sally Milo, Tucson, Arizona; eBay user ID "going1nceamc"; trading on eBay since April 29, 1999

We live in an Internet world. You're starting an Internet business. Selling yourself with a website will help promote your new business, and you will want your website to explain your services to, and thus reduce the number of questions from, prospective new clients. Developing a website can be simple, inexpensive, and fun.

Fortunately, you don't need to be a techie to start a website. Many domain registrars, Web hosting companies, and online services offer build-your-own website templates. You select a design, add your photos, video and text—and you're done. Such websites are not particularly "portable" if you change hosting companies. When you're evaluating hosting companies, you might want to check out their website templates.

My vendor of choice is GoDaddy (www.GoDaddy.com). If you need a site with five or less pages, they will charge you $1 per month for it. They offer hundreds of customizable designs as well as the domain, hosting and marketing assistance. Their support team is on call 24/7 by telephone.

Tell the World

As your business grows, more people will want to know about what you do. Having a website that outlines your services, terms of service, and fees and includes testimonials from happy clients and buyers, compelling examples of items you've actually sold for others on eBay, and other company information will give your firm credibility and generate more business for you. I use photos and video to tell my story.

You will be busy running your company and juggling many tasks. Giving prospective clients the opportunity to read up on your business before walking in the door will reduce the amount of time you have to spend articulating your business processes and fees. A simple, easy-to-understand website will shorten the time needed to convince people of the benefits of your valuable services.

Your site should have the following basic elements:

- A home page that greets the visitor when they arrive at your website
- A page that explains the process of what you do and how you do it, selling the client on the convenience and value of your company's services
- A page that outlines your fees
- A page with some testimonials from other clients (the number of testimonials will grow as your business grows)
- A page that shows some examples of items you have sold and their selling prices
- A link to your eBay listings
- A contact page which includes your company name, address (and e-mail address), and telephone

Pages can be combined based upon your personal preference and vision.

Home Page. The home page of your site can be simple or very fancy. Either way, it should engage. Maybe your home page can have some wow stories such as, ". . . this old film camera sold for $550!" Your website's first impression needs to really sell you and your business, and it must garner enough instant interest to keep them reading. The links to other pages should be easy to locate, and the colors and fonts should be clear and easy to read.

Services Page. This page explains your company's overall process—how you handle the clients' items from start to finish. Just like a dry cleaner or car wash, you provide convenience and value. You provide a service that anyone could provide—anyone can sell on eBay. What sets your company apart—what makes it more professional, trustworthy, reliable, and efficient—will sell you as the right choice for listing a client's items on eBay. I caution you to avoid making your service seem complex. You're simply providing convenience to your clients and helping them use eBay, not offering some techie service. You're providing a personalized service, with a high level of integrity and expertise, and your Services page should shine light on this. Help prospective clients trust and believe in you— this page should accomplish that.

Fees Page. This section of your website will explain the cost of doing business with you. And this page should be decidedly simple. Non-eBay users do not normally understand the fees charged by eBay and PayPal. Most successful eBay drop-off stores have a very simple fee structure.

Testimonials Page. Success generates more success, and a page full of testimonials will share that success:

eBay Drop Stop sold my unwanted china for $650! I thought it would never bring more than a few dollars at a yard sale . . . I'm amazed!
—Candy Johnson, Sioux Falls, South Dakota.

Your testimonials page should only include individuals who have given you written permission, by letter or e-mail. The testimonials page will grow and grow as you add more people to your list. I prefer to use the full name and city of the testimonial. If I have received permission, it's more credible that way.

Hall of Fame Page. This page could be called Hall of Fame or Items We Have Sold. This is a showcase of photos, sale dates, and final prices of actual items you have sold for clients. When preparing this page, show examples of not only your highest-priced sales but also the types of items you would like to see clients bring in to you. If you're an expert on numismatics, then show the sale of a rare coin. If you know clothing, show some high-end shoes. People tend to relate to what they see.

My eBay Listings Page. Clients will want to see the quality of your work. Having a link to your live listings is invaluable in convincing people to use your company. This link will serve double duty, because some clients are also eBay buyers, and you may pick up some extra sales along the way.

Contact Page. On this page, provide your full company information. Make it easy to reach you. Provide your name and a list of employees' names and what they do, your company name and address, telephone numbers, and e-mail address. Your contact page should include your hours of operation so that clients can know when they can reach you, and if you observe specific holidays, mention them on this page as well.

You will attract more clients with a simple and high-quality website. If you're not an Internet expert, don't worry—there are plenty of ways to get a website up and running with zero programming knowledge. WordPress has been gaining popularity for websites and they offer hosted solutions to get you up and running quickly.

A Happy Home for Your Website

Your website must be fast and reliable. The Web hosting company you choose will determine the speed and uptime of your site. The uptime is the percentage of time that your website can be expected to be available and working properly. Most Web hosting companies will tell you their uptime statistics, and this figure should be very close to 100 percent. The speed of the hosting company's services will affect the time it takes for a Web page to load. The server (the computer upon which your site will reside) should be a modern, fast computer. Most major Web hosting companies have state-of-the-art equipment, and you can expect great service. Choosing a good Web host is not complicated, nor should it be a difficult decision.

Here are some of the factors you will need to consider when selecting a Web hosting plan:

Domains. Your Internet domain name is the address used by anyone wanting to visit your website. Although the Internet is really run by the numbers (like telephone numbers) called IP addresses, people find that the numbers are hard to remember and, well . . . boring. The purpose of a domain name is to point a Web user to your site quickly and easily. A memorable name, typically the exact name of your company, will make the process of finding you easy. Domain names are cheap these days, and you will probably get a discount on your domain name registration and annual fees if you buy the domain name along with a hosting package. My favorite domain name registration company is www.GoDaddy.com. They provide extremely low-cost domain names, high-quality Web hosting, e-mail, and many other services. If your company name is Acme Auction Listing Helper, you might want a domain name called www.acmeauctionlistinghelper.com. On the other hand, this is long, so shortening it to acmeauctionhelper.com will make it easier on the fingers. As of July 2013, a domain name from GoDaddy can be registered for $0.99 for the first year (plus ICANN fee of $0.18 per domain name per year) when purchased as part of a three-year deal. The second and third years will cost $7.99 per year (plus ICANN fee of $0.18 per domain name per year). Domain costs vary depending on the extension and time period selected. For example, a .com may more expensive than a .biz. A domain name is currently free if purchased in conjunction with GoDaddy's Web hosting services.

Setup Charge. This is usually a one-time charge for setting up your account with the Web hosting company. These days, this fee should be close to zero because of the stiff competition among hosting companies. Look for companies offering free setup.

Monthly Fee. This is the fee you will pay for the Web hosting plan, and rates will vary greatly, depending on the amount of disk space (see the next section) and level of service you want from your hosting company. At this writing, the non-sale monthly fee for Web hosting ranges from about $6 to $20 per month.

Storage Space. This is the amount of physical space you're allocated on the Web hosting company's servers to store your files. For an information site, this can be a very small amount of space—as little as a few megabytes. Most hosting plans offer gigabytes of storage, far more than you will need for an information site. If you plan to host images and video, expect to need more, but you can always upgrade to a larger plan later. Keeping your site clean and free of unwanted or unused files will also help in managing disk space. Remember to keep copies of your files on your own personal computer for backup.

Monthly Data Transfer. A Web hosting plan is like your car—the more you use it, the more it costs to operate. Data transfers are uploads and downloads. Uploads includes moving photos, videos and files from your computer to your hosting plan. Downloads occur when visitors navigate your site and view pages and multimedia.

Most hosting plans place a limit on the maximum amount of data you can transfer each month. For a simple site, this figure will be very low, probably well below the host's maximum. In a single month our company's server had 76,982,190 kilobytes of transfers. This means that more than 73 gigabytes of data were transferred into and out of our host's server. You can always monitor your usage with your hosting company and decide when it's time to upgrade your plan.

E-mail Accounts. Your hosting plan should have free e-mail accounts, which will allow you and your staff to have branded e-mail with your own company's domain name. These e-mail accounts should have built-in spam and virus protection as well as a Web interface that allows you to check your e-mail from anywhere in the world on any computer.

Tip: If you'd like branded email, you can setup a forwarding email from your hosting to a Gmail inbox. Gmail offers faster email and superior spam filtering. It has a built-in feature that allows you to manage other email addresses and still have them appear to come from that email when replying through Gmail. It's how I manage multiple email accounts in a single inbox.

SSL Certificate. You probably won't need one, but if the Web hosting plan includes a secure sockets layer (SSL) certificate, you can allow users of your website to transmit personal information securely. This is typically used when sending credit card or other sensitive information via the Internet. With most buyers now paying via PayPal, the SSL certificate may be superfluous, but if it's free with your hosting plan, why not?

Databases. I'll discuss content management systems later in this chapter, but for now, I'll just mention that you'll want to have database capability with your hosting plan. This is usually offered as part of the hosting package, and you will want to have at least a handful of what are called SQL or MySQL server databases (see below) with your hosting plan to maintain and update your website. These databases are easy to install and use, working with simple and automatic Web interfaces, and they will be useful in developing content, image galleries, blogs, message boards, and other features that you may want to add down the road.

Server Operating System. Typically, your Web hosting company will offer a choice of two types of servers, Linux or Windows. I myself use a Linux server, but many people prefer Windows. We're not talking about the Windows operating system that may run your computer. Most of the free software that will help you develop your site is compatible with a Linux system, and you will find that Linux is the economy choice without compromising the features you need. I would suggest using Linux. If you do so, your hosting plan must support a computer language called PHP, as opposed to ASP for a Windows-based hosting plan. These options will come under standard language support in your hosting package.

Forums. This is a great service that's free with most hosting plans, allowing you to set up community boards for users of your website to share ideas and make comments. Having a forum, as well as a page hit counter, lets you check your website's "pulse."

Blogging. Blog is a shortened term for Web log, and is a frequently updated journal intended for reading by the general public on the Internet. Facebook is a type of blogging service. This popular format is typically informal and personal and can be a great way for you to chat with the public. You can set up a blog that links to your website for free. You can also develop a page on Facebook and Twitter and embed the stream of information on your site.

Facebook, Twitter and LinkedIn can provide exposure for your business. Set up a page dedicated to your business, as opposed to your personal page. Many firms now use social media accounts to sell their services and handle customer support.

Photo Galleries. Your hosting plan may include photo gallery support, and this would be helpful for you in setting up your Hall of Fame page. You can use a photo gallery to engage visitors who come to your site.

Popular photo and video sharing sites also permit you to embed content. YouTube, Instagram, Flickr, Imgur, Picasa and dozens of other social media sites permit uploading multimedia and then embedding it into your site. You can explore the Wikipedia article on photo sharing sites at this link http://en.wikipedia.org/wiki/Photo_sharing.

Dedicated or Shared Hosting. You may see the terms dedicated or shared hosting when selecting a hosting plan. You won't need a dedicated server to run your company. A dedicated server is a computer at the Web hosting company's location hosting only a single client, while with a shared hosting plan, as the name implies, your website resides on a computer shared by other users and maintained by the hosting company. A dedicated server is more expensive and requires an administrator to maintain it.

If you're very technologically inclined, you can rent dedicated server instances on the Rackpace Public Cloud at www.rackspace.com/cloud. I've used this service and it's amazing. They offer fully scalable servers for affordable prices. You pay only for what you use. If you don't have an IT background, this isn't for you.

When comparing Web hosting plans, look for a company that won't charge a set-up fee or require a minimum annual commitment or contract. GoDaddy.com's basic $5.99 Web hosting plan includes 100 gigabytes of storage, unlimited band width, a choice of Linux or Windows operating systems, 100 e-mail accounts with anti-spam and antivirus protection, 10 MySQL databases, forums, blogging, photo gallery, and more. This deal, for the price of a premium coffee drink, is hard to beat. Don't let the low price fool you; this total package will run your business with great bandwidth and uptime. But shop around—there are thousands of Web hosting companies out there.

Tip: Avoid expensive Web design packages. Keep yourself on a tight budget and keep things simple, until you become proficient in setting up a site for yourself. You'll want to be able to update your site quickly, so don't delegate too much control (if any) to others

More Freebies

Content management systems is have become very popular as the Internet has attracted non-tech people who want to set up websites easily and quickly. A content management system allows you to setup and update your website without a single bit of computer code or programming knowledge.

After installing a content management program you will be able to design your website rapidly, adding pages, images, and links with a bit of typing instead of complex coding. If you want the capability to maintain your website from anywhere in the world, allow user-level access for your employees to contribute content, create e-mail, generate your own "press releases," and a lot more, you will want a content management program. Wikipedia offers this article that lists the content management systems that are currently available and many are free and open source en.wikipedia.org/wiki/List_of_content_management_systems.

Among the best is Drupal. Drupal is feature-rich and is definitely worth a look. If your Web hosting company does not provide automatic installation of a content management script, you can find Drupal at www.drupal.org.

Formerly associated mainly with blogs, WordPress is now a fully functioning content management system which will enable you to develop and manage your website. GoDaddy offers special hosting deals in conjunction with WordPress. I have used both Drupal and WordPress and like them both.

You can easily find more free programs simply by going to Google.com and searching for "free content management software." The software development community has really stepped up to the plate with these free systems. As long as the content management software is easy for you to understand and use, any program will do the trick. GoDaddy has an inventory of free content management scripts that you can install instantly with zero programming knowledge.

The Dark Side

The reality is that the Internet is teeming with scammers and thieves who want to steal your private, personal information, account numbers and passwords, and then use this information to transfer funds from your accounts and/or steal your identity. Hackers seek out and exploit websites with security vulnerabilities. Some viruses come in e-mail, install themselves on your computer, and then log your keystrokes to capture the passwords that you use to log onto your accounts on websites such as eBay or PayPal.

Fraudsters send out phony e-mails by the millions that are known as spoofing or phishing. A spoof looks like a legitimate e-mail from eBay, PayPal or some other well-known company and is designed to convince you to click a link within that e-mail and compromise your personal information. You should never click any link in an e-mail to sign in on a website. Banks never ask for account information, or for you to verify account information, in an e-mail. I receive at least two messages a month on Facebook from a beautiful fair maiden in a faraway land offering to be my best friend or wife.

Offers from the widow of an assassinated prince to move his fortune out of her homeland with you as the trusted friend aiding in the legal process, claims of overseas lottery winnings, fund requests for sick relatives and whatever other tall tales you hear are scams. Report them to the site from which they came.

eBay has a secure system called My Messages, part of their effort to combat fraud. This system allows you to see any e-mail sent to you by another eBay member or staff person right on the eBay site, without an external e-mail program.

Your Web hosting company provides spam and virus protection for your e-mail, and have systems to thwart hackers in attacking your website. It is critical to understand, however, that nothing can stop a con artist if you accidentally give up your password to them. Having a good antivirus software program on your computer will help to identify and delete dangerous viruses that may attempt to steal your login. Many high-quality antivirus programs were mentioned previously in Chapter 13 and more can be found via a Google search. Gmail does a stellar job of removing viruses from emails. Keep in mind that most security problems are caused by lax security practices.

Security Checkup

Here is a quick security checkup review to make certain you remain safe on the Internet and that your business information is secure:

- Ask your Web hosting company about their security and anti-hacking procedures

- Determine if your hosting company has redundancy. If a server goes down, a backup server should automatically kick in. Ask if they perform a daily backup of files, in case they have an equipment failure or a security violation that results in the loss of or damage to your data.

- Find out how much your Web hosting company will charge to provide automatic daily backups of your data and the cost of restoring your data in the event of data loss

- Keep a backup of all files on your own computer

- Activate the firewall feature on your personal computer to keep intruders from hacking into your computer while you're connected to the Internet

- Install an antispyware program on your computer (Microsoft offers a free one on their website, or use Google to find available free or low-cost programs)

- Install an antivirus program on your computer

- Keep all passwords secret and do not share passwords or user IDs with others

- Change passwords frequently and keep a written record of your passwords in a secure place but not on your computer

- Maintain constant physical security of computers at your home and office. If you share computers with others, you increase the risk of accidental or intentional data destruction.

- Avoid giving your business e-mail address when registering to use websites (to avoid spam), and be cautious in general about to whom you give your e-mail address, to avoid spammers who send malicious viruses

The Internet Crime Complaint Center is an alliance between the Federal Bureau of Investigation and the National White Collar Crime Center. They have additional tips on how to avoid being the victim of Internet-related crimes at www.ic3.gov/preventiontips.aspx.

With a bit of knowledge, common sense, and caution, you can operate a safe and secure website and keep your business out of the hands of fraudsters.

Keeping Your Website Fresh, Fantastic, and Frequented

It is important for you to maintain accurate and current information at all times on your website. You can generate excitement for your website by using these methods:

- Update your site as frequently as time permits to keep people interested and coming back

- When you sell notable items, add a photo and the sale price to your Hall of Fame page

- Have your website's address printed on packing slips, business cards, letterhead, and any other printed documents

- If you have a retail drop-off store, include your Internet address on your store's signage

- If you have a yellow pages listing, be sure to include your website's address

If you're listed in your local telephone directory, most of the Internet telephone directories will pick up your business listing from it, but it's important to check if you can add additional information, such as your website's address. Here is a list of some of the more popular free online telephone directories that people use every day to find businesses such as yours:

- www.google.com/local/add

- www.superpages.com

- www.switchboard.com

- www.yellowbook.com

- yp.yahoo.com

You should take advantage of any free listing options in other business guides Millions use search engines each day to find all kinds of information on the Internet. You can register your website with virtually all of these search engines free of charge, or you can use the "paid search" feature, where you purchase targeted advertising on the search engines for your company's site. Usually you pay for each click—each time a user links from the search engine's site to your own site after they type in keywords to find what they seek. The link to your website (and others) will be prominently and separately displayed as a sponsor at the top of the search engine results page a/k/a the SERP. Most search engines automatically pick up the content on your website. In the past you had to ask them to do so, but that's no longer the case.

If you choose paid search, be certain it is highly targeted. Because your client base will be limited primarily to businesses and individuals within no more than about 25 miles from your business, you don't want to pay to attract customers beyond this trading area. Google.com, at present the most popular of the search portals, does offer this kind of pay-per-click, performance-based advertising that can be targeted to display your ad only to users within a specified number of miles from your business—very handy!

A cost-effective way to submit your site to thousands of search engines and other sites is a program called SubmitWolf (cost as of July 2013: $199), software that will automate the submission process for you. It's a one-time cost, because you're paying for the software, not permission to submit to the many websites. You can accomplish the same thing by hand, submitting to one site at a time, but this tool will pay for itself many times over in time saved. You can find this software at www.trellian.com/swolf/.

I also suggest promoting your new site on craigslist.com, if one of its many sites is in your area. Craig's List has a section where you can post free classified ads for business services, and it is very popular.

Hiring Talent

Hiring a Web designer can be an expensive proposition, and once you turn over your virtual storefront to an outside contractor, the critical ongoing maintenance of your site can be a perpetual cash drain.

You may try the following happy medium for a new site:

- Develop all the textual content yourself
- Provide all the edited photos and graphics
- Provide the designer with a clear idea of how you want the site to look and function
- Require in your contract that the designer train you on content maintenance and uploading and have a basic HTML reference handy. (Most website creators loathe the update and maintenance function, anyway, and are happy to be out of the ongoing maintenance loop.)

15. Streamlining Strategies

A client dropped off a Masonic apron that was encased in glass, with a few notes on the back that dated it to the Civil War. She told me that she had paid $40 for it at a garage sale and that she wanted me to sell it on eBay. Shortly after the bidding started, I was flooded with offers of up to $500 to sell it offline. When I relayed this to the client, she said 'Do it!' Well, I didn't, because my experience has told me when you get offers like this, it will go higher. The apron ended up selling for $1,100, and the client was very pleased. She brought me some additional items that generated over $5,000.
—Tom Shanley, Allen, Texas; eBay user ID "treeline2"; trading on eBay since February 24, 1999

Just as you use a business plan to help define your business and present it to investors and banks, you need to have systems in place to keep your business running smoothly. Being organized will pay off in a number of ways, including higher productivity and reduced stress for you. A well-oiled machine will make you profits. Being badly organized will cost you in lost time and frustration.

De-Clutter

Are you a naturally organized person? I'm not. And knowing this, I have to work hard at being organized. When I was the only person working for me, it was actually harder to stay organized than now. As my business grew and I added employees, who are very organized themselves, I was able to see and define the big picture of my company, and together we keep things in order and operating to my great satisfaction.

Now it's time to get out your pen and paper and add some work flow strategies to your business plan, to help you define how you will actually operate. Being a smooth-running, organized business will take some time and a ton of discipline. You will find many distractions along the way, but you can never be too focused when running your very own business.

You can start getting organized by shedding as many of the unnecessary and undesirable activities in your life as possible. This is not off-topic. Look at your daily routine and see what you presently do that consumes your valuable time without benefiting you. Do you wash your own car? Do your own laundry? Clean your own house? Are you running errands that could be delegated to someone else? Finding ways to delegate tasks will free you up to mastermind your business and help to bring that sharp focus to what you really want and need—tremendous financial success! Before you reject these remarks as some sort of rah-rah motivational speaking mumbo jumbo, realize that highly effective people are highly organized—constantly avoiding unnecessary activity, instead planning each minute of their day. Think about the additional time you will free when you delegate chores to other people.

Divine Planning

Please don't be in a rush. Rushing will lead to mistakes and cause havoc. You're playing a very important game of chess that requires strategy and intelligence. If you're used to punching a time clock, keep in mind that you're now your own boss and are no longer paid by the hour. Though you may be proud of how hard you work, focus instead on efficiency—how much you can accomplish with the least amount of effort. Ideally, owning your own business will give you the luxury of being able to do what you want, when you want. A well-thought-out plan for managing your business will allow you freedom to enjoy more time with family and friends—taking a vacation when you feel like it and not having to wait for the boss to say you've earned it.

You can help days go smoothly by thinking of all of the tasks you have to accomplish each day and compartmentalizing them. You don't need to prepare listings or pack orders every single day. You should write down all the tasks you need to accomplish and place them into buckets of time when you will complete them. It's very tempting to try to get everything done all at once, and many new business owners make this common mistake.

Here is a sample weekly list of tasks for a store that operates Monday through Saturday.

Monday	Tuesday	Wednesday	Thursday	Friday	Saturday
Answer buyer questions	Answer buyer questions	Answer buyer questions	Answer buyer questions	Answer buyer questions	Answer buyer questions
Pack and ship orders	Photograph items	Process payments and deposit checks and money orders	Pack and ship orders	Photograph items	Process payments and deposit checks and money orders
Inventory and order supplies	Prepare eBay listings	Pull and check paid orders	File documents	Prepare eBay listings	Pull and check paid orders
Compress and reorganize shelves	Store items	Clean and vacuum store	Compress and reorganize shelves	Store items	Pay clients
Clean and vacuum store	Clean and vacuum store		Clean and vacuum store	Clean and vacuum store	Clean and vacuum store

I am assuming that most clients will come to your business at unscheduled times—so these largely random visits aren't on this daily schedule.

Sunday is a day of rest on this sample schedule. Because Sunday is a good day to end auction-style listings (because more bidders are at home and on their computers), you may choose to list auctions ending on Sunday and, therefore, will need to answer bidders' last-minute questions from home. This also means that you will be scheduling the seven-day listings to start on a Sunday, even though your listing days shown here are Tuesday and Friday. With software or using eBay's scheduling feature, you can easily start listings on any day you decide. If you use listing software you will be launching them at your leisure. You will need to answer buyer questions on a daily basis, so I have placed this at the top of each day.

Depending on the sheer volume of merchandise you receive each week, you can be flexible about scheduling the photography and listing tasks, but you want to have at least two days dedicated to preparing listings.

Processing payments and pulling items for shipping can be done the day before the actual shipping. This allows time to develop a strategy about which packing materials you will need and which shipping carriers you will use for which items, as well as estimating the amount of time required to pack the paid orders. To become a Top Rated Seller on eBay, you have to ship within one business day. This is something that may change your proposed shipping schedule.

I find packing and shipping a relaxing task. I suggest doing packing no less than twice a week to keep your buyers as happy as possible. But I have done shipping as infrequently as once a week when I used Priority Mail (for lighter items) only—when I didn't send out any heavy shipments, for which I usually use UPS. After each shipping day, it's helpful to reorganize and compress your merchandise storage shelves to utilize the additional space left by the shipped items. Once I became a Top Rated Seller, I had to ship every day of the week, except weekend.

You can inventory and order shipping and office supplies just once a week. Filing can be done twice a week. Stay on top of your filing so that you can quickly put your hands on a contract or paid bill. If the filing gets behind, it will snowball, and you can get burned when you really need to find a specific document fast. The time spent foraging for unfiled or misfiled documents will quickly amount to more hours than you would have spent just doing it right the first time.

Keeping a clean and orderly store will attract repeat customers and also helps you stay efficient and organized—so I put this task down for each day.

The weekly tasks can be rearranged any way you feel is appropriate. If you have full-time employees handling specific tasks such as photography, listing, and/or shipping, you would obviously add this task to every day.

You'll be paying your rent or mortgage, bills, and possibly taxes monthly. And if you see your business growing steadily, you'll want to plan your spatial needs, staffing requirements, and equipment purchases in a fairly long timeline. As I type these words, my warehouse is full to the ceiling with merchandise. I had to give up my personal office to store client items. We could move to a bigger location, but because the flow of client merchandise does not always fill our store, we are conservative about long-term expansion planning. We can control the volume of our work by being even more particular about the value and nature of the items we accept for listing. You may decide that you don't want to be huge but you do want to make great money. Selling higher-value goods is a work flow strategy to help you reduce volume and maintain revenue.

Handling the Stuff

Always keep your client contracts handy and maintain a generous work space to receive new items. If you offer to clean client merchandise, you should have an area dedicated to this chore. And I do mean chore: cleaning is a major time bandit and normally we don't do it—we actually turn down items if they need more than just a quick dusting. It's difficult to turn away people, but we aren't in the cleaning and restoration business. If someone brings you a rare piece of art or a spectacular sterling tea service, you may offer to do the cleaning, but I suggest you refuse bins of filthy common items. It's your decision and your business, so make the call.

You might remind the client that cleaning antiques and collectibles can significantly reduce their value to collectors. This is especially true for silver and other metals, wood, fabrics and fiber, Lucite, and similar degradable items. When in doubt, don't clean. Wipe off dust with a soft cloth. Clearly state in the auction that you have not cleaned the item because it could decrease its value, and that the buyer should seek professional help if they wish to restore these items after purchase. Some items such as coins should never be cleaned and should only be conserved by an experienced professional. Coin grading services PCGS, ANACS and NGC will not provide grades for coins with visible signs of cleaning.

You should have small labels for numbering client items (inventory control numbers). I use a Dymo label printer to generate sequentially numbered inventory stickers on the one-inch by one-inch self-adhesive labels, Dymo part number 30332. You can always buy small labels at the stationery store or online and simply write your item numbers on them by hand. You have to do a pretty hefty volume to justify a printer dedicated to this task. I opted for the Dymo Twin Turbo because it will hold and print two different types of label stock at the same time.

The labels will help you track your consignments, and you should also keep a log of your incoming client merchandise. You can do this with software, but when you're starting out, it's just as easy with a spiral-bound notebook or steno pad. The information you want to capture includes:

- Client name
- Date of receipt of the item(s)
- Brief description of the item(s)

- Status columns to show date of photography and then listing (to help track what is still unlisted)

You need a good supply of bubble wrap bags or bubble wrap for storing fragile items. You should have various sizes of these bags, and you can find them on eBay by searching the term bubble bags. You don't want the self-seal type, and don't confuse bubble bags with the padded or bubble mailing envelopes often sold under the Jiffylite brand name. These are great for shipping but not good for merchandise storage.

Plastic bins will come in handy. They can be used for storage of client items before, during, and after making listings. I buy the large, heavy-duty, stackable type with the hinged dual flaps that form the lid. I number each bin to identify it and also tape an index card with the client's name on the bin. But until you start making money selling on eBay, you can always use free boxes from your local supermarket or department store. As your company grows, you can label the bins with numbers or letters and track the storage location of things from your tracking software or documents.

A high-quality, plastic, resin-top folding table works well for sorting and even photographing items. I don't suggest the bigger six- or eight-foot tables, as they are heavy and hard to handle. For petite women, this would be an undue burden.

We find that four-foot tables are inexpensive and easy to move around, and we can easily make an eight-foot table out of two four-foot tables. I use them for temporary work tables, desks, staging areas, shipping tables, and photography. We even use them at small events and trade shows, because covered with a tablecloth, they look great. The best part, you can reconfigure your store at any time.

Office Supplies—The Basics

You'll need some basic office and store supplies:

- Stapler and staples.
- Manila file folders. For filing paid bills, client contracts, and other documents.
- Manila envelopes (9 inches by 12 inches). For storing flat items such as photos, postcards, magazines and small books.
- Pens. And lots of them. They're cheap, and you will have clients borrowing them all the time and forgetting to give them back—you can never have too many.

- Sharpie brand permanent markers.

- Scissors and box cutters. For making custom box sizes along with all the usual tasks. Get a couple of each as they are cheap and will be used a lot.

- Calculator. Get the solar type so you'll be battery-free, and look for one with large buttons. You'll have a lot of math problems: calculating commissions, adding up shipping and handling charges, etc.

- Lighter fluid. A miracle product for removing residue and old labels from plastic, glass, and other surfaces. Have it on hand always.

- Pure denatured alcohol. A great product to quickly remove grime. It's potent, so use only on unpainted surfaces. Not the alcohol from the drug store which is mixed with water, buy this at the hardware store and make sure it's 100% denatured alcohol with no water added.

- Acetone. This is nail polish remover without the fragrance added. A great way to remove residues when lighter fluid does not work.

- Glass cleaner. For quickly touching up glass items and a lot more (and cleaning your store windows, of course—and try a squeegee for that).

- Ammonia. This is a miracle product for bringing back the shine to gold plated items. Dilute with one part ammonia and one part water.

- A huge supply of index cards. For writing yourself quick notes, identifying large or sticker-resistant items, and to accompany items with notes for writing the listing.

- Re-sealable sandwich and larger freezer bags of various sizes. For storing items on your shelves such as flatware, jewelry, small porcelain or crystal items—anything delicate that will fit. These are also handy because you can number the item by placing an index card in the bag instead of using a sticker on the delicate item itself. I use the two gallon size for storing rare magazines. I also buy these at the dollar store.

- Large clear plastic trash bags. You can put your outgoing mail in them to allow for quick transportation to the post office or to make your postal carrier or FedEx driver's job easier. Get the clear type so no one mistakes them for trash and accidentally throws them out!

- A good selection of basic tools. This includes screwdrivers, pliers, hammer, and rubber mallet (the tool for assembling and taking down those locking metal shelving units) as well as a standard, compartmentalized plastic toolbox. The dollar store in my neighborhood stocks all these tools.

- A good vacuum cleaner with a full array of attachments. For quick cleaning of dusty merchandise, not just your floor! I purchased a Bissel PowerForce Helix bagless upright vacuum at www.walmart.com for $43.84 plus tax. The shipping was free. Despite the low price, it's a powerful full size vacuum.

- Super Glue and two-part epoxy adhesive. For quickly resetting loose stones in costume jewelry or reattaching parts that may have fallen off of an item with age.

- Clear tape and masking tape. Use the latter for labeling virtually anything. Comes off cleanly and easily.

- Air compressor. I have found my small air compressor is amazing for dusting items quickly. Keep it by the photography table. These are available at any big hardware store and not expensive, but it will probably be a down-the-road purchase, depending on the volume and nature of your listings. Try Harbor Freight Tools for a good price on one. They have an oilless pancake air compressor that routinely goes on sale for $39.99 and is item number 95275.

- Paint brushes. Also available at the dollar store, these are perfect for gentle dusting and cleaning of fine antiques. I keep one on the photography table at all time for a quick de-dusting.

Your business may be completely different from mine, and you may find that you need other tools for your own specialties. If you sell a lot of computer equipment, you may want to set up a test bench with an open-case computer for testing hard drives, expansion cards, and peripherals. Your particular tools and supplies will reflect your own unique needs.

Under Your Thumb

Staying on top of a growing inventory of merchandise is challenging, and I suggest that you start using inventory control numbers. At my store, each item is issued a unique control number. We call this the item ID number and track it in our inventory system. Using such a number system with eBay's Selling Manager Pro or whatever solution you choose, you will easily be able to keep tabs on the merchandise. If you don't use listing software and are listing items on eBay manually, you can enter the unique item ID number at the end of your eBay description as a way of tracking the item through its sale and shipment. Keep your inventory in numeric order, neatly arranged on your storage shelves so that you can put your hands on any item in a matter of seconds. Your store will be the height of organization and efficiency, very handy when a prospective buyer calls with a question minutes before the auction ends.

Think of your items as having different statuses and keep them segregated in different staging areas. New items should have a dedicated table or shelf for examination, cleaning, and listing. Items waiting for photography should have their own committed area. Items being stored after listing will have a dedicated listed item shelf. For after they sell, have an awaiting shipping area.

Be disciplined, and you will find that everything flows well and stays very organized. Trying to locate misplaced things, whether a client item, a contract, or that darned screwdriver is a time bandit. Staying neat, tidy, and organized will maximize your time and improve efficiency.

There are so many ways to set up a system and work flow. You will settle into your own personal methods as you gain experience. You can also change your system at will if it does not work for you—developing new systems to replace the old is part of running an entrepreneurial enterprise.

Tip: I include a photograph of the item location and unique number tag on my eBay listing. This allows me to quickly locate the item when answering questions on My Messages.

16. Staying Fit and Trim

I sold a Greek amphora dating back to around 250 B.C.E. Amphoras are ceramic jars that were used to transport wine and olive oil in ancient Greece. The owner of this relic was a deep sea diver in the 1950s, and he had exhibited this in his house all these years. He was forced to sell it because he was downsizing, and he had been given an approximate value by Sotheby's of $800. I listed and sold it for $1,575 to an Italian buyer who paid an additional fee to crate and ship it back to his country. We collected a commission of $525, and the buyer paid all of the transportation and crating charges.
—Wayne Lehman, Portsmouth, New Hampshire; eBay user ID "cogebi"; trading on eBay since July 20, 1997

Even the most successful athletes have personal trainers to get them into shape for a competition. Many of us don't get enough exercise and I'm one of them. As a business professional, you need to embrace fiscal discipline. I would like to be your financial personal trainer helping you keep as much of the money you earn as possible.

As you look at different ways to purchase the supplies necessary for the successful operation of your business, you will often find differences in prices from one vendor to another. Learn to be frugal.

Be a Miser

It's okay to be stingy. Not tripping over dollars to pick up pennies. When you walk into a post office, you'll pay $1.50 for a shipping box at the retail supplies counter, while you can go online and obtain free shipping boxes and envelopes of various sizes from the same U.S. Postal Service—including free shipping of these supplies to your home or office.

When you work for another company, worrying about the cost of everything the company purchases is probably someone else's problem. You own your own business and you will have to analyze every purchase to ensure you're getting the best possible price.

Do you enjoy saving just to see if you can? Being frugal can be lots of fun. Companies spend a great deal of money figuring out ways to separate us from hard earned money. Extravagant advertising campaigns and colorful packaging are designed to persuade you to buy their products. In this society based on consumption, even our government encourages us to spend, with tricks like lower interest rates to help spur spending when the economy is struggling. In your new position as the CEO of your own company, you may feel a sense of greater spending power, but for practical purposes it's an illusion. We all need to stay focused on our real financial goals. My good friend Kathy Ireland says that "No" is a complete sentence.

In our society, temptations to dive into more debt are everywhere. Here are some tips for you to stay fit and trim financially:

- Before making any purchase, ask the question, "How much will this investment return for me in actual dollars?" or, "Is this purchase absolutely necessary for the successful operation of my company?"

- Never finance anything unless you're sure that it will generate additional profits— otherwise, pay in cash or wait until you can afford to do so.

- Compare three different vendors' prices for every item you purchase. When contacting vendors for prices, be sure to let them know that you're price shopping and that your company's policy is to buy from the cheapest vendor (given, of course, that the product is the same from vendor to vendor).

- Shop on the Internet and pay reasonable shipping costs to save time, as a result allowing more focus on what makes you money—selling, not shopping.

- Pay all credit cards off in full at the end of each month. Keep a record of all charges so that you know exactly how much you have spent and whether or not you can pay for those items when the bill comes due. Interest charges on an ongoing credit card balance can eat up any savings you may have realized from careful shopping. Paying with a debit card linked to your company bank account is an even better idea. There's no bill to pay at the end of the month.

- Pay in cash if you can receive a substantial discount for it.

- Buy any items you use frequently in volume to get the best discount possible.

- Maintain impeccable credit so that you can obtain the absolute best interest rates for any purchases that you can reasonably argue must be made on credit.

Being frugal does not necessarily mean settling for generic brand or inferior products. It means finding the best possible wholesale or discounted price for the brands and products you use every day.

At my company, one of our most frequent purchases is shipping boxes. One major office supply superstore who shall remain nameless sells 12- by 12- by 12-inch cardboard boxes in packs of 25 for $34.68, which comes out to $1.39 per box. Another vendor sells the same box for $0.51 each. I can get free delivery from the first vendor with no minimum purchase, but the second company with the lower price requires a minimum order of $300 for free delivery. Because of my volume, I can always get free delivery, and I am saving more than 63 percent on this box. We stock up on many low-cost supplies from this discount vendor and order much less frequently, perhaps once a month or less, to get our order up to at least the $300 minimum for free shipping, ultimately to get the best prices.

No Harm in Asking

Certainly not everything in life is negotiable, but most companies offer some form of discounts. And even if they don't, there's no harm in asking. Being a member of AAA affords discounts from many vendors. Using an American Express will secure a discount at FedEx Office locations. As a veteran in the United States Navy, I am extended discounts from many merchants by simply showing my ID card. There are many ways to save a little money here and there, and trust me—it adds up. Find all the discounts you can muster.

At any business establishment or when I shop by telephone, I always ask for a discount. And I receive a discount surprisingly often. Employees of various businesses are empowered to grant discounts to customers on a discretionary, per case basis, and from my experience, will do so if they like you. So be sure to pour on the charm everywhere you go, and you will be amazed at the results. You won't get a discount at your local 7-11, but there are many, many ways to save.

Follow these tips for garnering discounts everywhere possible:

- Maintain a current AAA membership and then use it by asking for discounts everywhere you shop
- Ask for free delivery when you shop online—it's the same as getting a price reduction
- Offer to pay in cash if the merchant will then agree to pay the sales tax
- Search Google and see if you can find coupon codes for online merchants—on one occasion, I was able to get a rental car for less than $10 per day this way

Develop powerful vendor relationships to earn more discounts. Never take the attitude that you're entitled to a discount, and always express great appreciation when you get one. Sending thank-you and holiday cards to vendors who allow you discounts and remembering key employees' birthdays—these are ways to keep the relationships you develop strong and fruitful. Express sincere thanks when any employee goes above the call of duty. Although it's never appropriate to give expensive gifts to vendors, I give baked goods. I enjoy baking and give the gift of sweets as a token of my appreciation for great service.

Power in Numbers

Co-op purchasing is the concept of pooling purchasing power with others to obtain quality products and equipment at significant savings. Seek out like-minded individuals with similar businesses to save big money. If, for example, other companies in your area use shipping supplies as you do, offer to work with them on making bulk purchases to get free delivery and volume discounts.

Shipping for Fewer Dollars

Did you know that most shipping companies have different prices for their customers depending on their volume? If you're a high-volume shipper, you can work with your account manager to get these discounts. Arrange a meeting with your shipping company ask them to discuss discounts with you. You may be required to meet minimum shipping volumes to qualify for these discounts, but as your business grows and so does your monthly shipping bill, you can realize huge savings when you maintain the volume needed to qualify. Ask and you shall receive!

You can also ask all your vendors to ship items to you on your own UPS or FedEx account, as a way to increase your overall shipping volume. Simply provide them with your account number and ask them to bill the shipping charges directly to your account. Be sure they use ground shipping to ensure the least cost method. Prepare and email your own labels to them to be sure.

You may be surprised to learn that even the U.S. Postal Service will give you discounts on shipping. Shipping online earns you a discount. We use the USPS Tracking service with all our parcels to provide online confirmation of delivery. Tracking is free with most classes of mail if you process the shipping label through eBay or online.

When you're just starting out and there's a lot of information to process, you'll most likely want to keep things as simple as possible. Since you'll be listing items on the eBay site, it might be easiest to go ahead and initially use eBay Labels for shipping. Once you've got things running smoothly, you can then shop for the absolute best deal as far as your particular situation is concerned. You should always evaluate your business and how you handle shipping. If you do low volume, just use eBay's integrated shipping platform. It works well.

> Tip: When buying shipping boxes, try to weigh samples to see how their weight will affect your overall shipping costs. Be sure to purchase a good variety of box sizes to provide options to comfortably fit various items— you want to avoid having too much extra space in the box, and thus a higher weight, that may push your parcel to a higher rate category.

Give Yourself a Break

One of my oldest and most cost-saving tips is to, "Remember the breaks!" I've preached this at nearly every seminar I've taught for eBay University since I started evangelizing the site years ago. You will recall that eBay gives every seller 50 listings per calendar month for free. (Technically, the Insertion Fee is $0.00.) If you do more than 50 listings, then the Insertion Fee is $0.30 per item for either auction-style or fixed price. If you list 104 items per month, you'll pay $16.20 in Insertion Fees (104 listings – 50 free listings = 54 listings @ $0.30 = $16.20). But the per month subscription cost to a Basic Store is $15.95 (if you pay on an annual basis). So 104 listings looks like your breakeven point ($16.20 - $15.95 = $0.25, which I'd say is close enough to call even).

But you can fine tune this break point even further. With a Basic Store you get 150 free listings, so you'll have another 46 free listings (150 – 104 = 46) to work with, and these extra free listings have a value of $13.80 (46 x $0.30 = $13.80). As a non-store subscriber,

150 listings will cost you $30.00 (150 listings − 50 free listings = 100 listings x $0.30 = $30.00. As a Basic Store subscriber, the same 150 listings will cost you $15.95 (the monthly fee, which is about half as much).

And there's another important break you need to consider. As a regular seller, you'll pay a 10% Final Value Fee on all items sold. Assume the final value of the items you sold was $2,000. The fee due is $200. But as a Basic Store subscriber, the Final Value Fee would range from 4% to 9%, depending on the category of the items you sold. Assume the average fee worked out to be 7%. If the total value of the items you sold was $2,000, then the fee due would be $140.00. This is a $60.00 savings over what you'd pay as a non-store seller. And this $60.00 would pay for almost four months of a Basic Store subscription.

The point I want to make here is that eBay offers you the opportunity to increase your profit margins as you do more business. After you've been in business for a while, you'll know how many listings you average per month. You'll be able to determine which category of eBay Store gives you the biggest break. Be sure to take advantage of it. And remember, you can change store categories at any time. If this section evoked a headache, pull out the aspirin and let's keep going.

Get It on eBay

I love using eBay. There are many things I can't buy for my business on eBay simply because I need them fast, but when there's a little time, there are many ways to save big money. With patience and planning, you can stock up on necessities at very low prices.

Here are just a few of the bargains I found for my company on eBay:

- Nikon digital camera. Paid: $135. Retail: $250.

- Credit card terminal for phone orders. Paid: $135. Retail: $650.

- Foam peanut dispenser. Paid: $76.50. Retail: $183.00.

- Novatron lighting kit model V240. Paid: $333.00. Retail: $996.80.

These are just four examples from the hundreds of items I have purchased. I refuse to pay retail for anything I can buy at a discount.

Some quick eBay buying tips:

- Research completed listings to make sure you're not overpaying

- Review the seller's feedback and avoid bidding if there are excessive complaints for non-delivery

- Always consider shipping charges as part of the total price, and if they aren't specified, always e-mail the seller before bidding to ascertain the shipping charges—some sellers do charge rather high handling fees

- Ask the seller if you can use your own UPS or FedEx account for sending the parcel (ask before bidding) and, if so, whether they will charge you a "boxing" fee

- If possible, purchase heavy and bulky items from a seller nearby so that you can pick them up or get lower shipping costs

- Bid on items you don't need fast to get lower prices, or use Buy It Now if you need it immediately

- Use software to bid at the last minute (called "sniping") and avoid a bidding war (I use www.auctionstealer.com)

- Look for items ending at odd times like 2:00 A.M. and then place your bid with the sniping software to assure a restful sleep while the auction ends—there is usually less competition for items ending at off peak hours

- Avoid getting emotionally involved—you will always find another one on eBay if you don't win the bid

- Use PayPal or a credit card for payment so that you receive the maximum protection possible for your purchase (never mail a check, money order, cash, or send a wire transfer)

- Use the "Save search" link on any search page to bookmark searches for items you buy frequently, and eBay will e-mail you when these items are listed

- Experiment with search terms such as "wholesale" or "lot" to find bulk of any particular item

17. Acquiring New Clients

I am a former commodities broker and decided to try something different and less stressful. When I used to live in New York, I always loved secondhand stores and decided to try selling for others on eBay. I loved the idea of going out for dinner and coming home to find I'd earned money while I was out! A client brought me a Chrome Hearts Biker jacket that is no longer in production. It was in immaculate condition, and she wanted to start it off at $1,800, knowing my commission was 50 percent. She thought I had gone mad when I told her I would want to start her listing at $4,999.99 because of the jacket's rarity. She was extremely pleased when it sold at my asking price.
—Debra Kent, Miami, Florida; eBay user ID "mightykismet"; trading on eBay since June 16, 2000

You will need business cards. Not the kind you print on your own printer but high-quality cards that convey an image. I usually have 1,000 printed at a time. That may seem like a lot, but if you're actively marketing and promoting your business, you use your business cards on a daily basis. The coffee shop where I get my daily brew has agreed to carry a large stack of my business cards. The lady who cuts my hair keeps a bunch at her reception desk. The man who services my three cars regularly hands out my cards. For the best deal on full-color cards, buy from www.nextdayflyers.com.

Fellow chamber of commerce members and local businesses will gladly display your business card if you reciprocate. Business cards are the effective and inexpensive way to market your company.

You can design your own cards or have someone else do it. The printing is only as good as the design, and some effort needs to be put into that if you want to make a great impression.

Realize that simply being good at what you do is not enough. The best product in the world will be a complete dud if nobody knows about it, and you must be a great promoter to run a successful business. Don't let this intimidate you. Self-promotion, or marketing yourself, is a developed skill, not something that comes naturally to everyone—certainly not to me! Anyone can master the basics of marketing without pouring over marketing textbooks or taking expensive courses.

Your total marketing package is a recipe made up of many ingredients. You've already started—your market research was a critical part of writing your business plan, and you have developed valuable contacts.

Big companies can hardly determine the tangible benefits of each ad they place, but they understand the value of consistent marketing as a core part of their financial success. With a small business such as yours, you will have a far greater handle on the results of your marketing efforts to acquire new clients, and with a little testing, you will find the ideal ways to promote your new business.

Marketing and promoting your business will require focusing on these general areas:

- Market research
- Pricing your service
- Advertising
- Promotions and tracking
- Public relations
- Brand awareness and protection

Who's in Your Crosshairs?

Who can use your service? You must identify your audience before you begin to market. Some of the possibilities are:

- Individuals who are retiring or downsizing their lives for some reason
- Estates of deceased individuals (a situation that often leaves a family with lots of unwanted items)
- Wealthy individuals who enjoy buying new things and want to shed used items
- Bankruptcy attorneys
- Divorce attorneys
- Probate attorneys
- Dissolved businesses or partnerships
- Nonprofits who need donated items sold for cash
- Local government agencies with surplus property
- Auctioneers with unsold items

- Businesses that need to liquidate excess inventory

- Banks and finance companies with repossessed merchandise

- Leasing companies with off-lease inventory

- Rental companies that need to retire their assets

- Insurance companies with damaged (but salable) goods for which they have already paid out claims

- Manufacturers with overruns, canceled orders, and factory seconds

- Custom imprinting companies with misprinted items

- Installers and movers who routinely come across unwanted client items

- Public storage unit operators

- Hotels and motels that are renovating

There are a zillion more folks who need your service. Identify individuals or businesses from whom you will receive a steady flow of merchandise. One of my clients is a busy probate attorney and a very consistent source of good material. Another client helps elderly individuals with downsizing and moving and has brought us hundreds of high-quality items. Another is an antiques dealer who uses us for ongoing high-end art and antiques liquidations.

You can't market to everyone at the same time—it will be best to focus in a few areas at a time and work your way down the list. Joining the local chamber will give your company immediate networking capability. If your chamber is an active one, they can be a source of constant referrals.

You can usually get free marketing information from your chamber or local newspaper, both of which normally have a ton of financial and demographic data, such as buying habits and preferences, which can help you understand your trading area. The economics of your community will play a significant role in the nature and quantity of unwanted merchandise available to you.

Happy Clients Spread the Word

Your rates are an important part of marketing your business. You'll want to steer clear of people who are much too sensitive about the starting prices of their items or the commission you charge. I have interviewed eBay sellers who are getting up to 60 percent commission on each sale, but their clients are happy with the fees because they are moving unwanted items. Your marketing should focus on this concept—you move items to which your upscale clients have no emotional or financial attachment. How do you reach them? Mostly by word of mouth.

You can adjust your rates if you find you're not getting enough high-quality merchandise or if you receive too many complaints about your rates. You need to be flexible with your rates if you're not reaching your audience.

Marketing Yourself

Budgeting advertising is tricky. Don't blow your money by advertising in the wrong places. Avoid advertising that requires a long-term commitment, unless you can get out of the contract easily by paying some form of nominal cancellation fee. If you agree to 52 weeks of advertising in your local paper to get the lowest possible rates from them, be sure that you can easily stop the ad if it's not bringing you customers. I tried printed yellow pages advertising and it was a dud.

There are so many forms of advertising, they might make your head spin. Be disciplined with your ad budget—frugally try different kinds of advertising until you find what works, then keep the successful ad campaigns running. Once it's not broken, don't fix it.

Strong ad copy is critical. Grab our attention right away and hold it, without extraneous fluff. Your ad copy should be direct and engaging—you want people to call you and stop by your store.

Advertise your business with these proven tools that have worked well for me:

- Telemarketing a/k/a prospecting for "gold"
- In-person sales calls by appointment
- Small, strategically placed classified ads or inexpensive display ads
- Fliers distributed strategically around town or on door knobs
- Sales letters to corporations, nonprofits etc.

Toot Your Own Horn

Before you spend a dollar from the advertising line item in your budget, grab your business cards and hit the pavement. The chamber will provide a complete list of all of their members. Start networking with them at the chamber's mixers and meetings. It will take time for people to get to know you, but as you distribute your business cards at these functions, your name will start to circulate and people will become familiar with you.

Follow up with the people you meet and ask them for an appointment to discuss your service. Visit each business you can, offer your printed brochure, and ascertain any possible need for your service. Just remember that everyone is a potential client.

Take the chamber's membership directory and start prospecting. Forget any negative image you may have about telemarketing. You're simply making phone calls. Call the members of the chamber, inform them that you're a new business and a chamber member, and ask them for an appointment to discuss your services. If you're turned down for the appointment, offer to mail a brochure and business card. Your goal is to become as well known in your local community as possible. This process requires a great deal of patience, because people are not always friendly to unsolicited calls.

Members of the chamber will be a bit more friendly than most, because they joined the chamber to develop their own businesses and understand that you're simply networking in the same way they do. You'll also find a warmer reception if you take the time to learn a little about your fellow chamber members' businesses and offer to network for them with others when you see the opportunity.

Be pleasant and natural on the phone—don't talk fast. Try to avoid a sales pitch tone, and you'll get a lot more appointments.

Here's a good way to approach an initial telephone call:

Hi, this is Jane, and I'm a fellow chamber member. I am calling you because I have recently joined the chamber and am networking with other members. My business sells unwanted items for other people on eBay. I would like to stop by your office and discuss what I do with you. Would you have time to see me tomorrow?

A Warm Reception

Asking for a specific day and time sounds professional. Gauge the tone of the other person. If you do not get a warm reception, thank them and go on to the next call. You only want to talk to people who want to talk to you, so focus on the calls where you receive a friendly and warm reception. When calling larger firms, you may need to speak with the purchasing agent, or whoever handles the acquisition and liquidation of the company's assets. At manufacturing businesses, this title may be production manager. Usually, whoever handles the purchasing for a company is also responsible for the liquidation of excess items.

You will notice that I am focusing on commercial clients in this discussion of prospecting and sales calls. The reason for this is simple—cold calling homes is not very productive. You will get a chilly reception from most people when you call them at home, and your efforts will result in few items. But when you score a new commercial client, you will receive a steady stream of merchandise from them as well as plenty of high-quality referrals to other businesses that may need your services. Companies have real inventory management needs and many are coping with excess.

After hitting up your local chamber, you'll want to start expanding your cold calling efforts to the list of different types of businesses mentioned earlier in this chapter. You will find that ads in the local newspaper will be a helpful tool in locating auctioneers, attorneys, and the other types of appropriate businesses. Try to set up appointments as before, to explain your services. When visiting a law office that handles divorce, bankruptcy, or probate matters, take a large stack of your business cards. Ideally, the attorneys will give them to clients when they feel it's appropriate. Be aware that giving a referral fee to an attorney may be considered unethical or even be illegal in some states, and you would do better to position yourself as a valuable service for these attorneys, to help their clients rid themselves of unwanted assets.

You can apply these networking concepts to many different kinds of situations. Show me the money!

Getting Published

Print advertising is expensive and poorly focused. You can burn up a lot of cash placing print ads in newspapers or magazines.

I suggest placing small and inexpensive classified ads to attract new clients. With print advertising, most of the new clients you reach will be individuals. If the ad is cheap enough mention that you help both individuals and companies liquidate unwanted items.

Place your ads in the most popular, widely read newspapers and magazines, but I rarely advertise in magazines unless they are the local weeklies. Magazines have very long publishing lead times and tend to have a broader distribution than local papers. This is changing as digital magazines become more popular.

Pay for advertising that will reach people in a radius of no more than about 25 miles from you. At least 90 percent of all of my clients are located within ten miles of my store. Consider using papers that are distributed exclusively in your town. The larger the circulation beyond your area, the more money you will be paying for advertising that is of no real use to you. You certainly don't want to have someone call up with great stuff to sell only to find out they are located 100 miles away.

Before placing a single ad, request an advertising kit and rate information from the publication. This information will provide insights into the demographics and financial profiles of the publication's readers. Study this information carefully. If you're seeking wealthy individuals with unwanted goods, you would want to advertise in a publication that they read.

Daily Miracles

Virtually all classified ads are billed by the word. To keep costs down, you want simple ads that grab attention and create a call to action. Here is a sample of such an ad:

We perform miracles every day on eBay! Sell unwanted items through us without the hassle—we do everything! Call today for more info: 818-555-1234, Trade-It-Away, Inc.

In this particular ad, you assume that the reader knows a little about eBay and maybe even has considered selling their items themselves. The clients you seek will be relieved when they see your ad, because they always wanted to find that spare time to sell their unwanted stuff but just never got around to it—but you're the hero who can do it for them—relieving them of a chore they were avoiding—and they'll call you. This type of marketing takes advantage of eBay awareness, while the short, succinct ad copy keeps the cost way down.

Familiarity Breeds Branding

When buying ads, repetition is key. It's a proven advertising axiom that people usually respond after seeing an ad over and over again. If you can run your ad for several months, you should see improved results over time as people read it repeatedly. As in the above example, include your company name in all advertising—you're building a brand, so be sure to reinforce that brand in people's minds at every opportunity.

You can also purchase display advertising. It's more expensive, because typically display ads are larger and the publication will charge by the size of the ad. These ads can really eat up your profits fast. But if you're going to buy display advertising, I suggest that you develop the basic message yourself, perhaps expanded from one of your classified ads. Then someone has to design the ad. Many newspapers will design your ad free of charge as a part of their service to you as an advertiser. And although I prefer to design my ads personally in Photoshop, I have found that quite a few publications have in-house design personnel who do a fantastic job. As before, frequency is important. And as always, you need strong ad copy to grab the reader's attention.

Be a great listener. Your ad sales representative will guide you. In advertising they want you coming back again and again. If you fail, you won't. They work hard to ensure you succeed.

Ad placement can be just as important as the ad copy itself. If I am trying to bring in clients with musical instruments, for example, I will place my classified ad in the section of the paper where such items are sold. If I want to attract commercial clients, I will write an ad touting my abilities to help liquidate excess inventory and run it in the business section of the paper. Your copy should focus on your desired demographic.

When you become an eBay PowerSeller (and you will if you're making enough to pay your rent), eBay's Co-op Advertising Program will reimburse 25 percent of your qualified advertising expenses, as of this writing. Qualified publications must have a circulation of at least 10,000, among other guidelines (including preapproval of ads by eBay), but under the program you can be reimbursed up to $8,000 per quarter at the Titanium Power Seller level. To learn more about this program, visit pages.ebay.com/services/buyandsell/powerseller/coopfaqs.html.

Frequent Fliers

A well-designed business card is an advertising flier in itself, but it would be effective to have a larger printed advertising flier for your business as well. I use four-by-six-inch, full-color (both sides) glossy postcards (also printed by Next Day Flyers—$147.95 for 5,000!) The postcard-size ads are easy to handle and distribute. Your message should be simple, catchy and compelling, and strong copy is critical. I use a large headline to grab attention and concise copy explaining what I do. Because most people are familiar with eBay, your message can be brief. You don't need to explain eBay; rather, focus on the fact that you sell items on behalf of others. In addition, your flier should include:

- Some sample sale prices of items you have sold for others (with photos if possible—you're paying for full color printing, after all)
- Testimonials from clients
- Your complete contact information
- A call to action, such as a discount for your services if the customer presents the flier

You can design simple fliers in Microsoft Word, but to produce a fancy flier yourself, you will need a graphics program such as Adobe Photoshop or Illustrator. Or you can look for a reasonably priced graphic designer, and here again, a post on Craig's List (if available in your area) may well do the trick. Through Craig's List, I have hired people all over the country to do various clerical jobs as well as more specialized tasks, such as graphic design. If you use a graphic designer, be sure you get your design's native source files so you can update or change the flier in the future. The basic template can be repurposed as often as you want, saving you money.

Buy a high volume color printer to save money on printing costs.

I distribute the fliers by having them dropped off at homes and offices and in our busy Burbank downtown shopping district. I also have them in various local shops. I find that most small business owners will display my flier if I agree to reciprocate in my own store. A flier is a good place to mention the nonprofit-related aspect of your service: people can donate to a good cause by giving you items to list on eBay and designating the proceeds, less your commissions to go to a nonprofit.

I also enclose a few fliers when I mail customer payments, using 9-by-12-inch manila envelopes. It costs a tad more in postage, but the benefits are worth it.

A co-op advertising company can prepare and mail another type of highly targeted flier for you. There are many of these companies, and we all know the packets of coupons they mail. I use Money Mailer (www.moneymailer.com). For about $325, they design, print, and mail 10,000 full-color, one-sided fliers to residents in my local area. This is called cooperative advertising, because a number of businesses with coupons in the packet share the costs, thus keeping them low for each merchant. These programs are highly effective, because the mailings target specific zip codes and Money Mailer also makes your coupon available for download on its website. For me, direct mail other than co-op or very focused lists (such as your own clients) is much too costly. An advantage that Money Mailer offers is its sheer size—my sales representative could quickly access their numerous other eBay consignment sellers' ads, which we used for ad inspiration. It was also reassuring to know that others were having success with Money Mailer's program.

> Tip: Mail out ten fliers to each person who calls in response to your advertising, along with a friendly introductory letter. Even if this person doesn't ultimately use your services, they will often refer others to you.

Measure What You Make

It's important to track and test any marketing program before making a significant long-term financial commitment. Testing involves tracking the success of your ads. If you use printed ads, fliers, and other printed media, be sure to include a coupon—for instance, for a discount on your services or for one free eBay listing—to see which ads are generating the most responses. The coupon should have a code that indicates the source of the ad. For example, your ad in the "Main Street Trading Times" would include a coupon coded "MSTT0613," indicating the paper's name as well as the month and year you placed the ad. A coupon can generate a positive sense of urgency—very productive with busy people who procrastinate in disposing of their surplus items.

I suggest pulling all the coupons and offers in the Sunday paper that really impress you and putting them in an ideas folder to help you create your own promotions. I love to look at other people's ads to get ideas for my own, and I'm constantly reading newspapers and magazines to get ideas for my business.

You're a Publicist, Too

Become a mini-publicist. Publicity is routine in most major and midsize companies. Issue a press release about your business when you open your doors. Free publicity in your local newspaper, radio and TV is the goal. Find a sample press release online. There's millions of them.

Our firm has been has been featured on the local news and in the *Los Angeles Times*, *Reader's Digest*, *Entrepreneur*, and *Time* among others. We've had lots of articles in major antiques periodicals, and on the Internet, about amazing prices we've realized for collectibles on eBay. The free publicity from these many articles and interviews resulted in a higher awareness of our business. After an article about us appeared in the Los Angeles Times, new clients were still mentioning it six months later. The goal is free advertising.

Fear usually stops people from writing a press release. Professional publicists will tell you that writing a press release is like open heart surgery—a very complex and specialized job that you couldn't possibly do yourself. This might be true for a Fortune 500 company's publicity, but for a small business like yours, there's no reason you can't do your own publicity. It soon will become just another part of your routine.

The media tend to be attracted to human interest stories, so if there is something interesting about your personal situation, you should include those details to help sell your press release to the media. Sally B. Donnelly wrote about me for *Time* after hearing about my business from one of my customers who knew her personally. You can never underestimate the value of networking for publicity—ask the chamber for a media list.

Before sending out a press release, it helps to call ahead and probe a bit to try to find out which reporters might be interested in your story. Directing a press release to a specific reporter will yield better results. Get their e-mail address and ask permission to send the press release electronically along with some high-quality photos of yourself and your business, in the format that they prefer. Sending the release in Word permits the person receiving it to copy and paste.

Many busy newspapers and magazines may simply print an article without asking for an interview. But if you're asked for an interview, it helps to have some talking points written ahead of time, addressing the benefits of your services. Media training and tips on handling interviews are beyond the scope of this book, but for the most part, if you're an outgoing and well-spoken person, you should find that doing such interviews will go smoothly. If you're having your photograph taken or will be on camera, it is very important that you're well groomed and look professional. If pictures or video will be taken at your business location or home, it's very important to organize and cleanup to portray the most positive visual image possible.

If you sense that a reporter is writing a negative story about eBay, decline the interview. You will be better off not participating in such interviews. I have never run into this situation, but it's good to be cautious. You have probably heard the adage originally spoken by P.T. Barnum, "There's no such thing as bad publicity," but personally I prefer not to get involved in anything that may be negative—I think it's bad karma.

If you're uncomfortable in front of cameras, then stick to print media. I would suggest doing some supplemental reading about media training and writing press releases.

> Tip: If you write well, you can literally write an entire article about yourself for the print media. More often than not, my published press releases are printed nearly verbatim, because I make a point of both writing the story as I think it can be printed and sending the text electronically to help the reporter get the story turned in without having to retype anything.

Don't Be Shy

Spread the word! I encourage you—no, I demand that you become a loudmouth! The greatest business (like yours) will fall flat if no one knows about it. Don't be shy in asking others to spread the word about your business. Hand everyone you know a bunch of business cards and fliers.

If they were pleased, even amazed, by your services, your existing clients will provide the bulk of your referrals. But don't just assume that these individuals will automatically think to talk up your services—ask them to do so. After you pay your clients, talk to them about their experience with you, and if it was a happy one, ask them if they know anyone else who might be interested and give them some of your business cards.

Referrals are worth money and if you want more of them, offer to pay for them. You can pay a flat fee or you can pay a percentage, but be sure to pay. I write down the name of the referring individual on the client's item submission form so I will remember to pay the fee, which of course I only pay when I have successfully sold at least one item for the new client. Smart and experienced businesspeople pay for referrals, just as they pay for any other form of advertising. If you want a consistent flow of new clients, referral fees will help.

> Tip: When networking with your business cards, use a felt-tip permanent marker to code the cards with a tracking number or initials matched to each person you give cards to. This allows you to track the card back to the person who originally gave it out and pay them their referral fee.

18. Handling New Clients: Their Items, Personalities, and Concerns

A resident in my town noticed that many wonderful and adoptable pets were being euthanized. This outraged her greatly, so she decided to establish a rescue shelter to help prevent these wonderful animals from being put down. After hearing about her efforts, I made the decision to use my earnings as an eBay seller to help her in this worthwhile cause. Today, my dollars provide the organization, Compassion in Action, with the much needed funds that help save the lives of hundreds of beautiful, loving pets.
—Elizabeth Ziegelbein, Elmendorf Airforce Base; eBay user ID "eczblack"; trading on eBay since May 29, 2003

Handling people is an art form and can be a daunting task. You're so eager to get clients for your new enterprise that you will invariably make mistakes. I will help you avoid this, but the unexpected will happen, and you must be prepared to make errors and learn from them. Be patient—dealing with people is probably the hardest part of being a businessperson. You have to juggle the different facets of your client interactions and determine what to do and when. Take a deep breath and put on your thinking cap. And don't worry—you will be great with each of your valuable new customers.

On any given day, my staff and I wonder who will walk in the door or call with myriad questions, concerns, ideas, and items for submission. Some days are so quiet you can hear a pin drop; other days, the telephone rings off the hook, and a small army of clients lines up in our lobby. All these individuals have special concerns and needs, and we have to be on our toes to assist them properly and quickly in any one of a hundred scenarios.

The Interview

The new client either stops by or calls. Evaluate each situation and use different strategies and tactics for closing them on your services. If you do not operate a convenient walk-in location, you'll be handling these new clients mostly by phone and sometimes by visiting their home or workplace.

The first thing you should do with a prospective new client is ask them for their contact information. Explain to them that you keep your client list confidential and that you will not share this information with anyone else. Individuals who are serious about using your services will give this information freely, and asking sets a tone that you're serious about what you do and that you value them as a potential new client.

You should get the following details:

- Name
- Address
- City, state, and zip
- Telephone number
- How they heard about you (As discussed in the previous chapter, this information is critical, because you will want to measure the success of your advertising, to track referrals, and to get a general idea of what kinds of marketing work well.)
- A detailed description of the items they would like to sell

An easy way to capture this data is on a three-by-five-inch index card, or if you type fast, you can enter it directly into a spreadsheet on your computer. I'm using salesforce.com customer relationship management which is an online subscription tool that helps me manage my business. I like it's access speed and the convenience of being able to retrieve client information from any device anywhere.

Some of your prospective clients will be competitors, tire kickers, and, in the case of a physical store, people killing time while their spouse is busy shopping nearby. Quickly identify the situation and determine who warrants your valuable time and who should simply get a brochure and be on their way. You should always deliver fantastic customer service regardless of the situation.

Be patient and help to educate. Not all prospects will immediately understand the value of your services, and you'll want to make sure that they fully comprehend exactly what you can do for them: all the great services you provide and the convenience of having an expert handle their items, thus maximizing their return.

For anyone who is new to eBay, explain how auction-style and fixed-price listings work and the strengths and weaknesses of each. Be sure they realize that, with an auction, there's the possibility the item will sell for much more than expected but it could also sell for much less, unless you set up a reserve price. With no or a very low reserve price, you can virtually guarantee the item will sell. With a fixed-price listing, the customer will obviously know how much to expect as their share of the sale. However, the item may not sell at all. Since 2009, fixed-price listings have outnumbered auction-style listings, which follows eBay's shift in marketing focus. (They want to compete more directly with Amazon.)

Explain eBay's fees and have a printed copy of them to show to your clients. If you charge the client for eBay and PayPal fees, this should all be on paper. You can easily put this together from the details available on the eBay and PayPal sites. If you accept direct credit card payments

You'll truly come across as a pro by having a breakdown on paper of what clients can expect to net on a sale of $50, $100, or $1,000, and you may want to include even higher-ticket sales figures if you're dealing with more expensive items.

Explain that buyers can bid up the auction-style listings and that the seller, your client, can expect to get a fair market value. Tell your prospective client that the amount their item will ultimately bring on eBay will almost always be higher, even after your fee, than what that item would have brought at a yard sale or flea market. Make it very clear that you're by far the best method for maximizing the money in their pocket, better than any other method of liquidation.

Closing the sale. There is no right or wrong way to close a sale. The old stereotype of the fast-talking, slick salesperson is history. To build your business, you must sell yourself, and that means that you should always be yourself when closing with clients on your services. Exude a comfortable style and clients will feel good about you. The key is to develop a relationship built on trust, respect, and appreciation. Relax, don't try too hard, and you will develop a routine and rhythm for dealing with prospective clients.

Questions, Questions, and More Questions

One benefit of referrals from existing clients will become evident immediately, as you will have fewer questions about your services from referrals. Without a doubt, your superior work with your existing customers will reach others by word of mouth, and these new clients will be eager to work with you, with few or no questions about what you do.

When questions arise then I would like you to be prepared to answer them powerfully. Here are some frequently asked questions and what you can say in each situation.

Q: Your fees seem awfully expensive. Are they negotiable?

A: We provide outstanding service and an extremely good value. Our fees are comparable to other eBay drop-off stores in (your city). We don't consider ourselves a cut-rate operation, because we don't provide lower-quality listings. I think you'll find our fees very fair considering all your options, such as a garage sales, local auctions, and pawnshops. With eBay, you receive the benefit of a global marketplace with millions of buyers. More often than not, you will get more money even after our fees than any other options you would have for selling your item.

Q: I already know how to use eBay, why should I use you?

A: If you prefer to sell your item personally, then you should. We provide excellent service, high-quality photography, and added value to you in terms of time savings. We often get more money for items because of our experience and excellent eBay feedback rating. A great many of our clients know how to use eBay but prefer the convenience of allowing us to do it for them.

Q: How much can I expect to get for my item?

A: In all but the rarest cases, our clients don't set a minimum starting price or Reserve price for their items. Our experience selling on eBay has shown over and over that the highest final prices are actually realized from auctions with low starting prices, such as $0.99 or $9.99. Bidders enjoy bidding items up and competing with other bidders, and starting at a very low price point attracts bidders and adds to the excitement. We let the marketplace determine the value, and therefore, the final selling price is unknown. If we do start an item at a minimum or Reserve price we charge a non-refundable fee to defray the higher fees eBay charges us for such listings. And if you do have a minimum price, it's important that it be realistic, because we would like your sale to be successful. The reality is that we cannot guarantee any particular item will sell at a particular price, but we will do the best job we can for you and hope that we get a buyer to purchase it on eBay.

Naturally, this response can vary, according to your own policies—you may choose to be more liberal in accepting items with minimum starting or Reserve prices. The above reflects my own company's policies.

Q: I have a [such and such] at home and would like to know what to expect on eBay. What would it sell for?

A: Well, we will gladly provide you with an evaluation of your item if you bring it in or allow us to come to your home [or office] and look at it.

The critical thing to remember here is to get the client to commit to bringing their items to you or allowing you to look at it in person. Many supposed new clients will eat up large chunks of your time asking you to look up final sales figures in completed listings on eBay, ostensibly for insights into what their own items would bring. Then they never bring the items in—they were just using you as a free research service. Give your time to someone who has actually let you look at the item in person. But be careful if you sense that the client has unrealistic price expectations—another case where you want to keep the research time to a minimum.

Q: How do I know you're going to be honest about what my item sells for?

A: That's one of the great thing about eBay—it's completely transparent. We provide you with the eBay item number, and you can see the results online yourself.

Q: How soon after it sells will I receive my payment?

A: We pay (weekly, biweekly, monthly) and we can mail your check, you can pick up your check or we can PayPal your money to you. Please keep in mind that even after an item successfully sells on eBay, we sometimes have to wait for payment from the buyer, after which we can pay you. Since we allow customer returns, we usually pay after receiving a positive feedback from the buyer or after the grace period for customer returns has expired.

Q: What happens if a buyer returns the item to you? Do I have to give the money back?

A: Ultimately, you're the actual seller of the item. We do our absolute best to list it accurately, based upon the information you give us and our research. We guarantee that the item will arrive as represented. If the buyer demands that we accept a return, we usually work with them to try to avoid this. But if the item is in fact returned, we will inform you, and it is your responsibility to make sure that we can give them an appropriate refund and hopefully relist your item for sale on eBay. Returns are extremely rare, but they do happen. We also have time limits and adhere to them unless the circumstance is truly extenuating.

Q: Can I keep possession of my item during this process?

A: We prefer to keep all items under our control to assure the fastest possible shipment to the buyer.

A bird in the hand is worth two in the bush. I urge you always to keep possession of items you're selling for clients on your eBay seller's account. Regardless of how good your relationship with a client, things can happen. Seller's remorse, sentimental attachment, a change in their financial condition, damage, and many other factors can cause problems for you. When their own eBay feedback isn't at stake, clients aren't always reluctant to change their mind about parting with their items. Of course, if you list on the client's own eBay account, this is not really an issue for you.

Q: What am I required to do as part of this deal?

A: Absolutely nothing! We handle the research, photography, listing, collection of money, and shipping. After your listing sells successfully, we mail you a check!

No doubt other questions will pop up from time to time, and it would be a great idea to keep track of the questions and of effective ways to address them. Jot down little notes on index cards related to customer interactions for reference and brainstorming. Take the time to discuss the details of these interactions with employees to help them better handle clients and any new topics that might come up.

Comfy Clients

If your new-found client chooses to start working with you immediately, this would be a great time to review final prices actually realized on eBay for one or two of their items (exact matches if possible, or closely comparable items if not) to give them an idea of what they might expect. You accomplish this with a search of completed items on eBay. Prices from completed eBay sales are not a guarantee of the same outcome for your client, so caution them about that as well.

You will need to gauge the level of research needed on a client-by-client basis. Some people really don't care what things sell for—they just want to get rid of them. Others will be hesitant to part with their cherished heirloom and might be very angry if it doesn't sell for top dollar. Be careful of the latter. Make sure you secure paperwork that clearly states the authorized starting price, which the client and you both sign. Be absolutely certain that the client understands that the starting bid amount or Reserve amount should be the minimum at which they will be completely comfortable in letting the item go. Even if it's just $0.99, it's always possible and does happen all the time that an item will sell for the starting price.

For more in-depth research tools use Terapeak.com, a subscription-based eBay research website. This site provides average price data, charts, time of day, and day-of-week sales trends and much more.

Stunned a Rug

I once listed a common, machine-made (and ugly) area rug for a client, and he authorized me to list it for a $1 minimum bid with no reserve. The shipping was so expensive that no buyer would bid more than $1, and the rug sold for that amount. The client was devastated. Now he told me that the rug was the joy of his life and a cherished family heirloom. I was stunned. My client was emotionally attached to this rug, and I shouldn't have agreed to list it at all, because he had undue expectations. Make sure your client truly understands your procedures and the possible outcome of an auction. The minimum bid set for an item should be realistic and low enough to leave room for the possibility of a sale. Remember that bad word of mouth is ten times worse in the long run than simply turning down an item that you don't feel is appropriate for your services.

Completed Only

As for your research, if you have a small number of things to look up on the eBay site, you can conduct the research while your client waits. When looking at the eBay listings, be sure to sort your search results by price, starting with the highest prices realized. And make absolutely certain that you only review the completed listings. If you're not readily familiar with the completed items search function on the eBay site, you should take the time to use eBay's help system to get a full tutorial on how to search for an item.

Remember that in Completed Auctions, you can search only the Subject words, the title of the listing, not the more detailed description, so you in many cases you will need to try different search words. Be very specific whenever possible and use make, model number, and any other specific words to narrow the search.

Thousands of Results

A search for a diamond ring will pull up thousands of results. You might try "1ct diamond ring" to narrow the search. For certain items, such as the diamond ring categories, eBay adds a Product Finder, a series of pull-down menus that allow you to specify the carat size, ring size, and other item specifics to aid in the search process. Be sure to look for these tools, as they vary from category to category and can really help in the research process.

Add date, color, brand, etc. to narrow a search. If you're looking up a hubcap from a 1970 Volkswagen, you would want to use a search similar to "1970 Volkswagen hubcap," or if you wanted simply to look for any Volkswagen hub cap from the 1970s, you could search "197* Volkswagen hubcap," in which the asterisk provides a wildcard. This would return any listing for the hubcap from that decade.

When searching, try plural and singular variations, for example, "Gorham Etruscan fork" and "Gorham Etruscan forks." You can learn about other advanced search methods by going to the help system on eBay. eBay's search engine is becoming more intelligent over time and will even predict what you meant if you enter the wrong search term or misspell a word.

Judgment Call

At this point, you should have a general idea of the value of the items you're dealing with. If you're unable to find similar items on eBay and have doubts about the value of what you're being asked to sell, you may be wasting time on something that won't be worth the effort.

But you also make a big mistake by rejecting an item simply because you don't know, or can't find out, anything about it.

You have to use some judgment. After all, your time is extremely valuable, and the last thing you want to do is fill your day listing junk. And frankly, junk is what about 80 percent of clients bring us. We literally turn down over three-fourths of what comes in the door. Often, individuals with junk have already tried to pawn it or sell it at a flea market or yard sale and have had no luck getting anywhere near the value they want. Believe it or not, until people really get to know you, you might be a target for folks who take you for a sucker, and they will try to waste your precious time listing their worthless stuff on eBay. Many people who come to us have already tried other eBay sellers who have turned them down.

Gold Mining

One eBay phenomenon is that many people unfamiliar with eBay have the perception that it's a gold mine. eBay has brought massive quantities of certain kinds of items out of the woodwork. Thus, the 1960s Life magazine issue on the moon landing might have brought $20 in a used book store or antique mall ten years ago (before eBay) but now might bring $1 on eBay, because so many copies of this issue have come into circulation on eBay. Supply and demand has driven the price into the basement. A woman once walked into my store and proclaimed: "I have 50 Beanie Babies, and I want to sell them on eBay." I sensed from her tone that she had extremely unrealistic price expectations thinking that they were now rare collectibles and that eBay was a gold mine for such things. I searched "Beanie Baby" in the Completed Listings on eBay, and turned our front desk computer monitor for her to see. The search results showed nearly 30,000 completed Beanie Baby auctions—almost all had started at $0.99, and most of the relatively few that had actually sold had fetched that price—$0.99. The woman was in shock. When she recovered, she said, "You know, I think I'll give them to the children's hospital." I quickly agreed with her.

Dodging the Deluge

Focus only on those things for which you can obtain good value. Try using different methods of valuation. You can tap into your network of knowledgeable friends for advice. It's always good to get help from others. I routinely confer with a local gemologist and jeweler whenever I'm asked to consign a piece of jewelry or a watch. He will tell me about the item's authenticity and value, and he often gives me gem weights and specifications. If he helps me write a description for my item, I pay him 5 % of the final selling price if the item sells. This is a great arrangement that works beautifully for both of us. I also send him appropriate clients who need money fast and want to sell their items outright and not wait for an eBay sale. He reciprocates and sends clients my way who want top dollar and don't mind waiting. I have similar relationships with experts on virtually every category. We keep a roster of experts all over the country (and even some in other countries) who can quickly identify and value items from a brief description and photographs.

Another defense against the legions of junky merchandise is a simple one—tell your clients you want good stuff. I keep a list of specific things that sell well, and I hand it to my clients. Part of this process is education. Just because someone paid $22.50 for a collector plate in 1975 does not mean it is worth $300 today. Most of the collector series editions people buy are so mass-produced that they don't hold their value.

But there are pitfalls to listing only items that can be easily researched. Sometimes you will have a sleeper item. Sleepers are things you would never imagine to be worth anything that turn out to sell for an amazing windfall. One such item was the 1930s Lenci figurine, described in the Introduction, which the client had almost thrown out because she thought it worthless and ugly. This ultra-rare porcelain sold for $17,000 on eBay.

Some amazing and unexpected sales at our store:

- An antique photo of Abraham Lincoln that sold for $5,000
- A four-inch Tiffany lamp shade that sold for $1,525

- An old Indy 500 felt pennant that sold for $1,414.87

- A set of Towle stainless flatware that sold for $1,136.11

- A two-and-a-half inch tall Wedgwood covered box that sold for $1,025

- A 1950s Nikon camera that sold for $1,000.03

- A rare Hummel figurine that sold for $917

- A nonfunctional vintage Fender tube amplifier that sold for $871

- An old and beat up cornet wind instrument that sold for $835

- An old Toby drinking mug that sold for $810

- A used storage tin from the 1800s that sold for $771.99

On the Collectibles Limb

Working with collectibles will require that you be willing to go out on a limb. A little intuition, going with your gut or playing a hunch may pay out big time. Avoid finding yourself bogged down with tons of unsold items that you should never have agreed to list for your clients but be willing to venture into the unknown when something grabbed your curiosity.

We sell in just about every category on eBay for our clients. The collectibles category is one area where prices are not easily researched and determined. Collectors are an interesting group who will often pay any price to get what they want. It's important with collectibles to have knowledgeable friends, dealers, and experts who can identify potential treasure. A terrific way to get this help quickly is by posting a photo of the item on one of eBay's great Community Boards and asking other eBay community members to give you their opinion.

When you're dealing with large lots or estates, you won't have the time to research each and every item while your client waits. It's important to explain this and assure them that their items will be handled efficiently and thoroughly at a later time.

Grandma's Broken Porcelain

Sometimes a client will have an inventory list of the items they have brought to you, and at other times, the items will arrive simply piled in a box. Regardless of how these new listing items arrive, go through them one at a time to note the condition and take a physical piece count. Write a short description of the item on your submission form or contract that is sufficient to identify it. If your client has their own list, you can simply check the pieces off this list. Carefully note problems with item condition. Don't be accused later of breaking Grandma's porcelain figurine. If an item has issues such as a scratch, a ding, or some other damage, be sure to make a note of it and make the client aware of it when you receive it.

You should try to accept only clean merchandise. Think back to what I said about cleaning in Chapter 15. We see so many boxes of dirty, dusty, and even filthy things that we simply have to draw the line somewhere. We ask our clients to bring items that are clean and ready for listing. Cleaning merchandise is no easy task, and eventually it leads to a dingy, dirty office or home. Sometimes it's hard to say no to a good lot of dirty merchandise, but unless you get a huge group of fabulous, dirty Steuben glass or a filthy three-carat diamond ring, you really need to ask your clients to come back when the cleaning has been done. Be careful also not to turn down items that should not be cleaned such as many antiques, collectibles, coins, etc.

Once everything has been inventoried on the submission form or contract, have the client sign it as evidence that you both agree on the item count and the condition of each item that is less than perfect. If you collect an up-front listing fee, now is a great time to total up what is owed and collect the money.

They Steal More Than Time

If this is the first time you have done business with an individual, you should request and photocopy their identification as due diligence to protect your business in the event that you mistakenly accept and list stolen property.

I once received a call from the Glendale, California, police department. They had found one of my company's check stubs in the apartment of a burglary suspect. Apparently, he had brought us some camera equipment to list on eBay. Because we had provided serial numbers on all of the equipment in our listings, the police were quickly able to identify it as part of the stolen property they were seeking. The great news is that this was the first such call we'd had in all our years in business. The transparency of the eBay marketplace, its easy search functions, and our good records helped to solve a crime! Fortunately we were not required to return the items as the victim was compensated through restitution in the court system.

Watch out for red flags. If you're offered a submission of ten brand-new, in-the-box, high-end cameras from a client you don't know well or at all, you should probably ask some questions. Where did they get them? Do they have a receipt? You also must get government-issued identification from 100 percent of your clients 100 percent of the time. Use common sense. You will find that 99.9999 percent of the time, the submissions you receive make sense and seem logical, but if something bothers you about a client's items or the circumstances, don't be afraid to inform them tactfully that you don't feel their items would be appropriate for your service.

Hopefully you will never have to face a situation where you have accepted stolen merchandise for listing on eBay. If you become aware that an item may be in question, it is your immediate responsibility to contact the police and discuss the item with them. If you follow some basic processes, such as always requiring government-issued identification and mailing payments by check (never paying in cash), you'll probably never have to face a stolen merchandise issue.

And you don't want to buy anything outright until you have checked the laws of your state and city regarding the buying of merchandise from the general public. As an eBay consignment service, you're acting as a listing service and a bailee—an individual or business organization having temporary possession of another's personal property without transfer of ownership. You're not the owner of the items you sell; rather, you're simply listing and selling them on eBay for others, for a fee, while providing interim storage until the items sell. The rules change when you start buying outright from the public.

Your Lifeblood

Referrals are your lifeblood. Give each of your clients at least ten of your business cards to distribute, ideally with their name or some code on each card to enable you to track referrals back to their source. I routinely give cash incentives for referrals, but to my wealthy clients, I prefer sending cookies or other tokens of appreciation rather than cash. Many of these high-net-worth individuals came to you primarily to declutter their lives. Don't underestimate the value of a thank-you card. Do something to show appreciation.

My dear friend Kathy Ireland is a Marketing Distributor for a powerful company called SendOutCards. With SendOutCards, you can send beautiful and affordable greeting cards and gifts by mail all from the convenience of your computer. To sign up through Kathy personally, visit her SendOutCards link at www.kathyirelandgreetings.com and you'll be able to audition the service by sending your first card free of charge.

Your best marketing tool is personal success. Success for clients with good merchandise will bring more clients. You have to be patient as you build your business, but when you get a great price for someone's item, the word spreads, and the referrals come in.

The Client Rainbow

Caution or even skepticism is natural with new clients. This is their first time dealing with you, and they may try to give you a few small, low-end items to test the waters. Be prepared for this situation, and be prepared to be firm in your position. Turn down the junk and explain why in a friendly way.

One of our former clients was an avid eBay seller himself who had put himself through chiropractic school with his earnings. He was an eBay veteran with impressive feedback. Busy with a new practice and seeking the services of a qualified eBay pro like himself, he had storage units filled with high-end merchandise, but because he didn't know us, he would give us a chance to prove ourselves by listing an initial group of low-ticket items. He gave us some fishing lures, surplus medical supplies, and a few other odds and ends to list on eBay.

I warned my store manager about the potential downside of accepting these test listings. Not only did we end up spending a lot of time researching, photographing, and listing these inexpensive things, but once they were listed, we were being second-guessed by the client on every listing title, description, and decision we had made on his listings. He was high maintenance on this low-end stuff, and I immediately got to the bottom line with him, telling him that this type of merchandise didn't warrant the time needed to give him the quality work he was seeking.

When most of these items sold and the client contacted us about test marketing some more things to see how we would do, I politely declined and asked for his best, high-ticket items. I realized that he was dumping the stuff he didn't want to bother listing on eBay himself, and that we would probably never get his best merchandise, no matter how good our work for him. I cut my losses and moved on, and this was the right decision.

Chatting You Up

Use caution with the extremely chatty people, too. Getting into long and unproductive conversations with clients is what I call the chit-chat rathole. An apparently lucrative one-item submission can quickly turn into a client you just can't get rid of. A $50 doll may have a history and pedigree that the proud owner must share in such detail you might start thinking, ". . . then the earth cooled."

Be professional and to the point, focusing the client and your conversation on the basics needed to put their item on eBay. Don't be afraid to explain politely that your work involves many other tasks and that you need to attend to them. If you're not a natural-born closer then practice this skill. If you're going to grow quickly, manage your clients professionally and politely while adhering to good time management.

When making appointments, set time limits and verbalize them. Your time is money, and you must consider how much time you can give each client based on the potential returns.

Some clients to avoid:

- Clients who try to cut your fees.

- Professional dealers who just want to unload their low-end, dead merchandise on you. You'll become their free storage facility, while they hope to move a few items that would not sell anywhere else.

- Profit maximizers who hope to buy something and resell it immediately for a quick profit. This plan only works if they have an exceptionally great eye for a bargain or extraordinarily good fortune. Usually, such people demand high starting prices that will result in few sales.

- Clingy people who really don't want to sell their items. They often make daily phone calls, asking if their item has been listed yet or if it has sold. Typically their sale price expectations are too high or they have remorse for selling something they really didn't want to part with in the first place. These folks carry undue expectations with them.

- Desperate individuals who need money today. Avoid these folks—they're trouble. Often a telltale sign, their first request will be that you buy their merchandise outright. You should have a nice long list of pawnshops and other cash buyers who can help them. But if you do have a listing agreement with them, they will behave much like the clingy people—calling daily to see if their item has sold.

- People who can't produce photo identification and insist on picking up checks rather than having you mail them. Don't take their stuff!

  Clients you should welcome with open arms:

- Wealthy individuals with too many things. They want to shed unwanted items and declutter their home.

- Corporations and businesses. They may want you to dispose of excess inventory, customer returns and open-box merchandise.

- Nonprofits that receive good donations. This group can be a challenge because they often want you to handle everything—the good and the bad. You need to make them aware that some of the merchandise won't be suitable for eBay, and you should have an agreement with them that any such items will be returned to them or donated to a thrift store.

- Any clients with quality unwanted items and realistic expectations.

A Quick Cheat Sheet

Here is a review of what to remember when handling clients and their merchandise:

- Be helpful, friendly and provide exceptional customer service

- Explain your service in detail for the first-timer

- Present prospective new clients your services brochure and fee schedule

- Collect the new client's basic information and note how they found out about you

- Ask that you see all items before you research more than one

- Try to accept only clean merchandise unless the items should not be cleaned such as rare silver and coins

- Research completed listings on smaller lots; do research for larger ones later

- Carefully and thoroughly review the piece count and condition with the client

- Fill out your item submission form or contract

- Hand your client ten business cards to give to others and ask them to write their name on them, and specifically ask for referrals

- Watch out for the tire kickers, time burners, and competitors seeking to pick your brain with no intention of listing anything

- Avoid the picky and difficult clients

- Avoid the chit-chat rathole

- Stay very organized—you're dealing with other people's valuable things!

19. Paying Clients

We had a walk-in customer bring us an 1870-CC Seated Liberty dollar coin to sell for them. We submitted it to a nationally recognized coin-grading company, because we felt it had a rare date and was in outstanding condition. It came back as one of the finest possible grades. We listed and sold it on eBay for $98,900. The client admitted that he was prepared to accept an offer of a few dollars or less. I think he was pleasantly surprised.

—Louis Palafoutas, Superior Galleries, Inc. of Beverly Hills, California; eBay user ID "superior"; trading on eBay since March 29, 1999

I really enjoy Louis' Seated Liberty dollar story. The CC stands for the government mint that once existed in Carson City, Nevada. The first six-ton coin press was painted with a large "1" to signify the first press located at the coiner's department. On February 11, 1870, the press struck the first coin bearing the infamous CC mintmark, a Seated Liberty dollar. All good things come to an end and as the Comstock Lode stopped bearing bountiful silver ore, the Carson City mint eventually came to an end in lockstep.

Press No. 1 was moved to the Philadelphia Mint in 1899 and then moved yet again to the San Francisco Mint in 1945. The antique press was sold to the state of Nevada for $225 in 1958 and was cleaned, painted and has become a favorite attraction at the Nevada State Museum which is now housed in the original Carson City mint building. No. 1 moved again to the Denver mint in 1964 and in three years she struck another 188 million coins. In 1967, No. 1 came back home and under the supervision of the wonderful volunteers at the museum, she mints the last Friday of each month. No. 1 may be the last operating coin press from that time period.

I've sold a few of these rare Carson City mint coins over the years and they always bring interest and big dollars.

Speaking of dollars, paying clients might seem a simple matter—you sell something, collect the money, deduct your commission, and pay your client. But there are some subtleties to this process, such as the frequency with which you pay clients and how to handle buyer returns. Keep good records and you will be rewarded.

Timing Is Everything

When your business is small, you can pay clients frequently plus you'll have happy clients. As you grow your business work smart so your workload will be as manageable as possible. Compartmentalize your tasks including paying your clients. As your volume of clients and their sold items grows, you will want to pay on a periodic basis that makes sense for your schedule and your ability to process the payments.

At my company, we pay our clients on a monthly basis for a very specific reason—we want to attract upscale clientele. By paying this way we accomplish three things:

- We weed out the desperate clients who usually do not have high-quality merchandise anyway.
- We allow time for the buyers to receive the sold items and leave us positive feedback. or let us know if anything was not 100 percent satisfactory to them.
- We reduce our administrative costs for handling these payments by streamlining payment processing into a discrete timeline.

If you plan to pay more frequently than we do, weigh the pros and cons of doing so. Paying quickly will thrill your clients and encourage them to submit more items. The downside is that you will spend more time dealing with payments. More important is the possibility that a buyer may wish to return an item for which you have already paid your client. To retain our eBay Top Rated Plus seller status, we are required by the company to extend a minimum 14-day money-back return policy to the buyer.

If you decide to pay weekly or every other week, you will have to micromanage each payment by monitoring the status of the shipment to the buyer. You can set up some check boxes on your item submission form that allow you to track some additional attributes of the sale, such as:

- Whether ten days have elapsed since you deposited a payment check, to ensure that the check hasn't bounced (only relevant if you accept checks)
- Whether the buyer has left you positive feedback for the transaction
- Whether the time allowed for returns has expired, if you have a returns policy

Tip: If your client has unsold items that must be picked up, you can hold
their check and unsold items together and ask them to pick up both at
the same time, as an incentive for them to remove the unsuccessful
merchandise quickly. I have found that items waiting for client pick-up
may sit at my store indefinitely if I mail their payments.

Move Those Funds

You can pay your clients by check or PayPal. PayPal does not charge a fee when you send money to family or friends. I certainly consider my clients good friends and use that option.

You should open a separate bank account where you will hold your clients' money until it's time to pay them. It may be tempting to spend money sitting in your regular operating account that actually belongs to your clients. Calculate what you expect to owe your clients after taking your commissions, and then move these funds to the client account for safekeeping. All banks allow you to make free instant transfers between accounts online.

If you're operating your eBay consignment company from within your existing retail business, you can offer your clients a store credit to make purchases in your establishment. You may want to offer reduced commissions for clients who opt for a store credit as a further incentive to receive payment this way, because you will make a profit on the items they take in credit.

Things Bounce Back

After shipping an order, track the status of that order's delivery. If you do not receive positive feedback immediately after delivery, send the buyer a quick e-mail asking them if they were completely satisfied with their order so that you can pay your client. There's a very good possibility that your clients will be looking at your eBay account to see if their items have sold, and in the rare instance that a customer service problem does arise, you should let the client know so that they realize their payment may be delayed until the problem can be resolved. Folks who don't routinely sell on eBay may not immediately understand that all sales are not final.

If you do receive a return, hopefully you haven't already made a payout for that item and you can simply relist it. You can also use eBay's Second Chance Offer feature to permit the under bidder(s) to purchase that item for their original high bid price when a deal falls through—including returns.

If you have already paid out on the sale, you will have the somewhat uncomfortable task of informing your client and asking for the return of the money. In the entire time I have been in business, I have only had to do this with clients who bring me large quantities of items. With such clients, there is an ongoing flow of payments against which I can make an adjustment. You may, however, run into a client who feels that the sale is a sale regardless of the return and refuse to repay you. Thus, you may wish to add some specific language to your contract that requires clients' cooperation in these situations. But if you're careful, this will rarely, if ever, happen, and you won't be stuck holding the bag.

At my company, fewer than 1 in 500 shipments results in any form of customer service issue or return. If you take care to be accurate and honest in your eBay listings and pack items well, you will rarely face return issues.

Keeping Existing Clients Coming Back for More

As the ambassador for your company, keep in touch with your clients' needs and work on ways to keep them bringing in more merchandise. I'm on one of my many business trips as I write this, sitting in my room at the Wynn Hotel in Las Vegas. Although the room costs what some might consider an astronomical amount, I'm quite impressed with the hotel's service—from the wonderful sundries to the little chocolates I find each evening after I receive turndown service—everything is brilliant and impeccable. Such exceptional service goes a long way in offsetting any sticker shock I would otherwise feel from such an expensive hotel stay. And though sticker shock won't normally be an issue with your clients, this is the very same type of service they should expect from you.

The Client Is King

Or Queen. Exceptional customer service keeps clients happy. It starts with your authentically great attitude, something that's deep within you as a person. Maintain positive energy at all times—it will definitely spill over into your professional behavior. Treat every client exactly as you would like to be treated, and you will find that real excellence surrounds you. Giving great customer service takes some practice, but eventually it will be second nature.

I love *100 Simple Secrets of Happy People* by David Niven, Ph.D. **Secret No. 73. Be agreeable. Make it easy for people to deal with you.**

Forging positive relationships with people will make your business thrive and turn first-time customers into a long-term clients. It's also critical that the quality of everything you do is consistent—do what you say you will every time, without making difficult-to-keep or empty promises, and people will judge you by your actions. Keep your word at all times.

In your eagerness to acquire a new client, you should never puff up the anticipated value of a client's items or promise something you may not be able to deliver just to score a deal. Train your staff to be helpful and knowledgeable. Every person who works for you should have the power and ability to make the decisions necessary to service your clients properly while still bringing profit to you.

Use Kid Gloves

From the moment you touch an item belonging to another person, you must handle it with the utmost care. Regardless of your own perception of the value, show that you value their cherished possessions to the same extent they do from your initial contact with the item all the way through its packing and shipping.

Their Call

Most of us are turned off by pushy salespeople. Even though you're selling yourself and your services, I urge you not to pressure clients to make any decision. Nurture your relationships with your clients and treat them like gold. Despite my normal policy of not listing items on eBay with minimum starting prices or Reserves, at a client's request, I once put a very fine set of sterling silver flatware on eBay with a $1,700 minimum starting price. I received no bids at that price, but several offers to purchase the item for prices several hundred dollars less. I presented all the offers to my client, but he declined them. I didn't try to pressure him, even influence him, or complain about his decision in any way. In fact, I told him it would be fine to keep the set in my eBay Store, because I really liked it and wanted to give it a fair chance to get more offers. And a few weeks later, it sold for the full price on eBay. I could have encouraged the client to accept one of the lower offers, but I didn't. I simply informed him of the offers without comment and deferred to his wishes. It was the right decision—when a buyer finally did surface, we both made money, everyone was happy, and my client brought me more high-quality items—he felt totally comfortable with me.

Giving Good Phone

A friendly voice on the phone welcoming prospective new clients is a must. Don't underestimate the importance of giving good phone. Train everyone in your organization to answer promptly and courteously. I don't screen my calls, and I tell my staff not to do so, either. I find it irritating when I call a business and hear *". . . and this is? What is this regarding?"* and I do not allow my employees to answer the phone this way.

Always return phone calls—even if doing so seems to be without benefit to you. Years ago, when I worked in the entertainment industry as a personal manager of actors, I once asked one of the most successful talent agents for her secrets of success. A key part of her formula, she told me, was that she returned every single telephone call every single day before leaving her office—without fail, without exception. Have a member of your staff do so when you're away or can't do it personally. The result will be professionalism on the highest level.

Make yourself available whenever possible. Have an answering machine to answer calls when you're not at work. This may seem obvious, but some companies don't have one. Your message should include your hours of operation to help clients in scheduling their visits.

Become an Oracle

Be an authority and let people know it. Providing advice to people about what you do will earn you more referrals. Numerous times, someone has declined my services, but because of my gregarious nature and willingness to be of assistance, they later referred others to me who then became clients themselves. Being charismatic and commanding attention with your great expertise and knowledge will attract people to you automatically. Success and confidence attract clients.

Speak at local organizations as a way of educating others about your business. I have spoken to many different groups, creating more business for me. Most people who fear sharing information will fail. Being generous with your time will attract other generous people to you.

Integrity Sells

You can't possibly know everything. As a seller of unwanted items, you will have to be able to assess complex situations related to the sale of a wide variety of merchandise. When you don't know something, it's important to be honest about it. You can't fake your way through—you must make every effort to find the answer. Take responsibility and never pass the buck.

Open Your Ears

Everyone is unique. We all speak and think in different ways, and it's very important that you listen carefully to your clients. While talking with them, never interrupt, and be thoughtful and open-minded. Maintain eye contact and ask questions about any points you do not fully understand. This is particularly important during initial client consultations to ensure that you understand your client's expectations of your services. If a prospect has never used an eBay consignment service before, guide them and teach them to avoid misconceptions.

Learning to listen effectively will bring you closer to the needs of your clients. Never argue verbally (or even mentally) with them; rather, try to understand how they think and feel—and try to relate to them. Because yours is a service business, customers are your number-one priority. This applies both to the clients who bring items and to the buyers who purchase them. Get to know the needs of each person with whom you do business. We speak to a lot of our buyers on the phone, but we also "listen" to them by keeping tabs on what they buy from us, and we keep lists of our buyers and their interests, so that we can notify them of specific upcoming sales.

Cross Your Ts

People appreciate efficiency, especially when it comes to getting paid, and your clients will feel more confident in working with you if your payouts and records are accurate. We can generate a list of both sold and unsold items for any client in a matter of minutes. Each time you pay your clients for sold items, provide them with a list of their unsold inventory and let them know if they are required to retrieve it from your place of business or if the items will be relisted. Keep copies of all your payout sheets so that you can refer to them in the event of an error. Generally, it's a good idea to keep a copy of everything you do for a client. Keep client-specific documents in their alphabetical file. Keeping everything chronological in the client's folder will help in finding documents quickly. There's a lot to be said for keeping a manual filing system. Although computer records are great, having hard copies is very handy in the event of computer data loss.

The "Wow" Report

Each successful sale is an opportunity to promote your fine work. Compile a list of your most amazing sales each month and include a copy of it (along with a photo, if possible) with your check when you pay your clients. Many people have items similar to those you have sold but may not have realized their true value or considered bringing them to you. Providing this wow report to your clients will help keep you and these items in the front of their minds.

When someone calls you and asks for more information about your service, offer to email more information to them. With permission, you can send these prospective clients a monthly update of your successes as well. Being a good self-promoter is a necessary part of being a businessperson. It's not rocket science, it's good people skills.

Tip: I encourage you to keep your item photos indefinitely. You never know when you may want to use them at some future date for publicity or marketing purposes. If you start running out of space on your computer's hard drive, you can always burn them to a CD or DVD and save them in a secure and safe place. Save the auction information so that you can match it up to the photos if needed.

Coupon Culture

Coupons and discounts are a part of American life. There's historically high unemployment and people watch their dollars. There's even a TV show called *Extreme Couponing*. The word sale strikes a chord that gets us spending. I certainly love to save money, and I've caught myself putting off washing my car until the Sunday newspaper arrived with the car wash discount coupon in it. Fortunately for me the cashier knows me well and extends the discount without a coupon or my asking.

Whether your business is going through a slow period or growing robustly, consider mailing out coupons to your clients. Make them fun and include a call to action. A coupon should provide enough value to get someone to act quickly. You can offer a discount on your commissions, for example 5 to 10 percent off your normal fee for a specific month, or if a client brings in ten or more items, etc.

Another coupon idea could be a nonprofit contribution program. You can work with your local nonprofits and get their permission to mention that a portion of the proceeds of every sale (taken from your commission, of course) would be donated to a specific nonprofit. People tend to respect and admire those who do good for their community. Cause marketing is an integral part of all large corporations.

Make it Personal

People appreciate awesome personal service more than ever in this increasingly impersonal world. It's always a good idea to give clients a call, and not just to let them know the status of their items. If one of their items sold for an amazing amount of money, you should call the client the same day and give them the good news. Touch base with your clients on a monthly basis, even when they don't have items in your care, to see how they are doing, check to see if they have more items that need listing, and find out if they have friends who may need you. Staying fresh in their minds is great marketing, and they will appreciate your personal service. Avoid being out of sight and out of mind.

20. Conflict Resolution: Handling Client (and Buyer) Disputes Effectively

I sold a collection of 35 match safes on behalf of a local minister whose grandfather had collected them. I sold one alone for $485 on eBay. Most of them sold to a California doctor who collected match safes and was willing to pay whatever he had to pay in order to get them.
—Len Smoke, Orlando, Florida; eBay user ID "superdealsusa"; trading on eBay since February 27, 1998

When the Going Gets Tough, the Diplomat Gets Going

Don't duck a complaint. It can be scary dealing with an irate person, but you have to do it. Be strong and wise in your solution to every problem that presents itself. On occasion, as we have discussed, someone may be unhappy with the price their item realized, or they may regret having sold it at all. Simply reminding them that they are bound by a legal contract will probably only further fuel the fire. Stand your ground and explain your obligations to your buyers but express sincere empathy and understanding for your client. Diplomacy and a spoonful of sugar will go a long way to calm nerves and get the situation under control. Bring the same kindness to all your business interactions and complaints will be rare.

And always follow through with your commitments. Once the bonds of trust are broken, it will take a tremendous amount of work to try to heal a soured relationship. An unhappy client can share one bad experience with ten other clients, impacting your reputation exponentially. So be very proactive with misunderstandings—clear them up as fast as possible.

As much as we might like to think otherwise, an attraction to conflict is part of human nature—conflict makes movies and television programs interesting. In real life, some people like to argue as a part of the fabric of their daily lives, while others prefer to acquiesce and avoid conflict. You will encounter many different personalities and cultures. Conflict looms whenever doing business with other people—both buyers and clients. The art of diplomacy is a discovery process, you aren't born with the skills. Work towards mastering the skills necessary to resolve conflicts as they arise to the satisfaction of all parties.

I believe that in general conflicts can be resolved using unemotional logic seasoned with a bit of understanding and compassion for your customers—whether a client or eBay item purchaser. Most conflicts arise either as a result of a misunderstanding or out of ulterior motives:

- Misunderstanding. In my experience, communication problems are the biggest cause of conflicts. Maybe your client didn't fully understand their contract, or perhaps some of the terms in your eBay listing terms were unclear. Usually such conflicts can be managed and resolved fairly easily. If you're careful, clear, and honest in your dealings with people, a conflict of this type that cannot be resolved is a rare event, because most people are fair and honest and have reasonable expectations.

- Ulterior motives. Some conflicts result from factors beyond your understanding or control, such as a person with ulterior motives who actively seeks conflict. Either a client or buyer may try to leverage a better deal from you after the fact by cooking up a conflict—commonly, for example, by claiming dissatisfaction with your service. These conflicts are much more difficult to resolve, because the other person will be playing games with you to obtain the results they seek.

Temper Tantrums

Remain calm. There is absolutely nothing to be gained from flaring tempers, and there's plenty to lose. I am a stubborn and, quite frankly, often rather difficult person by nature. It's very hard for me to remain calm during a conflict incident because of my personal programming. I have blown a number of business deals over the years because of shortsighted stubbornness and a lack of vision. Remember that you're a businessperson now, and being right doesn't necessarily always work in business situations. You have to approach every situation with confidence that you can resolve any conflicts that might arise. Keep in mind that one vocal individual can do tremendous damage to you and your business' reputation, even if you're completely innocent. Your goal is to have satisfied clients and buyers, and although you can't make everyone happy, you can achieve a high success rate with bad situations if you follow some basic ground rules.

Have you ever seen a small disagreement escalate into a big fight? Have you ever suddenly found yourself caught in the middle of a verbal battle? How did the situation get out of control? What were you feeling and thinking? Did you feel badly afterwards? What could you have done to avoid the conflict in the first place?

Conflict Management Tips

- Don't let any conflict escalate by allowing yourself to get angry; stop and take a mental time out to allow yourself to think.

- Determine the cause of the other person's problem and mentally inventory their objections and concerns so that you can address them individually.

- Put yourself in the other person's shoes and try your best to see their point of view while coming up with ways to come to an understanding and resolution.

- Be a great listener and remain open-minded about the possibility of a compromise.

- Think of any and all options that might allow both parties to get what they want and walk away happy.

- Be extremely truthful—do not simply tell the other person what they want to hear but instead be honest in your handling of the conflict.

- If the conflict is face-to-face or on the phone, do not interrupt the other person— take turns talking.

- Don't engage in finger pointing—blaming the other person will only escalate the conflict further.

- Be a lightning rod for the other person's anger—take some of their pain away by saying things such as, "I understand your feelings and want to help resolve this situation . . ."

- Increase your understanding of the other person's concerns and be an active listener.

- Lighten up. It's not appropriate to make light of another person's feelings or problem, no matter how absurd you perceive them. Be congenial and friendly. This goes light-years farther towards conflict resolution than being stern and hardheaded. People are by nature intuitive about others' moods and feelings, and projecting an affable and genuine attitude will help to bring any conflict to a swift conclusion.

Undue Expectations

Because you will have many clients with different personalities and levels of business experience, at some time or another, you will no doubt run into a conflict with one of them. The most common issue that will arise is that of a client's inflated expectations for the amount of money their item will bring on eBay. If you list clients' items with the minimum bid price they specify based on their expectation for the item taking into account your commission, then you shouldn't have a problem. If you charge for this minimum bid service with an up-front listing fee, some clients with inflated expectations of the value of their items may opt to save on these fees. But their treasures may not be as valuable as expected. This can cause, to put it mildly, disappointment.

As with my client described previously, whose family heirloom rug sold for $0.99, some clients may experience seller's remorse after the sale. It turns out that they had a strong emotional attachment to the item and, deep down, never really wanted to sell it and probably never should have. Now that their item has another owner, they're miserable and may, in rare cases, try to block the sale. As always, you must be understanding and empathetic but firm—you have a contract!

Some folks are so excited about being able to sell on eBay that they lose sight of the fact that things can sell for low prices. Inflated expectations are not uncommon, especially when based on the original purchase price of the item. Always let clients know at the outset that there is a very real possibility, without a high minimum bid or reserve price, of an item selling low. I make a point of trying to head off later client disappointment by reinforcing to them that eBay should be their venue for selling unwanted items—items for which they have no emotional or financial expectations or attachment—at a low starting price that encourages bidding interest. And if an item sells for more than they expected, there will be nothing but smiles.

Taming the Unruly

What happens if you present your client with their accounting statement and check and they become irate over a low selling price? It's critical that you and they understand your role as the liquidator of unwanted merchandise. Always under promise and over deliver. You're at the mercy of the eBay buyers and what they are willing to pay for an item. The marketplace sets the price.

Protect yourself throughout the process by saving critical e-mails between you and your clients and documenting everything. The contract is only the first step in this—any important decisions that you and your clients make together should be on paper and initialed by both parties, or in saved e-mails, to ensure that you have proof if a dispute arises later. Gmail is awesome because it allows you to archive every email and rapidly search for it by keyword.

Be patient, understanding, and clear about your role throughout any disagreement. Don't allow an unruly client bring you to the point of becoming jaded—keep a positive attitude and things will sort themselves out.

Educate your staff on the risks involved in performing services for a difficult client so they can conduct themselves in ways that minimize conflict. Often difficult people are more difficult with the staff than they are with the owner. If a client accuses an employee of poor service or improper conduct, present this information to your employee for their response. If it is a onetime complaint, then you should be prepared to support your employee, as you can easily lose a valued staff member over a client's ranting and unreasonable behavior. Never let the difficult client treat your employees in an abusive manner.

A difficult client is also likely be unhappy about your fees and may ask you to take a lower commission on a poor outcome. Stick to your guns and your contract in these situations.

Know when to fold—it's not always possible to service everyone's needs, and your sanity is at least as important as servicing the client. If you find that the client is angry, hostile, overly involved, obsessive, dependent, or otherwise high maintenance, you should complete whatever work you have outstanding for them and then end the relationship. The client who feels that they know more about eBay than you do is to be avoided, too, because they will constantly be telling you your job and second-guessing your decisions.

If you surround yourself with great clients, they will refer more great clients, and eventually your business will be based on people who are positive and appreciative of the fantastic results your eBay business provides.

Unhappy Happens

You have carefully crafted your eBay listing; taken wonderful, clear photos; sold the item and collected the payment; and packed and shipped the item with great pride. The world looks bright, and you're elated with your eBay transaction. But the buyer, on the other hand, receives the item and sends you an e-mail tersely stating that they are not pleased. The vase is smaller than expected, the shoes are a bit too loose, or the painting doesn't really look like it did in your listing. Perhaps Mary Homemaker thinks that she's still a size two twenty years out of high school.

What do you do? Take a deep breath—it happens. Even with the most incredibly accurate description and pictures, buyers aren't always pleased. So what do you do now? Here are the steps to take in making the buyer happy:

- Acknowledge their dissatisfaction by saying something like, "I'm very sorry to hear that you were not completely satisfied with your eBay purchase."

- Ask the buyer what would be required to resolve their complaint and decide whether you feel their requests are reasonable and if you're willing to comply.

- Depending on the nature of their request for resolution, ask if a partial refund would be acceptable, even if it means losing your profit or possibly a few dollars more; or assess the cost of taking a return of the item (your time and return shipping costs) and determine if it would be better to accept the return and simply relist the item.

- Take it back. If a return is the final result, be sure to pay return shipping as a good faith gesture—assuming the unhappy buyer is without ulterior motives, you want to retain their good will for possible future transactions.

Stripping Midge

There are some dishonest buyers out there, and you have to deal with each situation on a case-by-case basis. Rarely, buyers will try to swindle you. I once sold a 1960s Midge doll (Barbie's best friend) on eBay, and the buyer claimed it was not as described and asked me to refund $30 of the $34 he paid for it. I politely explained I felt it was unfair to practically give the doll away, and I asked him to return it for a full refund. The buyer promptly declined my offer and then disputed his payment with PayPal. In my response, I informed PayPal that I would accept the doll back as a return giving the buyer a full refund and they mediated the issue in my favor. But when I finally did receive the doll back, it was completely nude! The buyer had kept the clothes, which obviously had some value. Although I was completely shocked by this conduct, I had to weigh the crime against the cost of recovering the property—it was obviously not worth pursuing, and I had to let it go. Realizing that situations like this will arise now and then, you must be prepared to walk away and move on—putting your energy into more profitable pursuits. If I were to dwell on such problems, it would cost me both emotionally and financially—not a good investment of energy.

Most people are good, and you can count on many happy and successful transactions. When a wrinkle does pop up, it's important that you provide incredibly good customer service to your buyer and resolve their issue to the best of your ability. Even if you cannot honor an unreasonable request, be cordial, professional, polite, and customer oriented.

Sellers have a handy tool to block buyers on eBay. Google the term "eBay bidder management" and you will find the page that permits you to block the worst of your eBay bidders.

Staying Positive

Negative feedback is normally the result of a buyer not receiving the service they expected. New members of eBay are more likely to jump the gun and leave a negative feedback comment for you before first attempting to resolve an issue directly with you. Your feedback score is the backbone of your eBay business, and maintaining the highest possible overall positive score will encourage buyers on eBay to purchase items from you. It's critical that you protect your feedback by taking measures to ensure total buyer satisfaction.

Here are my pointers for keeping your feedback free of negative comments from buyers:

- Review your eBay listing descriptions for complete accuracy—from the wow to the warts.

- Research items and elaborate on their provenance and any other pertinent details you can provide.

- Be comprehensive and conservative in your description of the item's condition, carefully pointing out any physical flaws or damage. In our photos, we often show such flaws with labels or draw attention to them with a well-manicured and clean finger.

- Use a ruler or a coin to provide scale and size reference.

- Ship promptly.

- Include a thank-you card or note in the shipment that also encourages the buyer to contact you immediately if they are not completely satisfied with their order.

- Send a quick follow-up e-mail after the shipment has been delivered to ask the buyer if they were completely satisfied with their merchandise. Tracking alerts are available with all major shipping companies.

Do all that you can to resolve disputes before you leave a buyer a negative. You should know that eBay did away with seller-to-buyer negative feedback and therefore you can never leave a buyer a negative rating.

When a dispute does arise, it may be helpful to review the buyer's feedback and also the feedback the buyer has left for others. You can see the feedback a buyer has left for other eBay members by going to the eBay member's feedback profile and clicking on the "Left for Others" tab. This will give you a good idea of the member's own reputation and how they treat other eBay members. If they tend to leave other sellers negative feedback, you should review their negative comments—maybe you have a habitual complainer. Sometimes, as unfair as it may feel, bending over backwards for these complainers will benefit you in the long run, because a negative feedback can result in lost sales when other buyers see the comment, even if it is unwarranted.

21. Hiring, Paying, Motivating and Managing Employees

I own a jewelry business and decided to start selling through eBay. My clientèle is mostly attorneys and estate trustees. I have four full-time and two part-time employees running my eBay business. In our last four months of business, our eBay fees were only 4.88 percent of our total sales. I look for employees with good computer skills, and then I teach them everything else they need to know. I presently use a software program called Liberty from a company called Resale World. We sell exactly 71 percent of the items brought into our store.
—Stan Shelley, Hendersonville, North Carolina; eBay user ID "shelleys_yes"; trading on eBay since October 5, 2004

It's difficult to find good help these days. I've been very fortunate in my hiring, consistently finding people who are superb at what they do. Hiring is an art that requires some vision on your part. You want a certain balance—happy employees who work hard and know how to follow your vision, anticipate your wishes, and follow your business style. Being someone's boss is an acquired talent that will require patience and time. Not everyone will think the way you do, but they can still provide significant value to your company.

Make an effort to be in service to your employees and they will be in service to you.

One great attraction for many of my employees, past and present, is the flexibility of working in an online business. My employees can work just about any day of the week to handle such tasks as photography, packing and shipping, and clerical work. Most of the tasks I delegate can be saved up if necessary and completed a few days later.

Here are the key points to identify when hiring great people:

- Employee honesty—do they have past employer references?
- Strong computer skills (even shipping requires a computer!)
- Prior eBay selling experience
- A friendly, outgoing personality—a must for great customer service skills
- Willingness to be flexible about days of work and hours
- Someone who's enthusiastic about your business

Employee honesty tops my list, because we are handling other people's items, some breakable and many of high value. I need to have total confidence in the people working for me. It's important to find out as much as you can about whom you're considering hiring before bringing them into a position of trust and responsibility.

Here are some tips for hiring employees:

- Write clear, thorough, and realistic job descriptions for your employment ads, and make sure your ads provide sufficient information about the job. Or, with the high cost of advertising, you may want to shorten your employment ads and provide your website address for a job description and further information.

- Advertise, but also put out the word to existing employees, friends, and family—referrals from people you know and trust can bring you great employees.

- Find out what other comparable employers are paying, to be sure you're competitive.

- Interview carefully, looking at the prospective employee's qualifications and attitude during the interview and listening closely while you let them do a lot of the talking.

- Ask current employees to sit in on the interview—the opinions of those who intimately know your business and your ways can be very valuable.

- Check all job and personal references carefully—call them. Everyone's on their absolute best behavior in a job interview. Be sure to check how they performed at their last couple of positions.

- With the applicant's permission, conduct a background check (www.sentrylink.com does them for $19.95).

- If your applicant will be running errands, review their driving record, even if they would be using their own car. You are liable if they injure someone driving for the company.

- When making offers of employment, specify all of the terms (hours, pay rate and frequency, benefits, etc.) in writing.

The Best Money You Will Spend

Timing is everything, and the time to start hiring is well before you become overwhelmed with work. As your business thrives you'll be getting client referrals in droves, and when you find yourself working more than about 40 hours a week, it's time to hire employees, whether full- or part-time. If you've never had employees, hiring can be a difficult decision. You'll find yourself giving up some of your profits to have help, and it can be hard to part with those dollars, but it's something you'll have to do to expand your business. Yes, I've cautioned you to be frugal, but great employees are an exception—their paychecks will be the best money you will spend.

When you're feeling extra tired at the end of the day, diffuse or unproductive, having other people helping and supporting you can make a humongous difference in your own productivity and success. And if your budget has been kept in order, you should be able to accurately project how much extra money you will have at the end of each month that can be allocated to pay staff.

When You're the Boss

When you hire others, you will have some legal responsibilities as their employer, and the Internal Revenue Service as well as your state government will impose some rules on you as well.

Different kinds of business relationships can exist between you and others providing services to you, usually either that of hired employees or of independent contractors. The latter status can be tricky, and I strongly discourage you from treating your help as independent contractors without first consulting a tax professional.

With employees, you must withhold and pay income taxes, withhold and pay Social Security and Medicare taxes, and pay unemployment tax. You're not normally required to withhold or pay any taxes on payments to independent contractors, but be careful: incorrectly classifying an employee as an independent contractor can result in your being liable for the payment of taxes and penalties.

Your liability insurance will cover nonemployee injuries at your place of business. But before hiring anyone, speak to your insurance broker about the required worker's compensation insurance, which covers your employees in the event of an on-the-job injury. A handy resource for information about worker's compensation laws for your state is located at www.workerscompensation.com.

To withhold and report taxes, you will need to fill out an SS-4 form for the IRS, which will provide you with a Federal Employer Identification Number (EIN) to be used with all payroll services. A visit to the IRS website's Small Business and Self-Employed Tax Center will provide links to the information and forms you will need. Another option is to enter "apply for FEIN online" at www.google.com to get the direct link to the form.

Some states do not levy a personal income tax and mine is not one of them. Contact your state to determine if they require withholding and payment of state taxes.

Payday

As a businessperson, you have to keep your costs under control. This means budgeting your payroll—and personalities are a factor. Some people love the comfort of a steady paycheck, while others prefer to work on commission. A few rare individuals who were naturally obsessive about getting things done have worked in my store. A person who likes to keep the ball rolling is ideal for jobs like photography and shipping, where the task is repetitive and you need to be very productive to keep things profitable.

Piecework is a great way to provide incentive to your staff to generate more productivity. You can pay someone for each item photographed or listed. Piecework still requires you to adhere to the minimum wage, overtime and recordkeeping requirements set forth under the Fair Labor Standards Act.

Finding fast, diligent, self-starter workers may be harder than you think—but certainly not impossible. I suggest bringing on all employees initially as temporary, part-time workers so that you can see the quality and speed of their work. If they impress you, then you can hire them full-time.

For photographers, simply hand them a camera and an item and ask them to light, present and shoot it. For someone preparing listings, ask them to take your item and prepare a title and description.

There are different ways to compensate employees with different talents and speeds. You can:

- pay a salary;
- pay an hourly wage;
- pay on a per piece basis, such as for photographing items or packing and shipping; or
- pay a commission or flat rate for listing each item.

If you hire creative people, such as photographers, you may find that they are perfectionists. You need high-quality work of course, but only up to a point. If the photography, for instance, is great but simply taking too long, the law of diminishing returns may be gobbling up your profits; and paying on a per item basis for this task may help to give your talented photographer much needed perspective.

Recently, I came upon a large estate of very expensive and rare antique pocket watches, and I know nothing about pocket watches. Looking for pocket watch experts on the Internet, I found a new friend, too, in Lance Thomas, who worked in my office for several days creating eBay listings for these valuable rarities. I didn't pay Lance a flat per-listing fee but instead a 10 percent commission on each final sale. If he could make a compelling listing that sold successfully, I would be happy to share a nice piece of the pie with him. Because he was only paid when an item sold and I received payment, the situation was truly win-win. I believe that this knowledgeable expert generated substantially more profit for my company than if I tried to muddle through making the listings myself.

Work on your communication skills with prospective and existing employees, because how you compensate people is really a matter of negotiation. You will want insights into their compensation wants and needs, and involving them in the process will help to make them feel appreciated.

Tip: Pay is not a subject for public consumption and should be discussed privately. Employees often compare notes, however, so don't play favorites, or it may come back to bite you.

Payroll Joy

Payroll is a pain in the . . . well, it can be a chore. I have tried many different payroll services over the years—I've even tried processing payroll myself without a payroll software program. But I've discovered that an online payroll service is a joy. You can't be a "Jack or Jill of all trades." Focus on your business instead of learning complex employment tax rules.

I recommend Intuit Payroll (payroll.intuit.com). I have found them to be by far the simplest, most reliable, and most cost effective service available. At this writing, Intuit Enhanced Payroll charges $29.00 per month plus $1.50/month per employee. This fee includes processing all paychecks, withholding and paying all taxes, making contractor payments, producing annual W-2 forms and 1099-MISC forms, and basically anything else you need to handle payroll. Their set-up process guides you through every step required, including providing forms or links to obtain your federal and state employer identification numbers. All taxes are filed electronically whenever possible, and you get phone support from real people. You cannot afford the high cost of penalties for failing to file on time or making a calculation error.

With Intuit payroll, you can handle your entire payroll online from anywhere in the world, and if your employees take the free direct deposit option, you don't even need to go near your checkbook or QuickBooks program to pay them. Intuit Payroll even allows you to run a sample payroll from their website so you can test drive the service. In any case, be sure to compare the costs and ease of use before choosing a payroll solution.

Why They Love You

Let's be realistic: most people won't come to work simply to experience your charming wit and enjoy your wonderful company—they're usually working for the money. If you hire a retiree or student, their financial requirements may be lower, but employee incentives are a viable way to increase employee satisfaction.

Offer a flexible schedule to accommodate your employees needs. Find ways to motivate and retain the great employees who do so much for you each and every day, and incentive programs are designed to award achievers. Having happy employees will result in amazing customer service, and it is very important that they feel a sense of belonging at your company—this invariably translates into a positive and upbeat attitude.

In today's highly competitive business environment, incentives show appreciation that a salary, no matter how large, can't convey. Most companies, even smaller firms such as yours, offer incentive packages to their staff.

Here are some basic tips for any incentive program:

- Separate incentives from normal pay so that they stand out as something special
- Consider monetary and nonmonetary incentives combined to keep things interesting for your employees
- Reward individual performance and avoid giving group incentives—people love to receive personal acknowledgement for their hard work

- Solicit frequent feedback from your employees to determine how they feel about your treatment of them—listen to them carefully and effect changes when needed

And here are some incentives to consider:

- Scheduling flexibility
- A bonus for bringing in a large new account
- Bonuses for referrals
- A substantial discount on your fees when employees list their own items for sale
- Gift certificates from local merchants
- Full or partial health insurance reimbursement or a group plan to which you contribute 50 percent or more of the premiums
- Baby- or even pet-sitting for employees when they need it
- Offering to drive employees home if they don't own a car
- Offering to match IRA contributions up to a certain limit
- Writing heartfelt thank you cards
- Remembering employees' birthdays and/or anniversaries
- Taking the staff out for a monthly dinner
- Holding holiday parties
- Providing constant verbal appreciation and acknowledgment

There is really no right or wrong way to give incentives. You should do what your heart tells you. Treat your employees the same way you would want to be treated if you were in their shoes. If you take good care of them, they will return the favor by doing a wonderful job for you.

Who will Clean the Bathroom?

The ability to delegate is a truly critical management skill. Effective delegation will save you time, reduce personal stress, and help you motivate employees, too. To get tasks accomplished in your business by delegating, you must first gain the respect of your staff. You won't get instant respect merely because of your position as the employer—you must earn it. Be consistent and ethical in all your dealings. Lead by example: if you expect honest, hard-working employees you must be the same. Simply handing off all of the work to your staff while you drink coffee and talk to friends on the phone all day will result in resentment and, ultimately, employee dissatisfaction. Lead by example.

Treat all employees equally and with great respect. Employees are the backbone of your company, and you will want to show them how important they are to you. You must be willing to do any task that you delegate. If you ask someone to take out the trash, you should temper this by doing it yourself as well. Nobody likes to clean the office bathroom, but unless you can afford a janitorial service, you will have to schedule the employees to take turns doing it, including yourself.

Here are some tips for delegating projects to others:

- Choose the right person for the job—don't give a computer project to someone who types hunt and peck

- Be very concise in your instructions—think over them carefully and write them down before giving out a job

- Train well if the project is new to the employee

- Provide all needed resources to complete the job

- Give advice and support at all times

- Give deadlines and ask your staff to keep them, but make certain you allow enough time to do so

- Keep it real—never ask for the impossible

- Ask for measurable progress, with reports both verbal and in writing (e-mail is okay)

- Ask each employee to keep a measurable record of their productivity

- Give honest and fair feedback on all work

- Always praise someone for doing a great job

Effective delegation may require some finesse as well. Sometimes, an employee may express resistance when asked to do something that they don't agree with. Never ask an employee to lie on your behalf or do something uncomfortable. You should explain and justify your reasons for delegating to them.

Delegate a variety of tasks to keep things interesting. If your shipping clerk is an amateur photographer, then be sure to hand her a camera. If you already have a full-time photographer, you will want to tell him why you're doing this and assure them that you're not trying to replace him. Who will shoot the items if your regular photographer is sick or on vacation? (If you want to have creative workers, give them enough time to play!)

> Tip: Create a wall chart showing your company's weekly and monthly progress. Put up total sales figures, number of items listed, and other fun facts to keep everyone focused on the business' success.

Running Like Clockwork

Like the routine tasks discussed previously, delegating requires scheduling. And if your staff is to achieve the highest productivity levels possible, you will want to write up a schedule. It's critical that you carefully outline what is expected and when. If you know, for example, that you're expecting a large drop-off of items at your store, you might want to schedule the entire staff to help receive, review, and store them.

Although employees often like to take breaks together, this may cause you to be without the personnel you need to handle multiple phone lines and various situations that come up. Schedule staggered breaks and lunches so that you will have the help you need when you need it. Be sure to communicate your reasons for doing this.

If you run a physical drop-off location and are open more than five days a week, you will want to overlap your staff so that you have help every day. If you're open Monday through Saturday and have two employees, for example, you can schedule the photographer to work Monday through Friday and the eBay lister/shipping clerk to work Tuesday through Saturday. If your employees want to work less than full-time, it's important that you do whatever you can to accommodate them, while still ensuring sufficient coverage for the work that needs to be done.

22. Bookkeeping, Accounting, and Taxes

Working from home can benefit you greatly—you can stop at any point and take a break—but working at an office really allows you to concentrate and focus on building a customer base. When you have an office, it is a place of business, and that is what you're coming in for. eBay is the best thing that ever happened to a lot of people—I recently sold a rare book published by Salvador Dali, number 27 of 39, which brought $12,600 for one of my clients. We only estimated its value at $7,000 to $8,000. We were extremely pleased. I made $1,260 commission on the sale. With the right clientele, you will do really well. I quit my job two years ago to become my own boss and sell on eBay full-time.

—Michael Rybak, Los Angeles, California; eBay user ID "ezbaywest"; trading on eBay since April 2, 2001

Frankly, I feel that this book demands a lot of the reader and that if you have made it this far, you have the right stuff to become successful with eBay consignment. That's good—because most people like bookkeeping about as much as a cold shower, but for a small business owner, keeping up with the books is necessary. You'll thank me later. In the past, cleaning up the bookkeeping messes caused by my lax attitude has cost me dearly in outside, professional bookkeeping and accounting help.

Don't make this mistake.

Learn the bookkeeping ropes yourself, even if you eventually decide to delegate this task to someone else. Small business accounting is different from that of a big corporation, and you should focus on keeping your accounting as simple as possible. With a basic understanding of bookkeeping and some help from software, you will be able to prepare a balance sheet, a profit and loss statement, and a cash flow statement for your company. The balance sheet shows your company's total assets and liabilities (its value), the profit and loss statement shows if your business is profitable, and the cash flow statement gives you a good idea of your future cash flow patterns. With these documents, you will feel the pulse of your company's financial well-being.

Counting Your Beans

If you decide to use a payroll service such as Intuit Payroll, you have already taken a big step towards keeping excellent records and staying on top of one of your most daunting tasks.

Set up a separate bank account for your business, even when you operate as a sole proprietor. Keeping business records completely separate from your personal finances will really help when it comes time to do your tax returns. Use accounting software to pay bills and keep track of general ledger (G/L) codes—used to group expenses into manageable categories that will later translate into line items on your tax returns.

Tax Liability Issues

There will be a number of tax liability matters that you and your accountant will need to address.

Income taxes. If you start as a sole proprietor, you will be reporting your business activity on a schedule that is attached to your IRS form 1040, called Schedule C. Not only will a sole proprietor pay income tax but also Social Security and Medicare taxes, reported together as a separate item on the income tax return. The Social Security and Medicare taxes can be quite a surprise for the new small businessperson, who usually doesn't expect to pay roughly 15 percent of net income on top of the income tax. Operating as a partnership or LLC doesn't relieve a partner of the obligation to pay self-employment tax. Your accountant can help set up estimated tax payments that will lessen the burden of your final tax bills.

Payroll taxes. If you have employees, you'll need a Federal Employer Identification Number, or EIN, to file payroll tax returns. Also, depending on your location, various state and other local taxes will be required. In California, for instance, you need a state identification number as well as your EIN, enabling you to pay the state tax and disability insurance monies withheld from your employees and a state unemployment tax.

This is a great time to tap your SCORE counselor once again for help, this time on setting up your new business' bookkeeping and accounting procedures.

When in Doubt, Automate

I use the de facto industry-standard accounting program for my business: QuickBooks (www.QuickBooks.com). Many business accounting software packages are on the market, but you will find that most people speak QuickBooks, and my accountant recommends it. The program's wizard walks you step by step through the process of setting up your company's accounts, including allowing you to quickly and easily set up those general ledger codes I mentioned.

QuickBooks offers the desktop software product or you can move into the cloud and use the QuickBooks Online version that allows you to access your records from any computer, anywhere. QuickBooks Online subscriptions start at $12.95 per month. Be very mindful of security and change your online passwords often when using cloud services.

Instead of ordering preprinted checks for my business, I purchased a software program called CheckSoft Home and Business (www.avanquestusa.com). This handy software was $49.95 and allows me to prepare bank approved checks on my laser printer, using the company's special check paper. Some banks may require that you use a special magnetic ink or laser toner (called magnetic ink character recognition, or MICR) for your checks, and you can obtain these supplies through CheckSoft's website, on eBay, or from any major office supply retailer.

Using CheckSoft, I never have to wait for checks to be printed and shipped to me. Any time I change banks or open a new account, I can prepare checks for that account instantly. CheckSoft does not integrate with QuickBooks Online, so you can only use it with the desktop edition.

Intuit QuickBooks Connect can help you import and store your eBay transaction history (including sales, expenses, eBay/PayPal fees) and can help you prepare for taxes. You can subscribe to this application at the Apps Center. (Note: The Apps Center is available only on eBay.com at this time.)

> Tip: If you use PayPal to receive money from individuals and businesses outside of your eBay sales, you can download the handy (and free) PayPal Payment Request Wizard for QuickBooks. This cool tool allows you to invoice your customers quickly from your QuickBooks program and receive payment in your PayPal account.

If you're using a listing management tool, you will be able to print sales reports and financial statements from this program as well. To avoid information overload, it's a good idea to map out your accounting plan ahead of time and use the simplest tools you can to manage your business.

Many savvy small business owners use TurboTax (www.turbotax.com) to prepare their own income taxes, which can be a help or a burden depending upon the complexity of your business. If you have a very simple business, no real estate assets, and nothing too fancy going on, you may want to consider using TurboTax or other tax preparation software. TurboTax integrates smoothly with QuickBooks, and there's a Premier edition that helps you prepare self-employment tax returns. Because I run a more complex business these days, I use the services of a CPA, but if yours is a small, start-up sole proprietorship, you can use software to prepare your own tax returns. TurboTax has software you can install on your computer, but it now offers online tax preparation solutions, too, so that you can prepare everything right on their website.

If your business is a corporation or partnership/LLC and earns no more than $250,000 a year, the TurboTax Business software will prepare Form 1120S (S corporation), Form 1065 (partnership/LLC), and Form 1120 (C corporation). If you're doing more business than that, you really will want to consult a tax professional. The downside of using any software is the lack of intuitive guidance that a human accountant with years of experience can provide.

Tip: You can now purchase a special edition of QuickBooks for eBay.

Pinch Those Pennies

Many people feel that debt is the American way—spend on credit and hope for a better tomorrow! I think that you should focus on becoming debt-free—that's not unpatriotic! And this is the perfect business because you sell other people's items on a percentage basis with no direct upfront costs except for relatively minor eBay fees. You can't simply incur bills in the hope of being able to pay them later without a clear understanding of your budget and cash flow.

Just as your business plan contained some specific financial projections, it's critical that you keep yourself on a strict monthly budget. You will know what your recurring expenses, such as rent and utilities, will be; to create a monthly budget, you will have to make estimates beyond these fixed costs. Most accounting software, including QuickBooks, offers a budgeting feature that you can use to prepare a projected budget for your business and to compare your actual expenditures against this budget.

You will be receiving substantial sums of money that belong to other people in the course of your business, and it's important that you keep this money separate from your fees. You can physically move these funds to another bank account, which would be your client trust account. You can also setup a G/L code in your software that will designate this money as a liability, that is, something you owe to someone else (your clients). Keeping the funds physically separate will help you stay disciplined, and until you become more experienced with accounting, I suggest that handling that way is the safest and most logical business practice.

> Tip: Save your money for a rainy day! When you get an avalanche of merchandise to sell and you make a bunch of cash, save your money. It's very tempting to spend it, but remember that you work on a percentage of what will probably be an unknown amount from month to month, so you need to save as much as possible.

Accounting Partners

A great accountant usually comes by referral. Ask someone with a business about the same size as yours for a referral to a good CPA. You can also seek an accountant through the local chamber of commerce or through the American Institute of Certified Public Accountants (AICPA). The AICPA has been serving the accounting profession since 1887, and you can locate a CPA in your area on their website: www.aicpa.org. The commercial tax preparation companies can do the work for you, too, but when using such firms, it's very important that you provide them with well organized, clean financial statements.

Organize your financial information to save you money. Most accountants charge by the hour, and their rates can be pricey (compared to those of a bookkeeper), so it really benefits you to give your accountant the most concise information possible to keep their hours, and thus your accounting costs, in line. Your accounting should be fairly straightforward. A great accountant will also help you plan legal ways to lower taxes or even avoid them altogether.

Just as with anyone you hire, your accountant must mesh well with your personality. You should sit down and talk with (in other words, interview) a prospective accountant, discussing your business and their fees and just getting to know them a bit before hiring them. It's helpful to get an estimate, based on your initial meeting, of your projected accounting costs so that you can factor them into your budget.

Avoid large accounting firms. You're a small business. Work with a small business accountant. It's common sense.

Deadline Sanity

Because my business is fairly simple in terms of accounting, I find that I can write checks, assign general ledger codes to them, and reconcile my own bank statements at the end of each month. Because I type very fast and have a pretty good working knowledge of accounting, I have chosen to do my own bookkeeping—I find it fun and a welcome distraction from my other daily routines. I also like to keep my business running smoothly with tight, personal control.

If you're not comfortable with software programs such as QuickBooks, you will find that hiring a full-service bookkeeper can help you greatly. Many bookkeepers work from home. You can fax or mail them copies of your checks, and they will do all the computer work on your behalf. If you need copies of your checks for the bookkeeper, you can order a checkbook with a carbon duplicate option. The bookkeeper can manage your finances for you, reconciling the end-of-month bank statements and sending your quarterly data to your accountant, who estimates your quarterly tax payments (when applicable).

Keeping Up with the Joneses

One thing that a bookkeeper or accountant will be able to do for your sanity is to keep you on top of your deadlines. And when you use a third-party payroll service, it will automatically handle your tax deadlines, lifting a great burden off your shoulders. This alone is worth the price of the service—hands down! Because the deadlines for filing payroll taxes are rather complex and I fully expect you to outsource it, I won't go into detail about them here (it would make your head spin). Use a payroll service!

Here are some of the common accounting deadlines you will need to meet if you operate on a calendar accounting year (one that ends December 31, as opposed to a fiscal year).

Federal Form 1040

April 15. A valid extension automatically extends the filing deadline by six months, to October 15, the maximum deadline for filing. If you're filing a return for a corporation, S corporation, partnership, or LLC, your tax return may be due based on your company's fiscal year, which may be different from a calendar tax year if your accountant feels that's helpful with your tax planning.

Quarterly Estimated Payment

Due dates (primarily for the self-employed):

- January 15
- April 15
- June 15
- September 15

Early in my business career, I fell behind on my taxes, and cleaning up my accounting mess ended up costing me a boatload in both time and money. I realized that I had been making my accounting much too complicated. With solid preplanning, a simple approach to accounting will keep your business running smoothly and paying the least in legally required taxes.

Make an effort to pay for all business-related expenses with a credit or debit card with online access to your account. From the card, you will be able to upload the transaction data directly into QuickBooks. This will save you a tremendous amount of time in assigning appropriate G/L codes to those expenses and will maintain a good accounting trail. And this procedure will reinforce your frugality, too, as you'll see what you're spending in real time, rather than in a statement at the end of the month. Avoid paying cash, as this requires tedious manual data entry of expenses into your accounting software. Also, receipts are often lost or forgotten—losing your precious tax deduction. Finally, remember that most expenditures for your business are tax deductible.

23. Disaster Planning, Prevention, and Recovery

I became an eBay consignment seller three years ago, and in my prior job, I worked at several museums in collections management, having previously owned an antiques store. My husband suggested that I try selling some of my antiques on eBay. I thought that I was doing well with eBay, and eventually I ran out of things to sell, so I wanted to start helping other people sell their items as well. I recently helped a client sell two very distinctive and valuable Pablo Picasso Madoura ceramics. He had paid $100 for both of them, and after researching them, I realized their great value. Both ended up selling for a total of $5,376 on eBay. I run the entire business from beginning to end by myself.
—Carol R. McGeehan, Miami Shores, Florida; eBay user ID "luvantiqs"; trading on eBay since December 14, 1998

When I started this book, I made a commitment to myself and to you, my reader, to be very frank and factual about the realities of running your very own eBay consignment company. As with any business, things can go awry. The world is your oyster, and with a great attitude you will be a very successful businessperson, but you must also be a careful one—to avoid or mitigate losses due to disasters, accidents, or emergencies that may arise.

You can't possibly avoid every unknown event that could throw a wrench in your day, but being prepared, both mentally and procedurally, can soften, or even dodge, the blow.

It Happens

Some possibilities that may ruin your day include:

- Loss of your Internet connection (yikes!)
- Power surges that damage equipment and data
- Theft of property
- Identity theft
- Acts of God (force majeure)
- Accidental damage to merchandise

These are just a few of the possibilities. Of course, I hope that you never have to confront any such situations, but although the odds are against it, it's best to be ready.

Here's what you can do to help keep things running smoothly.

Internet

Not all Internet carriers are created equal. Be sure to pick yours wisely. Not only do you want to have fast Internet, but reliability is critical. Be sure to ask around before settling on a provider and learn as much as you can about the various Internet service providers' (ISPs) track records. If you use broadband (who doesn't?), you should have a backup means of getting on the Internet in case of a total loss of your primary connection. Set up a dial-up account, and make sure it's useable at all times. Virtually all broadband providers will give you free dial-up access to their network if you use their broadband service. Setup a dial-up connection on your computer and test it periodically. Most ISPs make an array of dial-up numbers available, leaving little chance you will be left in the "virtual dark."

Power Surges

The quality of the power you receive can vary greatly. I've had several power outages over the years, and power surges (and even brownouts and blackouts) are not uncommon. Therefore, having surge protection is important. If your city has very inconsistent power and you're prone to blackouts due to heavy power usage during the summer months when people really crank up the air-conditioning, or because of bad weather, it might be prudent to get a battery-based, uninterruptible power supply that kicks in when the power fails. These power supplies are readily available at your local computer store or on eBay, and many brands have a special software program and computer connection that automatically closes your open programs and safely shuts down your computer when the power fails. Do not buy a used one. Too much is riding on your data.

Theft of Property

A major reason I moved to Burbank was that I mistakenly believed it was virtually crime-free. Just two days before I wrote this chapter, the bank two doors down from my office had a failed robbery attempt. Oddly enough, I was not at all alarmed, surprised, or stressed-out about this situation, because we have a great police department here. More importantly, my office is secure, and I am confident we are not at much risk for a break-in.

Here are some additional tips:

- When items come into your store, put them in bins out of view until you're ready to list them.

- Keep a good physical barrier between your clients' merchandise and the public—avoid temptation.

- Never leave your store unattended, even for brief periods of time. If you work alone, lock up when you have to use the restroom or step out (keep an "I'll be back at _____" sign handy to display when needed).

- Deposit checks, money orders, and cash daily, and try to bank as close to your office as possible so that this is convenient.

- Check an eBay buyer's feedback before considering taking credit card charges by phone (if you offer direct credit card payments). Ask buyers with questionable feedback, and any buyers of items costing more than you would be willing to lose in the event of a credit card scam, to fax proof of identification. This situation demands a judgment call, because without hard copy proof of the transaction, the buyer can deny the charges.

- Always insist on picture identification from buyers who pick up merchandise.

- When accepting PayPal, ship only to the confirmed address on the PayPal payment to avoid the possibility of a chargeback, and make certain to ship by methods that allow tracking and proof of delivery.

- If you have employees, require two members of your staff (you can be one of them) to inspect every item before it is shipped. My company's packing slips require that two staff members physically sign off that the merchandise was verified to be the correct item and packed in the box.

- If you have employees, file a police report when items are missing, so that the incident is documented both for your files and for possible insurance claims. Showing that you're serious about such matters will also discourage employee dishonesty.

- Conduct a criminal background and credit check of employees. Employees with horrible credit have had trouble handling their own finances and may have trouble handling your business, too.

- Install an alarm system with remote monitoring notifying the police when the alarm is tripped.

- Immediately report any suspicious activities to the police, even if they seem trivial.

> Tip: You will do well to be security conscious at all times when you run a business. Don't leave anything valuable lying in plain view. Smaller, high-value items should always be locked away out of sight.

If you're handling merchandise of extremely high value, you may want to consider installing security cameras that record on a continuous basis. With the advances in computer technology, recording to a hard drive with lots of storage space is cheap, and you can store massive amounts of camera footage on them. But make sure the juice is worth the squeeze—that the cost of security is not higher than the potential loss you might suffer without it.

Identity Theft

You will be privy to other people's important personal data during the course of your business. Operate your company much like a law firm or doctor's office—keep sensitive client information secure. Designate which employees are allowed to handle and view client folders, and be sure to keep these files locked up if they contain sensitive information about your clients. Never throw any documents containing such information into the regular trash. Use a shredder or have a box for document destruction (we use a bonded company for this).

Acts of God (Force Majeure)

If you live in an earthquake or hurricane zone, it will be very important to secure shelving units to the walls so that they won't tip over. Put heavy merchandise towards lower shelves. In a heavy rain, our company's back door tends to allow a small flood, so we keep merchandise off the floor to prevent water damage. Check your building's roof regularly even if you're a tenant to make certain it is not leaking. Fix leaks or report them immediately to your landlord regardless of how minor—little ones turn into big ones. Check any trees that might cause damage to your windows, façade, or sign on a windy day, and keep such trees trimmed to control limbs that could spoil your day. Inspect plumbing regularly to check for leaks, and if you live in an area that's cold enough to freeze pipes, keep your items as clear of these pipes as possible and off the floor.

Accidental Damage to Merchandise

If you're handling very delicate or breakable items such as china, crystal, etc., consider prepacking them after you photograph and list them. Putting these items into bubble wrap and boxing them ready for shipment will prevent the accidental breakage that happens in a busy environment. Items with small, breakable appendages, such as porcelain figurines, are very likely to meet their doom if left unprotected. We use Ziploc bags for non-breakable items to keep them free of dust and coffee spills. Don't allow employees to eat or drink beverages when handling clients' merchandise. It's not a matter of if, but simply when, a coffee or soda will spill and ruin something expensive or rare.

You Need Backup

It is very important to your business that you protect the data on your computer. Computer data can inadvertently be lost for many reasons, including a power surge, equipment failure, file corruption, or even operator error. You need to be able to back up this critical data regularly and keep the backups in a separate place in case of data loss. In small companies, a regular backup can easily be neglected among the myriad of other tasks to be remembered each day. A daily checklist of must-do tasks that includes making a backup of critical, business-related files would help.

The data you may wish to back up regularly can include:

- Digital photographs for your listings

- Software that you have purchased and downloaded from the Internet

- Data files for software that you use in your business

- Your address book for e-mails, business calendar, and Internet browser bookmarks

- All business-related documents and files

You can store this data on another hard drive on your network, or a removable drive. I use a very small, removable USB drive, called a thumb drive or flash drive. A USB drive is very inexpensive these days and can rapidly store huge amounts of data.

Many third-party backup software programs and Internet storage services are available to help with your data protection needs. The cloud is currently a very popular option. Many providers offer inexpensive data storage. Mac users can use the subscription-based Mac services to move files to a secure, off-site Internet storage vault for safekeeping.

You may also wish to look at the various software solutions available by visiting www.download.com and following the link for "Utilities." There, you will find hundreds of free and inexpensive software programs.

Symantec System Recovery is a software program that takes a snapshot of your system, creating an exact copy of your entire hard drive at the moment you make the backup. This image of your computer's hard drive will come in handy if your entire system crashes due to hardware failure. You can store the backup copy on your network, another hard drive, or removable media such as the USB hard disk mentioned earlier.

Having a good backup plan will save you money. It only takes one incident of data loss to cost your business hundreds or even thousands of dollars in lost data, time, and frustration. Cloud computer services such as online backup are becoming more cost effective over time. Use them and ensure peace of mind.

Getting Back on Your Feet

If you planned carefully, recovering from a disaster will be a smooth process. The first thing you want to do is stay calm. Regardless of the nature of your disaster, you're still alive and healthy, and you will recover from it.

If your disaster was the result of theft, accident, or force majeure, then the first thing you should do is contact your insurance company. If you intend to start putting your business life back together, you should videotape or photograph the damage before you start repairing it. Speak to your insurance company about the steps required for you to process a claim successfully.

It's important that you pick up the pieces carefully. If your loss involves computer equipment, don't panic, even if the equipment has been damaged due to fire or natural disaster. Don't assume that the data is a total loss. If the equipment is intact, there's hope that data can be recovered. For data recovery projects, getting professional help is important. Don't try to do it yourself. If your system is damaged, forensic computer service companies can assist with data recovery. Choose this specialist carefully, because your company's entire data will be in their hands.

It is estimated that only 40 percent of companies recover from a total catastrophic loss of their business data. For your company to be among the living, you should run regular drills of your disaster recovery plans. For your computer data, try restoring your data onto another, non-mission-critical computer to see if you can successfully put it back into action during a simulated emergency drill. Do a monthly drill to ensure that you and your employees are ready for anything.

When a viable backup is not available in the event of equipment failure or data corruption, you can seek guidance from your computer's hardware manufacturers for assistance in data recovery.

Conclusion

I moved from Los Angeles to Las Vegas in 1995, and I had to start my life over here. Being a single mom was challenging. I knew nothing about the Internet or computers, but in 1997, I bought an old telephone modem and went online for the first time, and I was absolutely astonished by this new frontier. I discovered eBay, but I could not afford a digital camera because at that time they were close to $1,000. I saw an ad for a scanner on sale for $100, and I learned how to scan jewelry and was selling it on eBay. We became eBay consignment sellers to help increase our sales without having to buy merchandise. We now operate a 12,000-square-foot antique mall in Las Vegas that includes an eBay drop-off store. We have quickly become PowerSellers, and we sell under several eBay user accounts. I can honestly say eBay has changed my life!
—Renee Poole, Las Vegas, Nevada; eBay user ID "notjustantiquesmart"; trading on eBay since August 22, 2004

Independence Day

You made it! It's Independence Day—for you. eBay is an idea whose time has come, and so has yours. Because now you have all the tools you need to start an eBay consignment business—and to be the success you've always wanted to be. Selling for others on eBay can give you the financial independence you've been dreaming of while you help other people, and with creative, varied, exciting work on the very cutting edge of the Internet and new technologies—what could be better? You can do it. I'm so certain of it that I'd like you to e-mail me at borntodeal@gmail.com with your personal success story. I want to hear it, and maybe you'll see it in the next edition of this book—by that time, you'll be an old hand at all of this!

You can do it—you really can. But don't just take my word for it—as Teresa D. Bankston says at the top of Chapter 14, "If I can be a successful eBay seller with six kids running around the house, then anyone can do this."

Appendix: Helpful additions for success

I've engaged some very insightful experts in their field to provide you with these helpful additions for great success with your eBay consignment business.

The Federal Trade Commission ("FTC") is an independent agency of our Federal government that protects consumers. The following are some excellent tips from Frank Dorman in the FTC Public Affairs office:

Avoid Scams

Scam artists use clever schemes to defraud millions of people around the globe each year. Being on guard online can help you maximize the benefits of the internet and minimize your chance of being defrauded. Learn how to recognize common scams and what you can do to avoid them.

Don't send money to someone you don't know. Not an online seller you've never heard of — nor an online love interest who asks for money. It's best to do business with sites you know and trust. If you buy items through an online auction, consider using an option that provides protection, like a credit card.

If you think you've found a good deal, but you aren't familiar with the company, do some research. Type the company or product name into your favorite search engine with terms like "review," "complaint" or "scam." See what comes up – on the first page of results as well as on the later pages.

Never pay fees now for the promise of a big pay-off later — whether it's for a loan, a job, or a so-called prize.

Don't agree to deposit a check and wire money back. No matter how convincing the story. By law, banks have to make funds from deposited checks available within days, but uncovering a fake check can take weeks. You're responsible for the checks you deposit: If a check turns out to be a fake, you're responsible for paying back the bank.

Don't reply to messages asking for personal or financial information. That goes whether the message comes as an email, a phone call, a text message, or an ad. Don't click on links or call phone numbers included in the message, either. It's called phishing. The crooks behind these messages are trying to trick you into revealing sensitive information. If you got a message like this and you are concerned about your account status, call the number on your credit or debit card — or your statement — and check on it.

The "Nigerian" Email Scam

So-called "Nigerian" email scams are characterized by convincing sob stories, unfailingly polite language, and promises of a big payoff.

The Bait. These messages are the butt of late night jokes, but people still respond to them. The people behind these messages claim to be officials, businesspeople, or the surviving spouses of former government honchos in Nigeria or another country whose money is tied up temporarily. They offer to transfer lots of money into your bank account if you will pay the fees or "taxes" they need to get their money. If you respond to the initial offer, you may receive documents that look "official." They may even encourage you to travel to the country in question, or a neighboring country, to complete the transaction. Some fraudsters have produced trunks of dyed or stamped money to try to verify their claims.

The Catch. The emails are from crooks trying to steal your money or your identity. Inevitably, emergencies come up, requiring more of your money and delaying the "transfer" of funds to your account. In the end, there aren't any profits for you, and your money is gone along with the thief who stole it. According to State Department reports, people who have responded to these emails have been beaten, subjected to threats and extortion, and in some cases, murdered.

What You Can Do. These emails can really tug at your heartstrings and appeal to your sense of altruism. Successful scam artists know exactly how to get you to give up your money. If you get an email asking you to send money to help out a stranger, delete it. Someone is up to no good, and trying to manipulate your emotions.

If you've lost money to one of these schemes, call your local Secret Service field office. Local field offices are listed in the Blue Pages of your telephone directory.

Hacked Email

You get a flood of messages from friends and family. They're getting emails from you with seemingly random links, or messages with urgent pleas to wire you money. It looks like your email or social media account might have been taken over. What do you do? For starters, make sure your security protections are up-to-date, reset your password, and warn your friends.

How You Know You've Been Hacked. You might have been hacked if:

- friends and family are getting emails or messages you didn't send
- your Sent messages folder has messages you didn't send, or it has been emptied
- your social media accounts have posts you didn't make
- you can't log into your email or social media account

In the case of emails with random links, it's possible your email address was "spoofed," or faked, and hackers don't actually have access to your account. But you'll want to take action, just in case.

What To Do When You've Been Hacked. Update your system and delete any malware. Make sure your security software is up-to-date. If you don't have security software, get it. But install security software only from reputable, well-known companies. Then, run it to scan your computer for viruses and spyware (aka malware). Delete any suspicious software and restart your computer.

Set your security software, internet browser, and operating system (like Windows or Mac OS) to update automatically.

Software developers often release updates to patch security vulnerabilities. Keep your security software, your internet browser, and your operating system up-to-date to help your computer keep pace with the latest hack attacks.

Change your passwords. That's IF you're able to log into your email or social networking account. Someone may have gotten your old password and changed it. If you use similar passwords for other accounts, change them, too. Make sure you create strong passwords that will be hard to guess.

Check the advice your email provider or social networking site has about restoring your account. You can find helpful advice specific to the service. If your account has been taken over, you might need to fill out forms to prove it's really you trying to get back into your account.

Check your account settings. Once you're back in your account, make sure your signature and "away" message don't contain unfamiliar links, and that messages aren't being forwarded to someone else's address. On your social networking service, look for changes to the account since you last logged in — say, a new "friend."

Tell your friends. A quick email letting your friends know they might have gotten a malicious link or a fake plea for help can keep them from sending money they won't get back or installing malware on their computers. Put your friends' email addresses in the Bcc line to keep them confidential. You could copy and send this article, too.

What to Do Before You're Hacked. Use unique passwords for important sites, like your bank and email that way, someone who knows one of your passwords won't suddenly have access to all your important accounts. Choose strong passwords that are harder to crack. Some people find password managers — software that stores and remembers your passwords for you — a helpful way to keep things straight. If you use a password manager, make sure to select a unique, strong password for it, too. Many password managers will let you know whether the master password you've created is strong enough.

Safeguard your usernames and passwords. Think twice when you're asked to enter credentials like usernames and passwords. Never provide them in response to an email. If the email or text seems to be from your bank, for example, visit the bank website directly rather than clicking on any links or calling any numbers in the message. Scammers impersonate well-known businesses to trick people into giving out personal information.

Turn on two-factor authentication if your service provider offers it. A number of online services offer "two-factor authentication," where getting into your account requires a password plus something else — say, a code sent to your smartphone — to prove it's really you.

Don't click on links or open attachments in emails unless you know who sent them and what they are. That link or attachment could install malware on your computer. Also do your part: don't forward random links.

Download free software only from sites you know and trust. If you're not sure who to trust, do some research before you download any software. Free games, file-sharing programs, and customized toolbars also could contain malware.

Don't treat public computers like your personal computer. If it's not your computer, don't let a web browser remember your passwords, and make sure to log out of any accounts when you're done. In fact, if you can help it, don't access personal accounts —

like email, or especially bank accounts — on public computers at all. (Also be careful any time you use public Wi-Fi.)

Securing Your Wireless Network

Understand How a Wireless Network Works. Going wireless generally requires connecting an internet "access point" – like a cable or DSL modem – to a wireless router, which sends a signal through the air, sometimes as far as several hundred feet. Any computer within range with a wireless card can pull the signal from the air and access the internet.

Unless you take certain precautions, anyone nearby with a wireless-ready computer or mobile device can use your network. That means your neighbors – or any hacker nearby – could "piggyback" on your network, or access information on your computer. If an unauthorized person uses your network to commit crime or send spam, the activity could be traced back to your account.

Use Encryption. Encryption scrambles the information you send over the internet into a code so that it's not accessible to others. Using encryption is the most effective way to secure your network from intruders.

Two main types of encryption are available: Wi-Fi Protected Access (WPA) and Wired Equivalent Privacy (WEP). Your computer, router, and other equipment must use the same encryption. WPA2 is strongest; use it if you have a choice. It should protect you against most hackers.

Some older routers use only WEP encryption, which may not protect you from some common hacking programs. Consider buying a new router with WPA2 capability.

Wireless routers often come with the encryption feature turned off. You must turn it on. The directions that come with your router should explain how. If they don't, check the company's website.

Secure Your Computer and Router. Use anti-virus and anti-spyware software, and a firewall. Use the same basic computer security practices that you would for any computer connected to the internet.

Change the name of your router from the default. The name of your router (often called the service set identifier or SSID) is likely to be a standard, default ID assigned by the manufacturer. Change the name to something unique that only you know.

Change your router's pre-set password. The manufacturer of your wireless router probably assigned it a standard default password that allows you to set up and operate the router. Hackers know these default passwords, so change it to something only you know. Use passwords that are at least 10 characters long: the longer the password, the tougher it is to crack.

Visit the company's website to learn how to change the password.

Limit Access to Your Network. Allow only specific computers to access your wireless network. Every computer that is able to communicate with a network is assigned a unique Media Access Control (MAC) address. Wireless routers usually have a mechanism to allow only devices with particular MAC addresses to access to the network. Some hackers have mimicked MAC addresses, so don't rely on this step alone.

Turn off your wireless network when you know you won't use it. Hackers cannot access a wireless router when it is shut down. If you turn the router off when you're not using it, you limit the amount of time that it is susceptible to a hack.

Don't Assume That Public Wi-Fi Networks Are Secure. Be cautious about the information you access or send from a public wireless network. Many cafés, hotels, airports, and other public places offer wireless networks for their customers to use. These "hot spots" are convenient, but they may not be secure. To learn more, check out these tips for using public Wi-Fi.

Comparing Products Online

Shopping online? A little research can save you a lot of money. Even when you know what you want, it can be overwhelming to choose among dozens of products, brands, and websites. Use these tips to help get the best deal – and to avoid a bogus offer posted by a scam artist.

Think Before You Shop. Think about your goals before you shop. Do you want the top-of-the-line product? A particular brand? Are there "must-have" features? What's your budget? If you decide what's important to you up-front, you're less likely to make an impulse purchase that could lead to buyer's remorse.

Get to know the products in the category. Often, the key features of a basic product and the top-of-the-line version from the same manufacturer are the same, and "add-ons" account for the difference in price. For example, you might have to pay extra for a toaster with a clock and fancy chime even if it turns bread into toast just like a less expensive model. Manufacturer sites often have the most information about product features.

Use Search Engines. If you think you've found a good deal, but you aren't familiar with the product or the company selling it, dig a little deeper. Type the company or product name into your favorite search engine with terms like "review," "complaint" or "scam." If you find bad reviews, you'll have to decide if the offer is worth the risk. After all, it's only a good deal if you actually get a product that works.

Check Comparison Shopping Sites. These sites connect you to many retailers selling the same product, sometimes at significantly different prices. Compare your total purchase price, including shipping and handling, and taxes, rather than just the selling price. Different sites also have different return policies. Check the policy and find out whether you'll be charged extra shipping or restocking fees for returns. Some sites let you sign up to get alerts when prices change.

Consider Coupons. Some companies offer discounts to online shoppers via email; other sites collect and list codes for free shipping and other discounts. Keep in mind that a coupon price isn't always the best deal.

To look for discounts, enter the web site or company name and "discount," "coupon" or "free shipping" into a search engine. Stay away from sites that make you download software or enter financial information to access the codes.

Read Reviews and Be Skeptical. When considering a review, think about the source of the information: is it from an impartial expert organization, one consumer, many individual consumers, a columnist?

You can get a good idea about a product's performance from reading user reviews on retail or shopping comparison sites. But they may not represent the experience of all purchasers: The FTC has sued companies that posted "fake" positive reviews. Some negative reviews may come from competitors.

You also can look for websites that specialize in reviewing products. These sites don't sell products but offer expert reviews and comparisons.

Evaluate what you see on retail sites. Some scammers set up "specialty" sites selling a particular type of product. Those can be full of glowing reviews from "shills" who are compensated for their posts, and may not include any mediocre or negative reviews because they've been deleted.

What do you know about the photo? A product photo is meant to cast the item in the best possible light. Could it have been doctored? Will it look as appealing in your home or office?

What If There's a Problem? Ask yourself a few questions: Does the brand have a reputation for good products and excellent customer service? What's the promised delivery time? How will you contact the seller if there's a problem? Will the company accept returns? If so, will you be charged restocking fees?

File A Complaint

Your complaint is an essential resource for local, state, and federal law enforcement officials. Law enforcers review consumer complaints to spot trends and build cases against hackers, identity thieves, scam artists, and other fraudsters.

Internet Scams and Fraud. In general, you can file a complaint about internet-related frauds, scams, and suspicious activity with the following organizations:

The Federal Trade Commission. The Federal Trade Commission is the nation's consumer protection agency and collects complaints about fraudulent, deceptive, and unfair business practices. If you think you may be a victim of fraud, file a complaint with the FTC.

Your State Attorney General. In addition to the FTC, you can also file a complaint with your state Attorney General's office if you think you may be a victim of fraud. Your state Attorney General's office handles a wide range of complaints related to consumer protection.

The Internet Crime Complaint Center. The IC3 is a partnership between the FBI, the National White Collar Crime Center, and the Bureau of Justice Assistance, whose mission is to serve as a vehicle to receive, develop, and refer criminal complaints related to cyber-crime.

www.bbb.org. The Better Business Bureau accepts complaints from consumers against businesses or services, and is dedicated to fostering an ethical business environment.

Spam. Forward spam emails to the FTC at spam@uce.gov. You can also forward spam to reportphishing@antiphishing.org. The Anti-Phishing Working Group is a consortium of ISPs, security vendors, financial institutions and law enforcement agencies that use this email to fight phishing.

The following content has been generously prepared and provided by Joseph E. Sullivan, legal counsel for eBay, Inc.

1. Auctioneer/Secondhand Dealer Laws

More than half of the states in the United States have laws regulating "auctioneers," and most states and many municipalities have laws regulating pawn shops and secondhand dealers. These laws require certain business owners to pay fees, obtain licenses, post bonds, take classes, collect and store certain records, and make filings with government agencies. Right now, questions abound regarding whether these laws should apply to eBay sellers. eBay takes the view that the laws should not, because the regulations generally were written before eBay existed and were created to deal with issues that do not arise in the eBay context. eBay's government relations team is working hard right now to convince local officials to not apply these laws online or, if unsuccessful in doing that, to convince legislatures to change these laws to make exceptions for eBay businesses. However, even during this unsettled time, sellers remain personally responsible for investigating and complying with all local laws to the extent that local authorities believe they apply to eBay sales.

a. Auctioneer Laws

While eBay transactions are commonly referred to as "auctions," there are several fundamental differences between traditional, regulated auctions and the transactions that are contemplated by the eBay platform. Traditional auctioneers control all aspects of their sales, from the members of the audience invited to the bids that get recognized, while eBay sellers conduct business very differently. A large percentage of sales advertised on eBay are fixed price sales or sales that provide that the "bidding" will end at a fixed time. eBay itself manages much of the interaction between sellers and buyers, eBay provides significant trust and safety services to buyers, and eBay offers buyer protection programs to protect buyers against loss. To recognize these large differences between auctioneering and eBay sales, eBay prohibits consignment sellers from using the term auctioneer to describe their businesses, unless the seller is licensed as auctioneers under traditional auctioneer licensing laws.

Important eBay rule. eBay sellers may not use the term auction or auctioneer in their name or advertising to describe their sales on eBay, unless they are licensed under their state laws as an auctioneer or auction business or conducting a traditional auctioneer business in a state that does not license traditional auctioneers. eBay sellers may use the term auction-style instead.

The current state of the law. As of this writing, the only state agency to hold affirmatively that consignment sellers on eBay need to be licensed as auctioneers has been the Louisiana Auction Board. eBay is currently working to try to change that interpretation or change the law. Regulators from North Carolina, North Dakota, Tennessee, and Wisconsin have issued statements concluding that their auctioneer laws do not apply to eBay sellers. Auction boards in Arkansas and other states are also reviewing the issue and may issue decisions in the near future. Because the interpretations of law in this area are changing so quickly, do not rely on what you read here—independently verify the standards required in your location.

b. Pawnbroker/Secondhand Dealer Laws

Storefront drop-off stores have grown in popularity around the United States as alternatives to pawn shops as places where people can bring goods for them to be sold on consignment. In response, pawnbrokers have argued that these stores should face the same regulations that apply to them—fingerprinting of all customers, reporting of all goods to local police databases, and, in some cases, application of holding periods before sale of the goods. However, on a closer look, drop-off stores offer a business model very different from pawn shops. Unlike when a person brings goods to a pawn shop and walks out the door with cash, a person who brings goods to a drop-off store only receives funds after the item sells on eBay, frequently over a month later. Moreover, pawn sales are not open to the world, whereas eBay is a transparent marketplace searched by millions of users every day. There has been little evidence of sales of stolen property via these drop-off stores on eBay, and eBay believes that application of the strict pawn laws would be overkill that would serve no valid purpose and instead have the unintended consequence of stifling small, local entrepreneurs.

In an effort to prevent stolen property from being listed on eBay, to provide a substitute for pawn laws that meets law enforcement concerns without overburdening eBay users with inappropriate regulatory requirements, and to provide efficient support for law enforcement, eBay makes all transaction listings available to law enforcement in the LeadsOnline (www.leadsonline.com) searchable database. LeadsOnline is the nation's largest online investigative system used by law enforcement for the investigation of crimes involving property. More than 42,000 businesses, including pawn shops and secondhand stores, in all 50 states electronically upload their transactions to LeadsOnline for use by local law enforcement. LeadsOnline's service is used by over 4,400 law enforcement agencies in 41 states. LeadsOnline will provide the service at no additional cost to listers, will ensure that this data is available only to law enforcement conducting legitimate ongoing investigations where the evidence relates to the ongoing investigation, and will also confirm that the records are provided in compliance with eBay's privacy policy. To recap: eBay is very pro-active when it comes to preventing stolen property from being sold via its listings. Law enforcement can directly search, without warrants, all eBay listings as they attempt to match the descriptions and/or serial numbers of stolen property.

Important eBay rule. Sellers who operate as storefront businesses must include accurate city and state item locations in their listings; must include item serial numbers if available in their listings; must record identification, billing, and listing information of all consignors; must retain those records for at least 60 days; and must make those records available to local law enforcement officials upon request during regular business hours.

The current state of the law. This issue continues to be debated around the country, and you must check with local and state officials on what is expected of you. In California, Michigan, and Florida, police have taken action against drop-off stores for failing to comply with local pawn and secondhand dealer laws. A Florida court rejected the police action there, but the issue is not settled. California's attorney general recently released an opinion stating that drop-off stores likely fell under the California definition of secondhand dealers and directing the legislature to clarify the situation.

2. Real Estate Laws

Real estate advertising services on eBay are offered by eBay Real Estate, Inc., a wholly owned subsidiary of eBay, Inc. ("eBay Real Estate"). eBay Real Estate offers two formats for the advertisement of real estate: auction-style format items and ad format items. Auction-style advertisements of real property do not involve legally binding offers to buy and sell. Instead, auction-style postings are simply a way for sellers to advertise their real estate and identify the most interested potential buyers. Following the close of the auction-style bidding, sellers and buyers are expected to contact each other to prepare and deliver the appropriate paperwork to transfer the property and to take such other actions as may be required by local laws and regulations. eBay Real Estate also offers sellers the option of advertising their property in an "ad" format that also does not involve legally binding offers to buy and sell. Sellers can specify their asking price, and no bidding takes place. Interested buyers fill out a contact form, and their information is sent to the seller.

Important eBay rule. Sellers may not post real estate advertisements on eBay on behalf of third parties, unless they are licensed real estate agents.

The current state of the law. Some local authorities have laws and regulations that may cover the types of services that eBay sellers provide to clients. Please take particular care in connection with the advertisement, sale, or marketing of real estate, because some government agencies may require that you first become licensed as a real estate broker or otherwise impose local regulation on your activities. Just as you're responsible on eBay to ensure that the items you sell are legal to sell, you're responsible for ensuring that the services you provide to clients are legal. A consultation with an attorney may help you clarify questions you may have.

3. Motor Vehicle Sales Laws

Please be aware that motor vehicle sales, especially across state lines, may carry higher legal liability than selling other merchandise on eBay. eBay highly recommends that you check with your state's department of transportation to understand licensing and liability issues before engaging in motor vehicle-related sales activities. Rules differs in a few ways because of the legal complexity of this area.

Important eBay rules. Sellers who are not licensed motor vehicle dealers cannot do the following:

- List vehicles under their own user ID
- Charge a fee for services based upon a percentage of the sales price
- Interact with bidders, filter, or otherwise control the flow of information between bidders and the owner of the vehicle

eBay sellers who are licensed motor vehicle dealers may do the following:

- List cars under their own user ID
- Charge service fees based on the final sales price
- Communicate directly with bidders
- Accept payment directly for the sale
- Arrange for registration and title transfer

The current state of the law. Most states require that anyone who sells cars or motorcycles for another to have a motor vehicle dealer's license. Laws and requirements vary from state to state (check with your state's department of transportation). Whenever required by law, eBay sellers must become licensed as dealers, brokers, or salespersons.

The following services usually require a dealer's license:

- Selling vehicles on consignment
- Auction management (responding to e-mails, calls)
- Negotiating final terms of the sale
- Collecting payment from the buyer
- Processing title transfer between seller and buyer
- Accepting a fee from the seller based on percentage of the sale

3. Nonprofit Sales

Charitable fundraising is a highly regulated area subject to numerous state and federal laws. eBay allows sellers to list items and collect proceeds on behalf of nonprofit either with eBay Giving Works, the dedicated program for nonprofit listings on eBay, or without eBay Giving Works, as long as the listings meet specific guidelines for charitable solicitations.

eBay selected PayPal Giving Fund to serve as the dedicated solution provider for eBay Giving Works. PayPal Mission Fund's valuable service and support includes: powering the nonprofit directory for eBay Giving Works, verifying that nonprofits are eligible for this program, collecting and disbursing sellers' donations, providing sellers with tax receipts, and tracking donations online. eBay features Giving Works listings on the website by differentiating these listings with a distinctive ribbon icon and including them within a specialized nonprofit search functionality.

Important eBay rules. Sellers may only list with eBay Giving Works if they:

- use the Sell Your Item form on eBay and enable JavaScript in their browsers;

- register with PayPal Giving Fund and maintain an account in good standing;

- agree to donate at least 10 percent of the final sale price or $10—whichever is greater—to a member nonprofit organization if the item sells (but the $10 minimum donation requirement does not apply to nonprofits selling items on their own behalf, called "Direct Selling");

- select PayPal or credit card as one of the buyer payment options (not required for listings in the Motors or Real Estate categories or for "Direct Selling"); and

- do not list the item in the Real Estate ad format or Mature Audiences category. Sellers may only list items for nonprofit without eBay Giving Works if they:

- are soliciting on behalf of recognized, tax-deductible, charitable organizations having 501(c)(3) status or equivalent with the IRS; and

- receive advance written consent for the solicitation from the benefiting nonprofit. To verify you received permission, you must include a scanned copy of the consent in your listing. It must appear with the nonprofit's letterhead, be signed by an officer, and include the nonprofit's tax-deductibility status as well as your name or eBay user ID, dates of event/listings, and donation amount (percentage of the final sale price).

The current state of the law. Most states have laws that require anyone who, for compensation, solicits funds for a nonprofit to be licensed as a professional fundraiser. If you sell items on eBay and a portion of the proceeds goes to a nonprofit but you receive a fee for the sale, these laws probably apply to you. You're independently responsible for complying with these laws.

Photo Gallery

Welcome to my personal Hall of Fame photo gallery. The eBay marketplace is an amazing way to connect with buyers across the globe who buy the most interesting and remarkable items.

This photo gallery represents some of my more notable sales on eBay and the photos are the actual images used to present these items to my eBay buyers. None were retouched in any way.

Some were forgotten memories. Many were simply collecting dust in garages or storage units. This gallery shows the amazing prices that can be obtained for items on the eBay marketplace. Perhaps these items will inspire you to become an eBay consignment seller like me.

You never know what treasure is lying buried in an attic, under some pile of clutter, hidden in a dark closet or perhaps in a warehouse. You can convert these unproductive items into cash for appreciative clients and *GROW RICH with eBay Consignment.*

$250 Magnificent Gilded Hand Painted 19th Century Plate

$595 Sandor Frog and Florals Costume Bracelet Circa 1930s

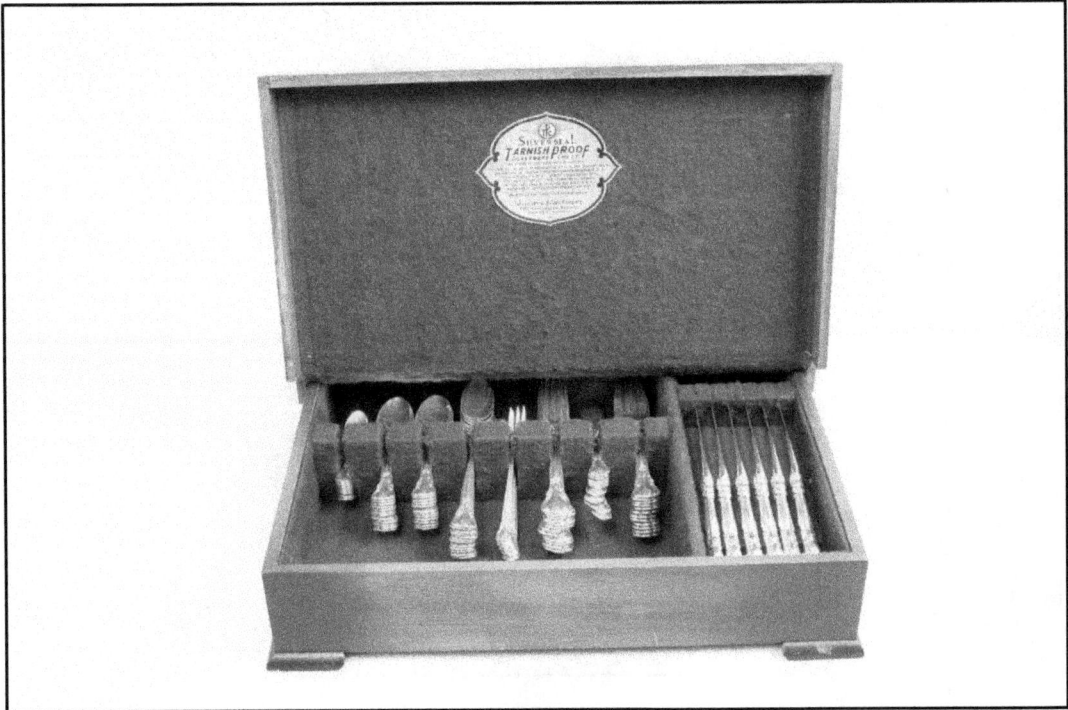

$3,400 108 Piece Set of Sterling Silver Gorham Chantilly Flatware

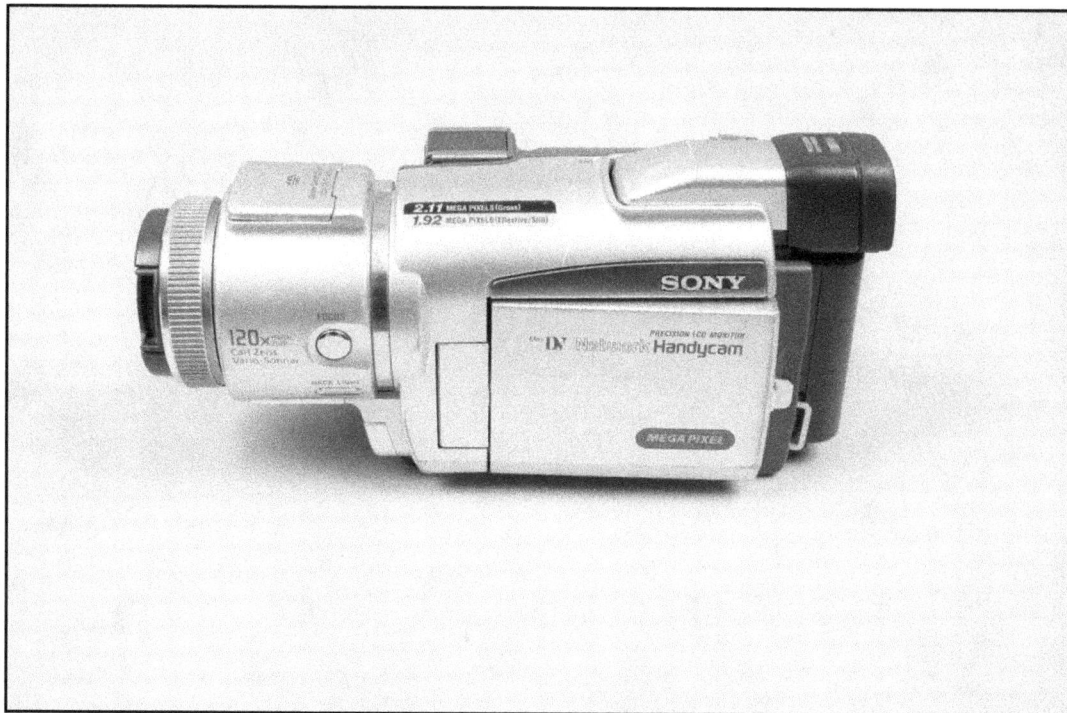

$100.90 Sony Handycam DCR-TRV70 Camcorder

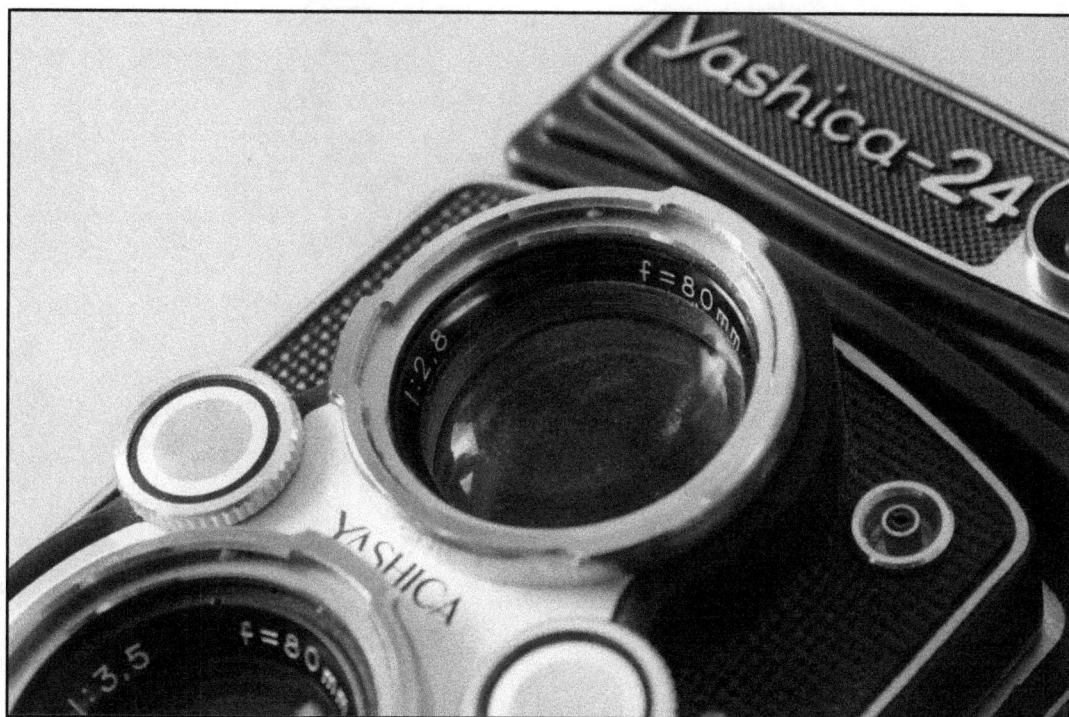

$125 Vintage Yashica Twin Lens Reflex Camera

$1,200 c. 1905 Antique Patek Philippe Pocket Watch

$299.95 Collection of Hot Wheels

$400 1987 United States Constitution Two Coin Proof Set

$495 Vintage Hewlett Packard 67 Scientific Calculator

$69.95 Vintage Rolling Stones Nylon Velcro Wallet

$175 Limited Edition Laddie John Dill Print

$572 Baltic Amber Necklace

$330 19th Century Mughal Indian Indo-Persian Cavalry Armor

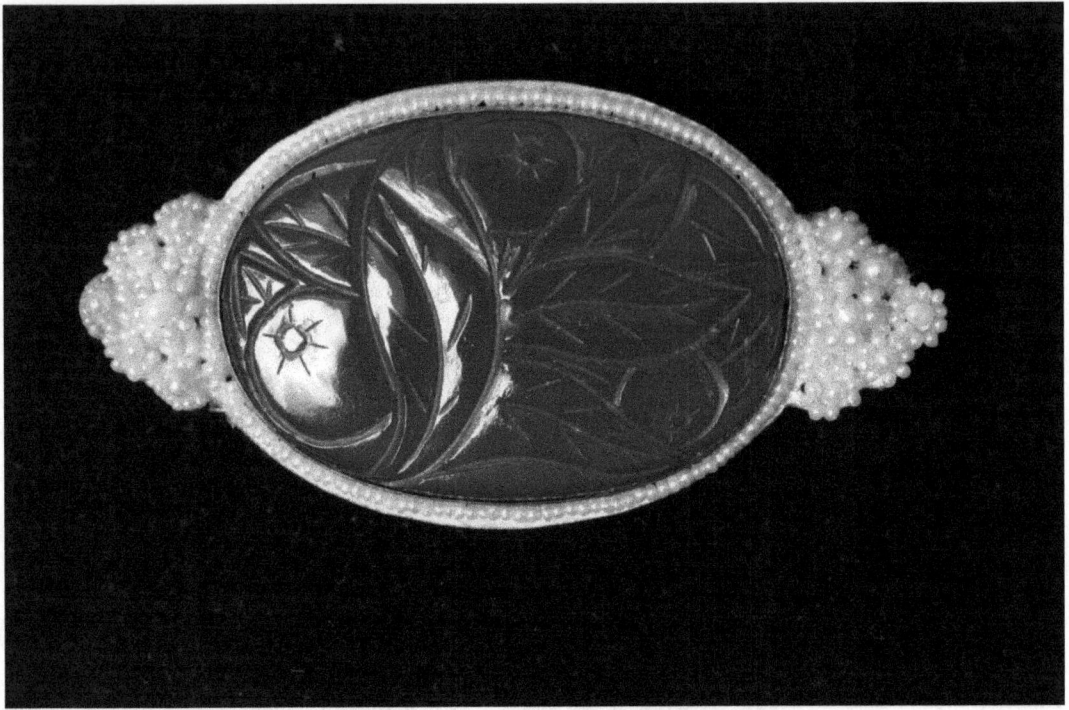

$274.50 Antique Victorian Carnelian and Seed Pearl Brooch

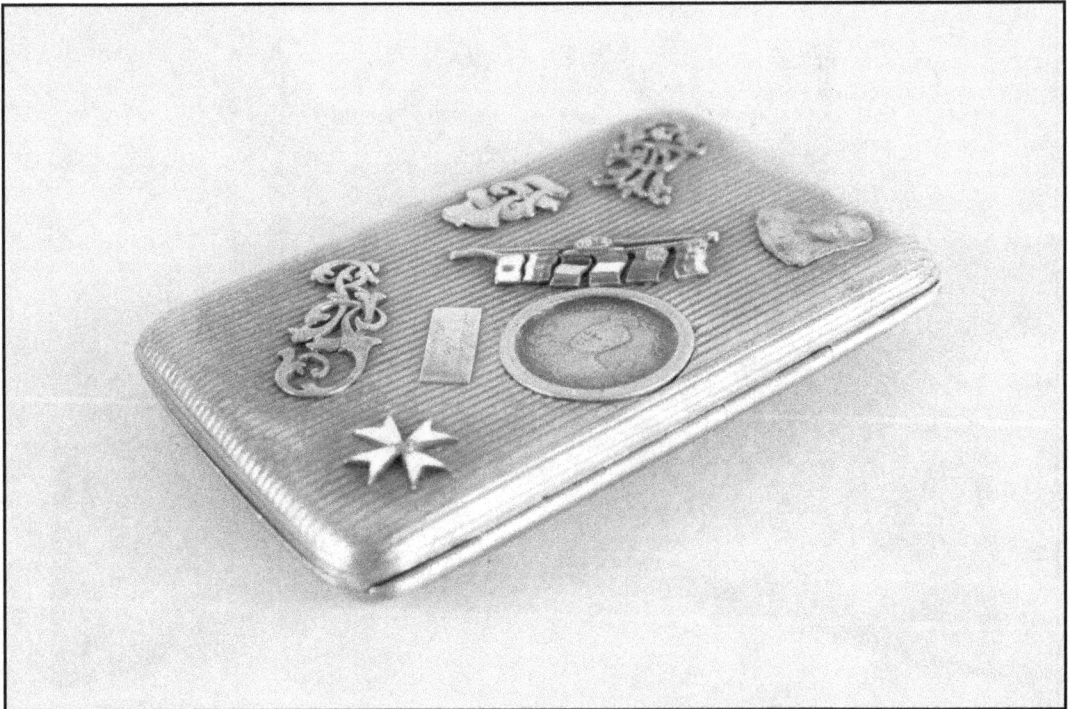

$2,000 Antique Russian Officer Tsarist Silver Cigarette Case

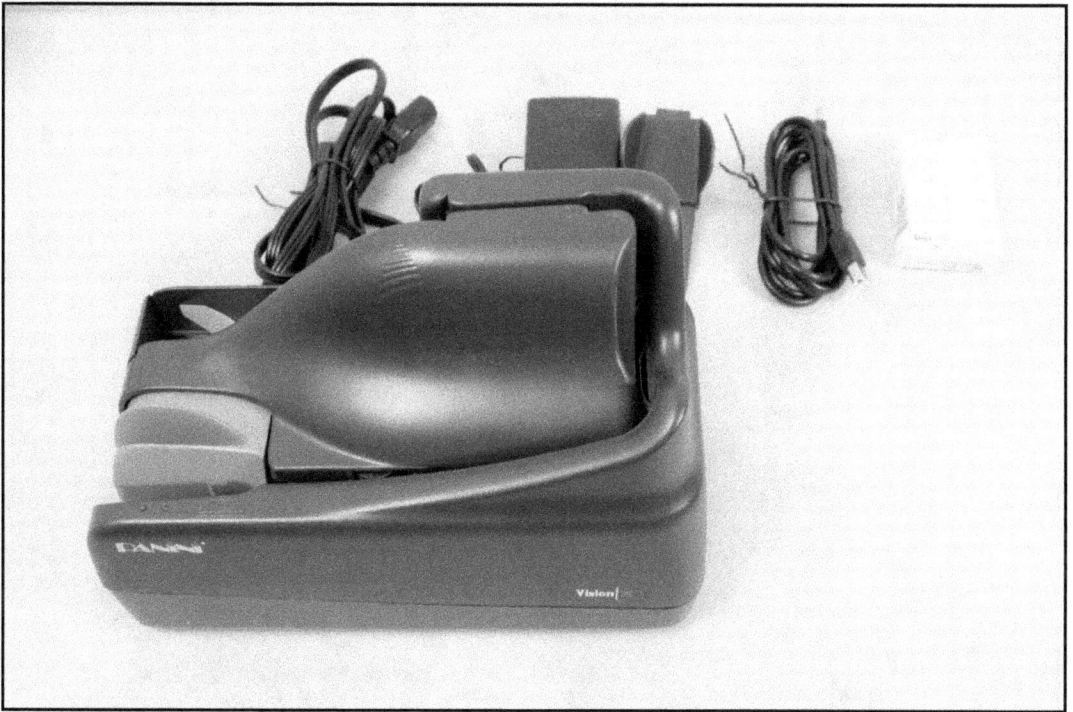

$200 Panini Vision X Check Reader and Scanner

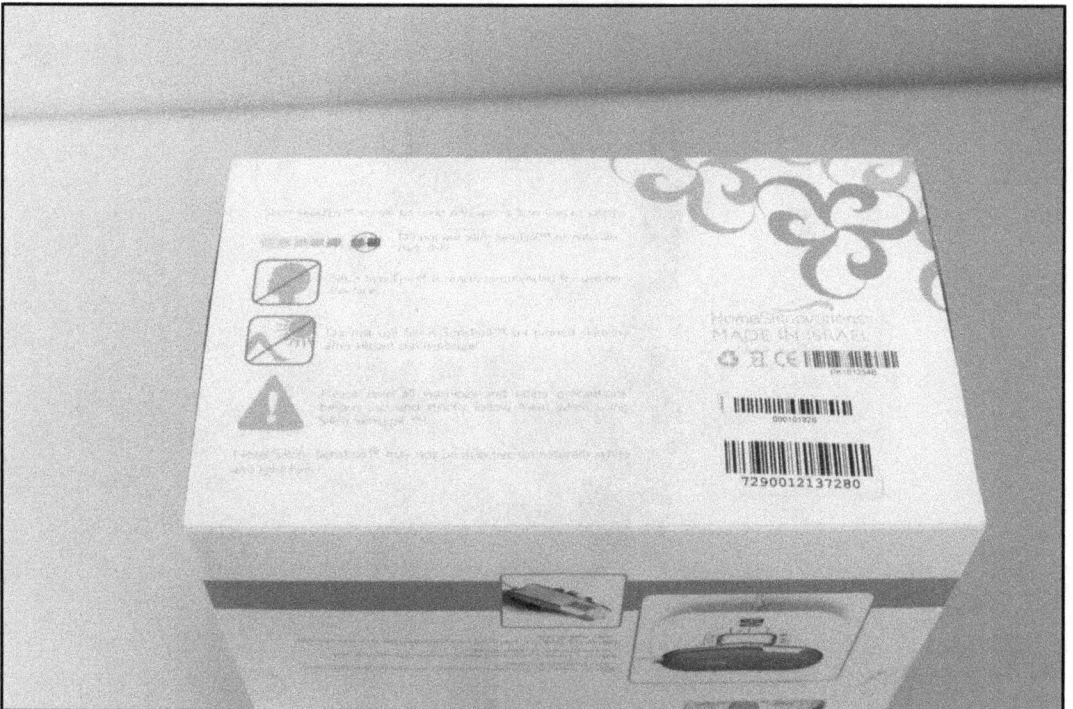

$270 Silk'n Sensepil Hair Remover

$7,896.54 Pre 1865 Antique French Napoleonic Cuirassier Uniform

$99.99 Icelandic Airlines Loffleider Captain's Hat Pin

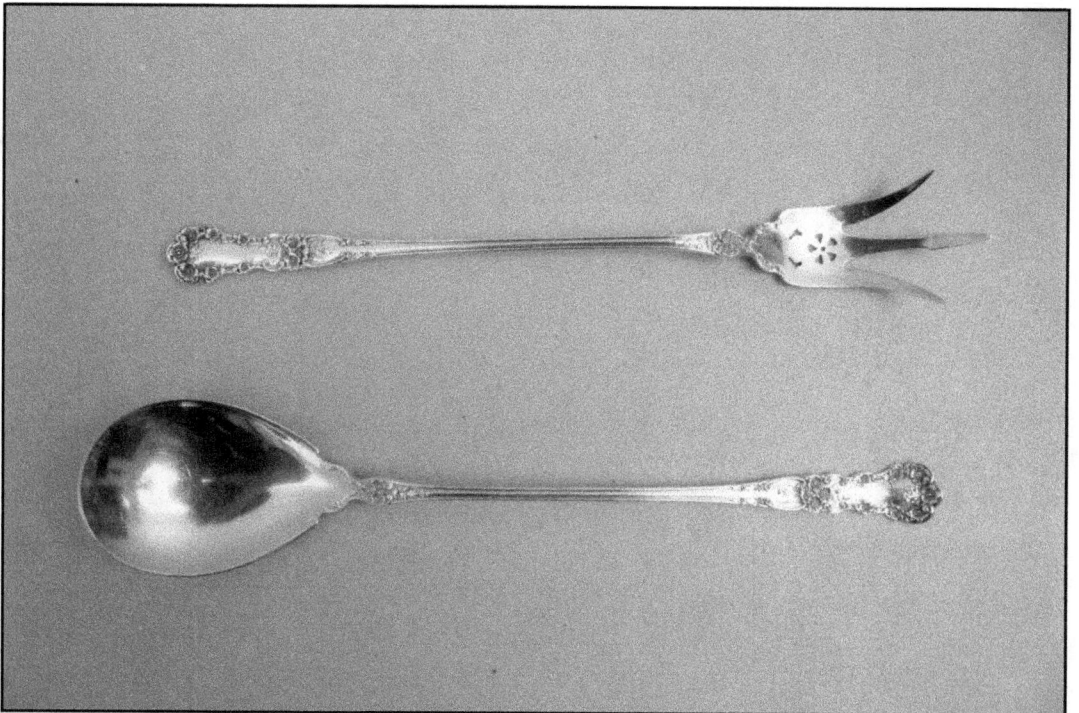

$250 Sterling Gorham Buttercup Salad Serving Set

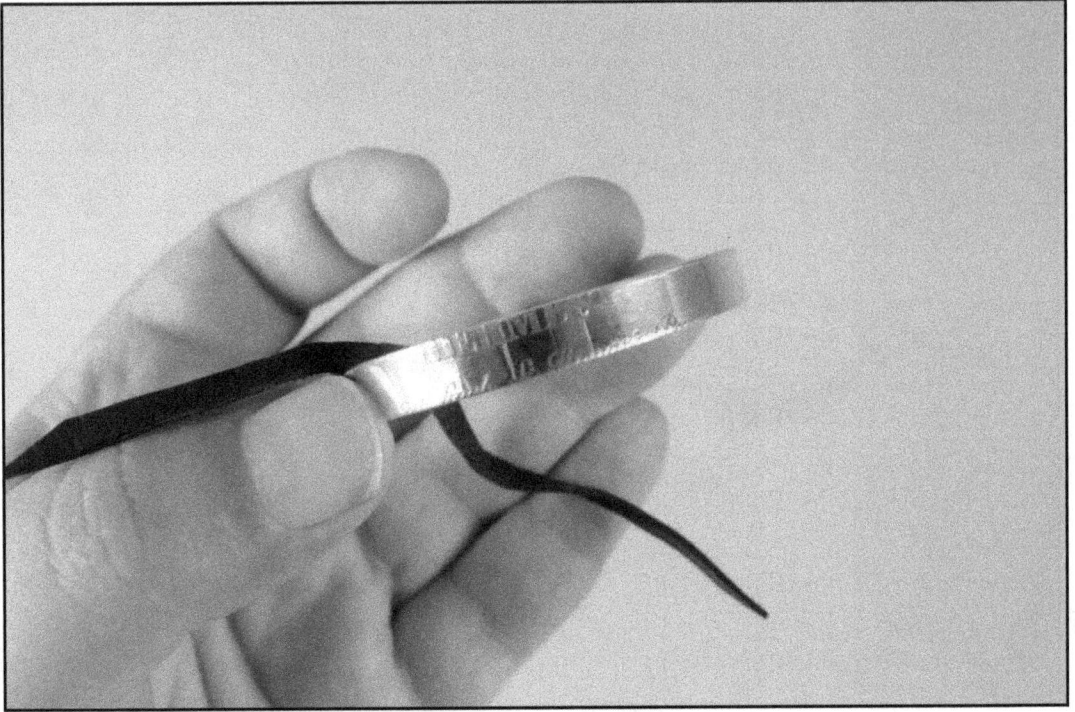

$242.50 Sterling Silver Hermes Bracelet

$355 Bon Jovi Signed Lost Highway Tour Leather Jacket

$631.38 Lladro "Will You Marry Me?" Figurine

$2,500 c. 1967 Gibson ES335 6 String Sunburst Vintage Guitar

$132.50 One Dozen Rawlings Official Major League Baseballs

$125 Fossil Nugget Ladies Ring

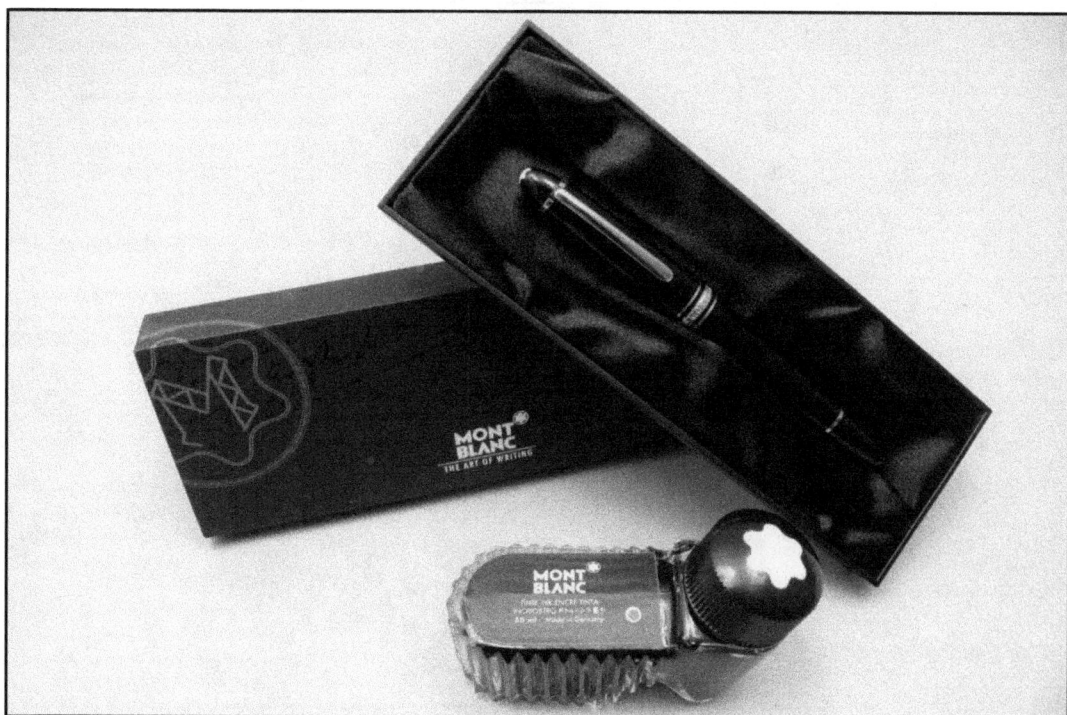

$280 Montblanc Meisterstuck Le Grand Fountain Pen

$415 Atomic Aquatics ST1 Scuba Driver's Regulator Set

$249 Lucky Brand Suede Multi-Color Patchwork Purse

$225 Catalina Island Pottery Set of 12 Party Trays

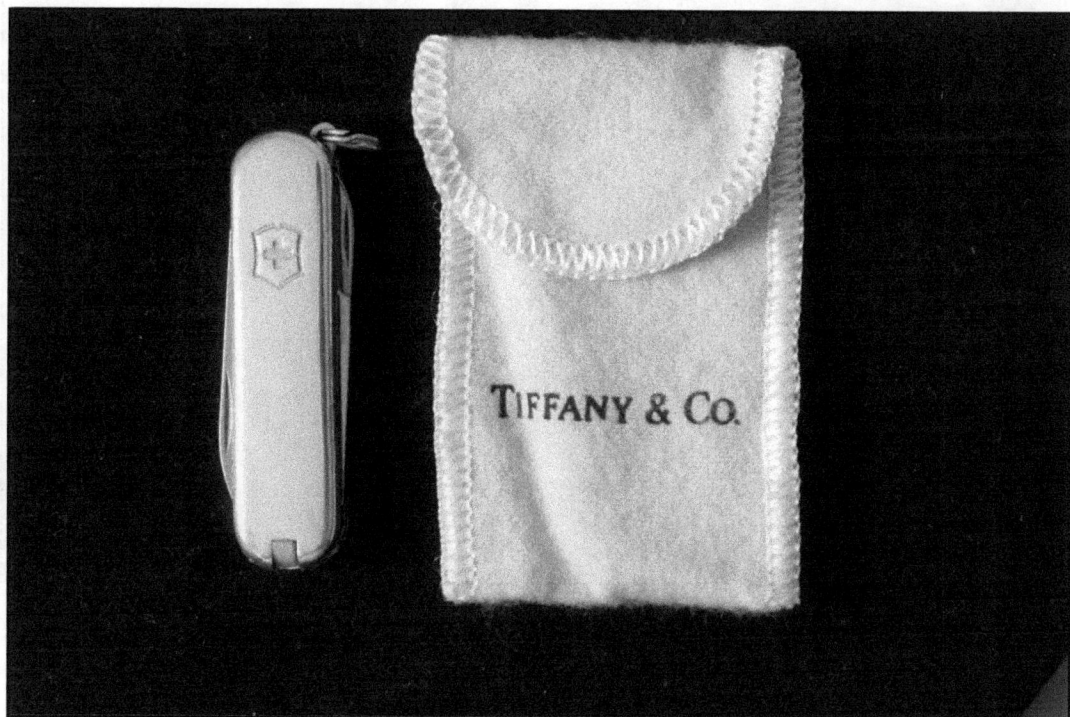

$190 Tiffany & Co. Sterling Silver Vitorinox Swiss Army Knife

$180.50 Antique Stereoviews 3D Slides

$107.50 Empire Sterling Silver Sugar Bowl & Cream Pitcher

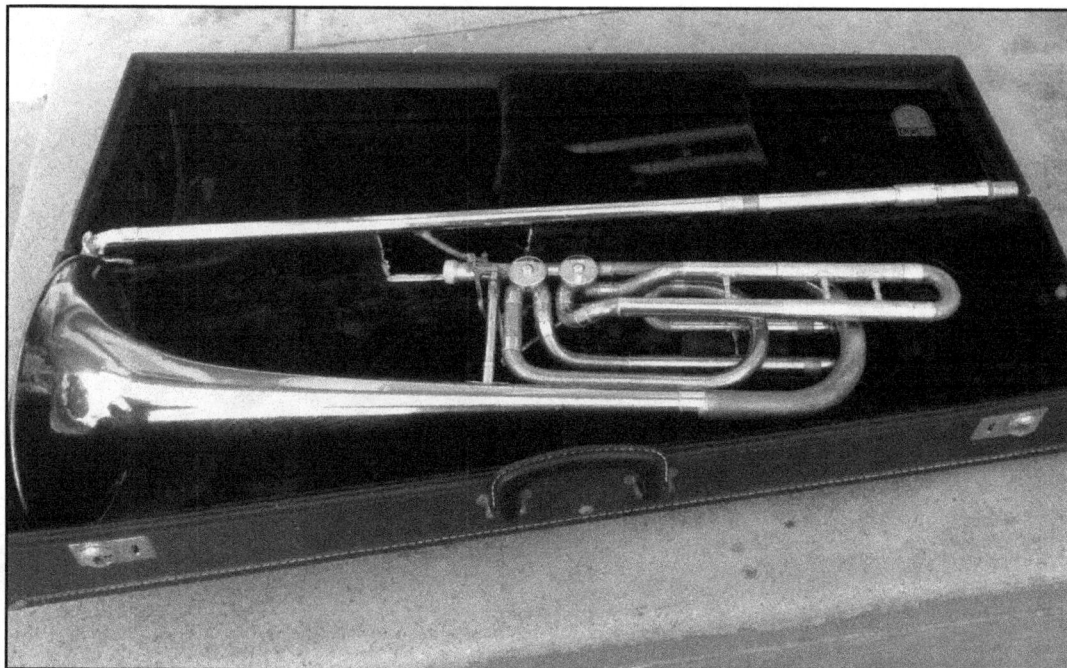

$2,750 c. 1970 C.G. Conn Selmer 62H Trombone

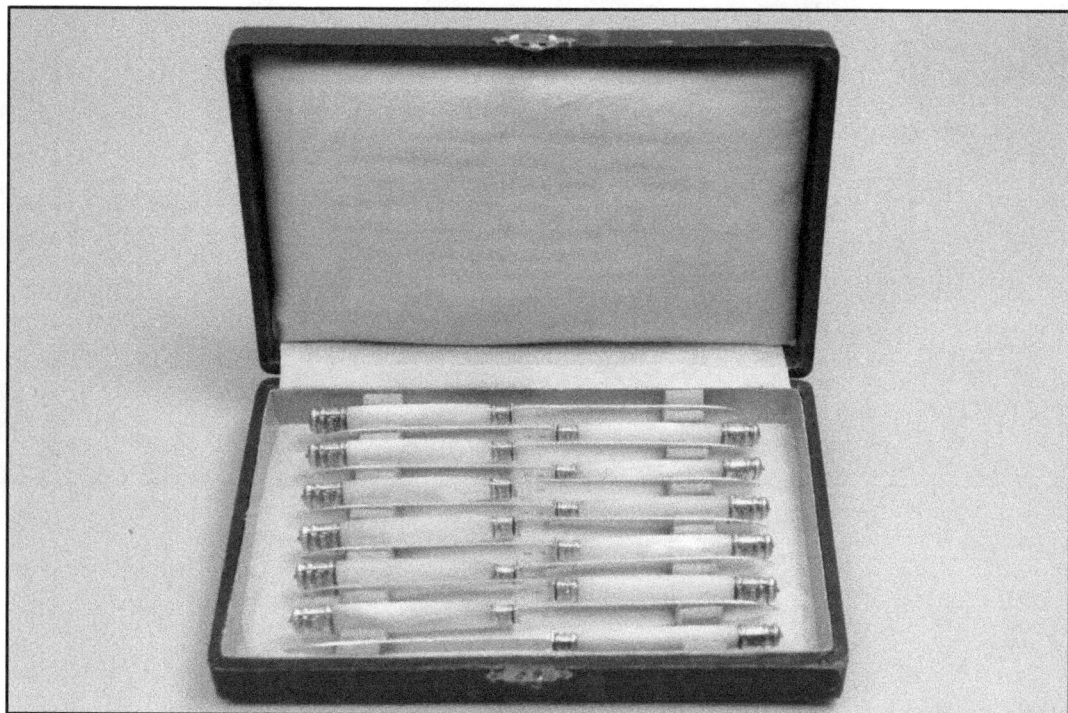

$250 Antique c. 1798 Paris France Mother of Pearl Knife Set

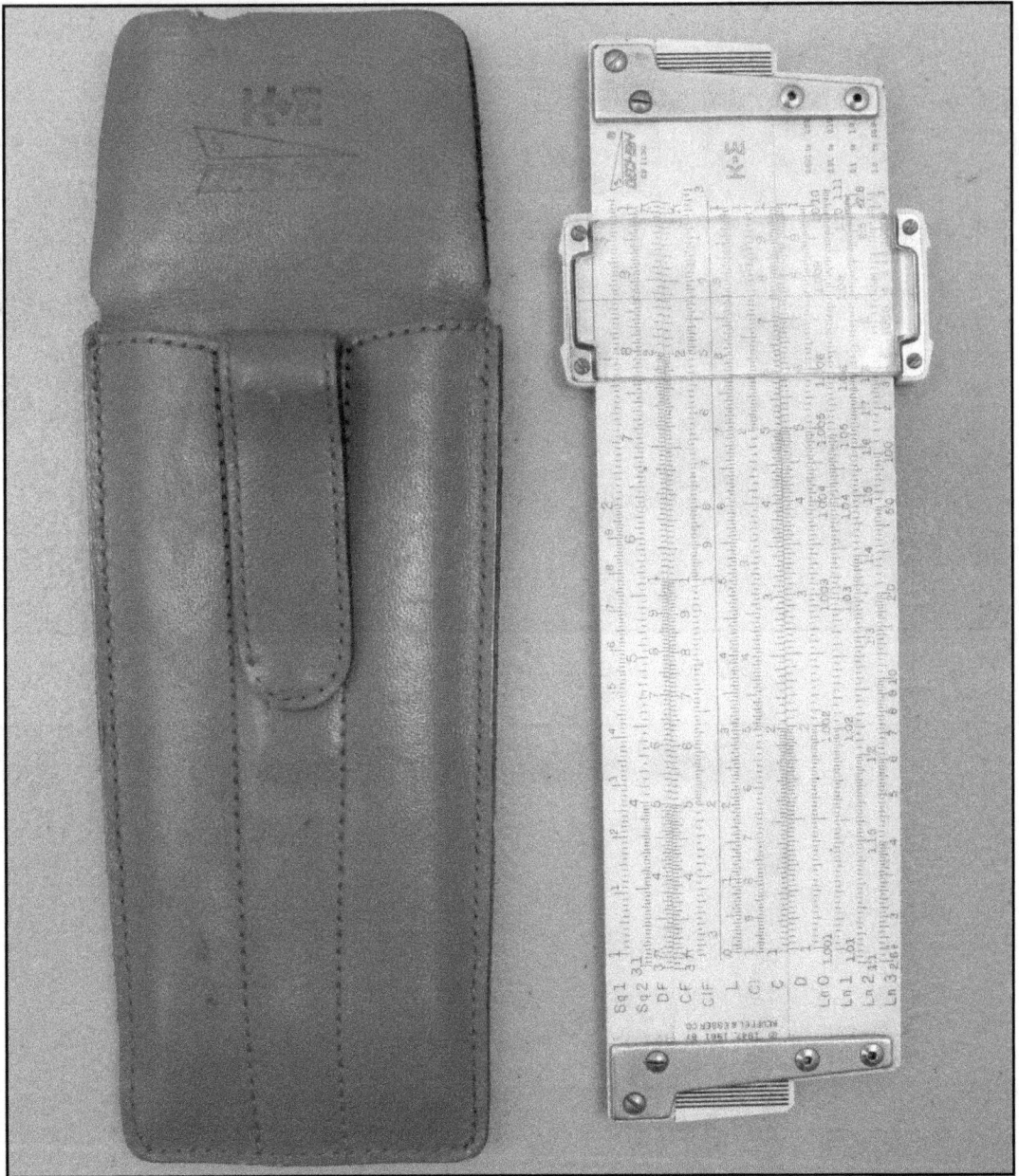

$225 Vintage K & E Deci-Lon Slide Rule

$960 Fine Vintage Silk Persian Area Rug

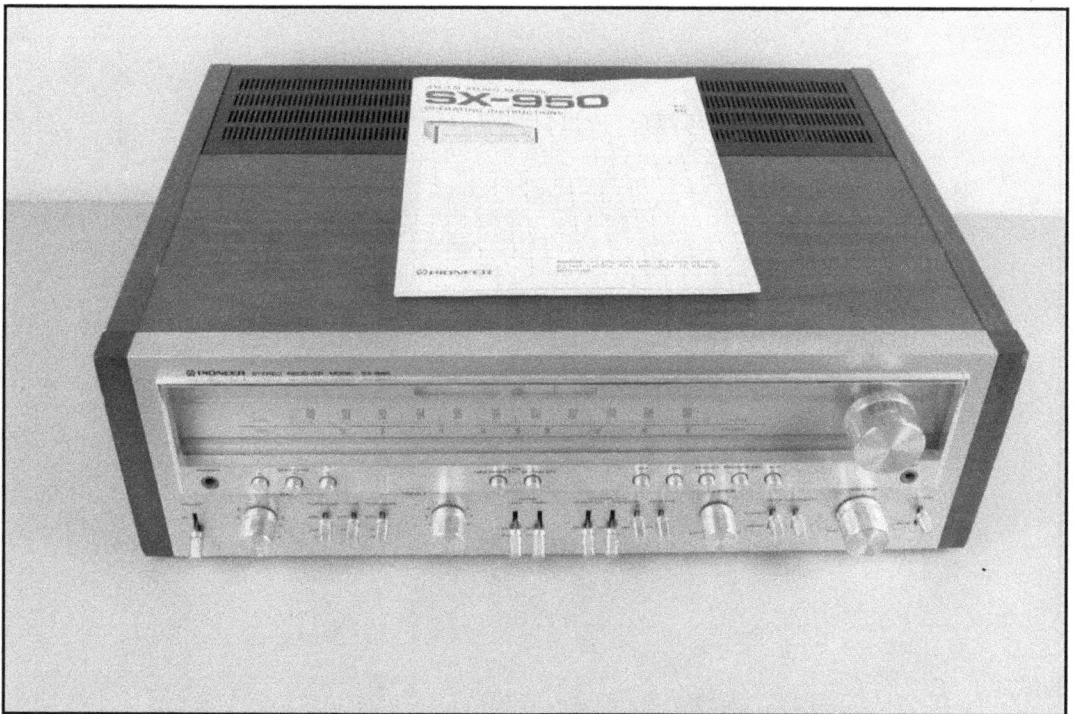

$499 Vintage Pioneer SX-950 AM/FM Stereo Receiver

$597.77 Hamilton 22 Jewel Wristwatch Movement

$295 Vintage Aquamarine and Ruby 14K Gold Ring

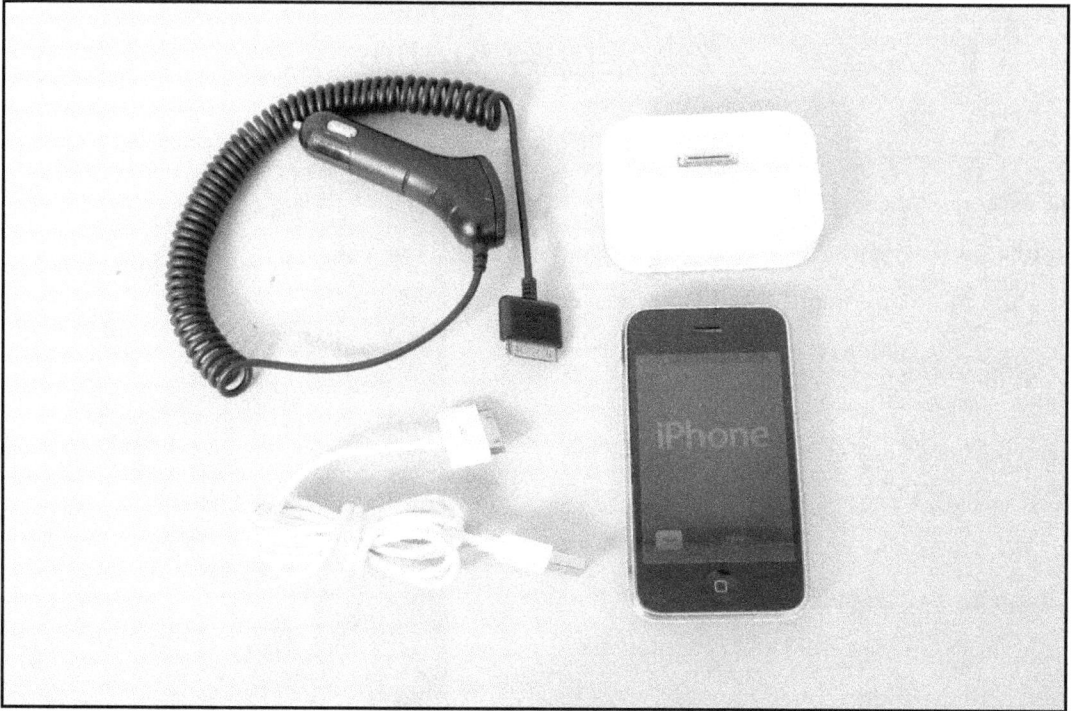

$159.95 White Apple 16GB iPhone 3GS

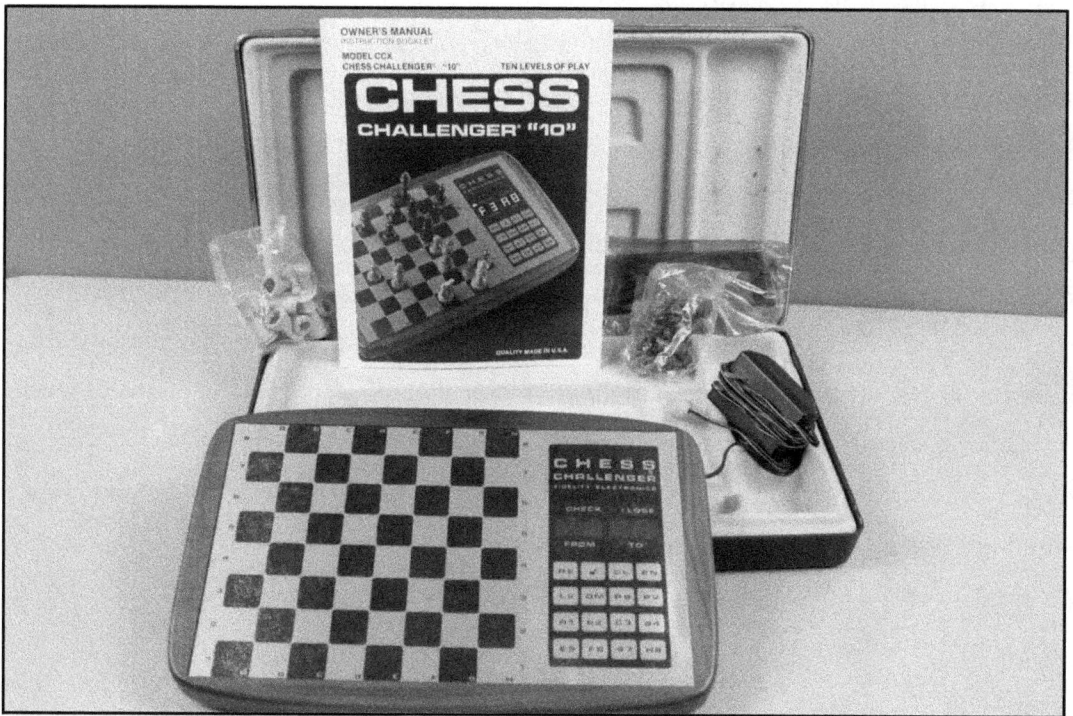

$155 Vintage Challenger Electronic Chess Set

About the Author

Christopher Matthew Spencer was among the earliest adopters of the internet. He's been writing books and articles and developing successful education for entrepreneurs and internet users ever since. He has sold over 200,000 items online and provided consulting to kathy ireland Worldwide and many Fortune 1000 companies, including eBay, NETGEAR, Visa, and Qualcomm.

Christopher Matthew has provided comprehensive training at more than 200 industry trade shows and has delivered keynotes and presentations at the top ten trade shows in the world. He served as an official product evangelist for eBay University for six years growing the brand in eBay's early years.

Christopher Matthew is the eBay and PayPal content author for Lynda.com, a highly-successful online software training library that provides education to millions of students.

Christopher Matthew has successfully bought and sold many companies and has run a bakery, an office products distribution company, a commercial fundraising agency, a television production company, a publicity firm, a celebrity brokerage, a hotel, a bar, a restaurant, and a real estate development firm. He presently owns and operates a full-service marketing, consulting, and technology agency servicing firms of all sizes. Christopher Matthew attributes his success to an optimistic attitude and the pursuit of all things fun. He is an insatiable learner and he loves sharing his knowledge with anyone who desires it.

Christopher Matthew received an honorable discharge from the United States Navy after eight years of loyal service.

Christopher Matthew lives in Burbank, California.

www.ingramcontent.com/pod-product-compliance
Lightning Source LLC
Chambersburg PA
CBHW062037090426
42740CB00016B/2930